Land Economics Monographs

Number 1

LAND

ECONOMICS

*A quarterly journal
devoted to the study
of economic
and social institutions*

Chile's Experiments In Agrarian Reform

Sponsored by
the Land Tenure Center
of the University of Wisconsin
and by the Agency
for International Development

Chile's
Experiments
In Agrarian
Reform

William C. Thiesenhusen

PUBLISHED FOR

LAND ECONOMICS

The University of Wisconsin Press
Madison, Milwaukee, London
1966

Land Economics MONOGRAPHS

PUBLISHED FOR *LAND ECONOMICS,* A QUARTERLY JOURNAL DEVOTED
TO THE STUDY OF ECONOMIC AND SOCIAL INSTITUTIONS, BY THE
UNIVERSITY OF WISCONSIN PRESS

DISTRIBUTED BY THE UNIVERSITY OF WISCONSIN PRESS
MADISON, MILWAUKEE, AND LONDON
U.S.A.: BOX 1379, MADISON, WISCONSIN 53701
U.K.: 26-28 HALLAM STREET, LONDON, W. 1

Dedicated To Ginny

Her Parents and Mine

TABLE OF CONTENTS

MAPS AND DIAGRAMS

Preface

THIS STUDY attempts to analyze several land reform experiments in Chile, a country where the traditional latifundia-*minifundio* agrarian structure still predominates. It is predicated on the idea that, when a more inclusive agricultural restructuralization comes, technicians will benefit from having studied how reform works on a small scale.

The Land Tenure Center, University of Wisconsin, and its cooperating institution in Chile, the Instituto de Economía, Universidad de Chile, have allowed me the enviable task of doing this research in a laboratory situation where social and economic change is taking place. To both institutions I owe a debt of gratitude.

To the friendly and hospitable people of Chile, forever patient with another student-gringo, I am deeply indebted: for their courtesy always, for their acceptance, for their kindness.

My purpose in this study is not to be destructively critical. The foreigner observing another culture has little reason to be arrogant. Should any of my statements appear harsh or disparaging, I have not meant them to be so. The reader will, I hope, keep in mind that the current generation of Chileans did no more to create their current social and economic difficulties than we as contemporary citizens of the United States have done to create the most critical problems our society grapples with today. However, to present-day Chileans in their culture, as to us in ours, falls the difficult job of evolving institutions to confront these problems and to accurately reflect the needs of the modern times. For this task there are no simple remedies nor quick solutions.

I must acknowledge the help of many people, although it must not be construed that they have any responsibility for my errors. Professor Peter Dorner, for his encouragement and ever-helpful comments, must be at the top of this list.

I also wish to thank Felipe Paúl, who accompanied me on all interviews and assisted in innumerable ways during the first half of 1964.

Furthermore, my debt of gratitude must be extended to the staff members of the Instituto de Promoción Agraria (INPROA), the Corporación de la Reforma Agraria (CORA), and the Compañía Italiana Chilena de Colonización (CITAL), who were always willing to share their information with me. I can only hope that in the presentation of information drawn from these organizations I have been worthy of their confidence.

Especially to be acknowledged in INPROA are Gonzalo Puga and Hugo Jordán who smoothed the way to the rest of the staff and read and commented frankly on some earlier draft chapters. I also received valuable information from Juan Soto, Fernando Irarrázaval, Carlos Avilés, and Juan Walker of the INPROA team. Those CORA staff members to whom I am indebted, in addition to Eduardo Silva Pizarro, its Vice-President under the recently concluded term of Chile's President Jorge Alessandri Rodríguez, are René Maluenda, Manuel González, Conrado Prorromant, and Fernando Grez. Cristóbal Underrichter, CORA's past Food and Agriculture Organization (FAO) Advisor also gave me valuable information.

I acknowledge the help of others who read drafts of some chapters and offered helpful suggestions: Professor Bryant E. Kearl, Department of Agricultural Journalism and Associate Dean of the Graduate School, University of Wisconsin; Professor Don Kanel, Department of

Agricultural Economics and the Land Tenure Center, University of Wisconsin; Father Gonzalo Arroyo, Centro para el Desarrollo Económico y Social de América Latina, Santiago; Professor Solon Barraclough, Instituto de Capacitación e Investigación en Reforma Agraria (ICIRA), Santiago and Cornell University; Professor Henry Landsberger, Instituto de Organización y Administración (INSORA), Universidad de Chile and Cornell University; and Fernando Fuenzalida, Economic Commission for Latin America (ECLA) and FAO, Santiago.

Professor Fritz Albert, Department of Agricultural Journalism, University of Wisconsin, took all photographs in February and March, 1965. Most of the diagrams were drawn by Mr. Mike Smith, FAO, Santiago.

Staff members of the Agency for International Development (AID), Santiago, have also been helpful.

My colleagues at the Land Tenure Center, Chile—Marion Brown, Daniel Stewart, Héctor Morales, Juan Carlos Collarte, Antonio Idiáquez, and César Carmona—have given constructive criticism and assistance in numerous ways.

The help of settlers on the colonization projects whose story forms the basis of this study, and who willingly consented—sometimes on two or three occasions—to being interviewed, was sincerely appreciated.

I also thank Msgr. Manuel Larraín, Bishop of Talca, for submitting to Felipe Paúl's and my own questioning.

The rationale behind these interviews and this monograph traces largely to the philosophy of Professor Raymond J. Penn, Director of the Land Tenure Center during its first three years.

Excerpts from this monograph (Chapters 2, 3, 4, 5 and 7) will be available in Spanish in 1967 from the Instituto de Economía, Universidad de Chile, Avenida Condell 343, Casilla 3861, Santiago, Chile.

Two 16mm. color films based on current Land Tenure Center research in Chile are available for rental or purchase. They are *Aspects of Land Tenure in Chile* (forty-six minutes) and *Chile's Experiments in Agrarian Reform* (thirty-two minutes). For details write to Professor Peter Dorner, Director, Land Tenure Center, University of Wisconsin, Madison, Wisconsin 53706.

All translations from Spanish to English have been made by the author unless otherwise noted. A Spanish word is italicized only upon its first use in the monograph.

The reader will find the following conversions useful:

1 US $ = E° 3.25 Chilean *Escudos*—as of 1964 when all conversions were made
1 Hectare = 2.471 Acres
1 *Cuadra* = Approximately 4 Acres
1 Cuadra = 1.5625 Hectares

WILLIAM C. THIESENHUSEN

Santiago, Chile
May 1, 1965

Madison, Wisconsin
December 1, 1965

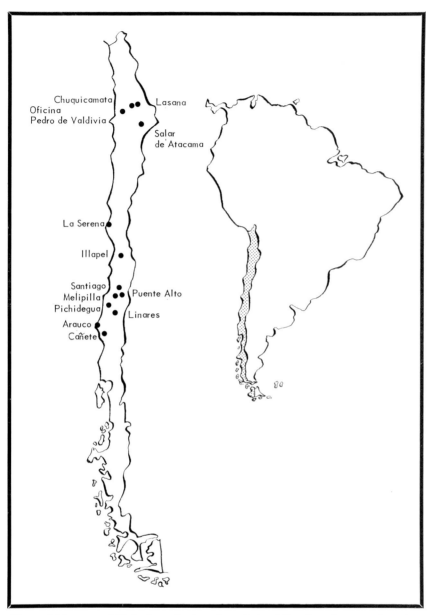

Above. This map of Chile keys the location of the following photographs, taken in February and March 1965, by Professor Fritz Albert, Department of Agricultural Journalism, University of Wisconsin.

Below. Chuquicamata—The world's largest open pit copper mine is found here in the heart of the Atacama desert. Chile is the second largest copper producer in the world. Seventy percent of Chile's export earnings come from her mines; over half comes from copper.

Left. Chuquicamata—This single mine produces more than half of Chile's copper—about 260,000 long tons annually. Locally, there are efforts to require that more refining be done in Chile. Legislation passed in 1966 will allow Chile to buy shares in joint copper corporations that will make her a partner in their operations and a participant in their profits.

Below. Salar de Atacama—In this salt field (*salar*) in Chile's northern desert, no plants can survive. In many areas of northern Chile rainfall has never been recorded. Clouds sweep in from the ocean, but the most they leave behind is a little moisture distilled as dew (*camanchaca*). Over one-third of the country can be classified as desert.

Above. Oficina Pedro de Valdivia—This is a *salitre* or saltpeter mine. During and after World War I a number of processes were developed for the artificial production of nitrogen. This, coupled with the effects of the depression of the 1930's, resulted in a steady decline in the value of Chilean saltpeter. Buoyed up only briefly during World War II and the Korean War, salitre mining, which includes the production of iodine, today accounts for about a sixth of the total value of Chile's export trade. At the turn of the century Chile supplied 67 percent of the world's needs for nitrogen. Today she accounts for only 2 per cent.

Right. La Serena—This family is one of about twenty brought to La Serena in the early 1950's from a then-depressed minifundio area in Italy. One of the major accomplishments of President Gabriel González Videla (1946–52) was the transformation of this beautifully situated coastal city. Slums were cleared, new colonial-style buildings erected, fine schools built, and the Pan-American Highway surfaced through the province of Coquimbo. González Videla also planned the establishment of a "green belt" around La Serena to supply some of its food needs. To bring new farming ideas into the region, González Videla recruited German and Italian farmers to settle here.

Below. Lasana—In the few areas of the Atacama Desert where irrigable bottom land is available, farming is very intensive. The Loa, that waters this land, is the only Andean river in north Chile that does not dry up and disappear before it reaches the west coast. Centuries ago this valley was guarded from attack by Aymará and Quechua Indians who lived in the dry uplands and were invaded by Inca tribes from the north.

Below. Illapel—South of La Serena, valleys begin to open up in which irrigation-by gravity-flow from the melting snow in the Andes is possible. Without this irrigation, all of middle Chile would be almost as dry as the northern desert during the growing season since rainfall is usually confined to several winter months. This farm encompasses about 160,000 hectares, but intensive cropping is possible on about 1,000. The rest of the farm consists of mountainous terrain on which some livestock graze. The area receives an average of less than 10 inches of rainfall annually.

Above. Illapel—Large farms in Chile are usually much larger than "family farms" and are called *fundos* or *haciendas*. About 30 percent of Chile's population live on farms. Many of Chile's farmers are landless wage laborers who live external to fundos (*afuerinos*), resident farm workers (*inquilinos*), or 50–50 sharecroppers (*medieros*). Others own extremely small farms called *minifundios*.

Facing. Santiago—In Santiago a shanty-town settlement of this kind is called a *callampa*, or mushroom. Most of Santiago's callampas are in an outer ring around the city. This one, however, is on Cerro Blanco, a hill near the center of the city overlooking the central cemetery. Some campesinos leave the land in sheer discontent at what seems to be a hopeless future. Others are forced off when landlords mechanize. Few of this disenchanted group find a real future in the city. Santiago's industrial economy is growing very slowly, and the new jobs that it creates require abilities these people cannot offer. Since most are uneducated and have no special skills, they are at the bottom of the labor market and usually must try to find employment in the service sector of the economy.

Above. Illapel—This resident fundo worker, an inquilino, threshes his wheat by spreading it out and running horses over it. The grain is his, not his landlord's. He sowed it, harvested it, and will market or use it. The land on which it was grown was assigned to him by his *patrón* (landowner) and he has borrowed horses to help with the threshing. Chilean inquilinos must work virtually full time for the landlord. But they are assigned a plot of fundo land on which they can tend crops of their own. In addition, in exchange for work, they may get housing, some grazing rights, a small cash wage, and sometimes other perquisites (*regalias*)—a loaf of bread a day, perhaps, or a regular ration of beans.

Right. Santiago—Wine produces about $700,000 a year in foreign exchange for Chile. But most of the wine from this harvest will be consumed in Chile. Excellent wines cost less than a dollar a bottle and wine accompanies the meal for most families that can afford it. Wine-grape production is rigidly controlled in Chile. A grower must have a license for the acreage he wishes to produce; the total authorized acreage is limited and licenses are expensive. This system is intended to give some assurance of quality and price but, in practice, it has also kept the wine industry in the hands of a few landowners.

Left. Puente Alto—Agrarian reform has made almost no visible impact on the enormous problems presented by Chile's traditional fundo system. Yet some exciting and impressive reform experiments have been undertaken. On Los Silos, settlers farm the bulk of the 182-hectare fundo communally. Besides, they have individual *chacras* (corn, beans, and potatoes). This settler and his son maintain vigilance on the herd of dairy cattle that colonists own privately as they graze the communal pasture. The Los Silos project is sponsored by the Instituto de Promoción Agraria (INPROA) which has undertaken to colonize five fundos formerly held by the Chilean Roman Catholic Church.

Above. Puente Alto—Of the sixteen colonists on the Los Silos fundo, eight lived on the farm prior to reform. Although it is communally operated now, it will soon be split into individual farms. By that time colonists will have had some time to gain the managerial experience they lacked when, as inquilinos, they were under the strict surveillance of fundo supervisory personnel.

Left. Puente Alto—Landowners usually live in a centrally located house frequently referred to by fundo workers deferentially in the plural—*"las casas."* It is often at the end of a grove of eucalyptus or poplar trees and surrounded by a garden (called a *parque*). Patrones usually spend a portion of their time on the fundos and part in their residence in town.

Below. Melipilla—Inquilinos often live on hillsides, less usable by farm owners for agriculture. Their standard of living is quite different from that of their landlord and recent studies show that with inflation the value of their meager government-established cash wage is declining in real terms. It is no wonder that pressures for agrarian reform are becoming stronger. Some economists believe that a well-conceived plan of agricultural restructuralization may be absolutely necessary if inelasticities in the supplies of agricultural products are to be remedied in the long run.

Left. Pichidegua—This family is one of seventy-six resettled on the former Church property, Las Pataguas, in O'Higgins Province, administered by the Instituto de Promoción Agraria. A dozen families in this project received subsistence plots of 1 hectare in size. Most families, including this one, were colonized on parcels averaging 16.7 hectares. Once landless, this man is now earning three times what he could expect as a day-laborer. He still faces some severe problems, however. He must pay for his farm and its buildings within twenty years. So far, his farm is simply not producing well enough to meet his annual schedule of payments.

Facing. Pichidegua—The first thing for settlers to learn on Las Pataguas is how to make managerial decisions. A more general reform in Chile would throw this necessity into sharp relief. Many of Chile's landless are farm laborers who do only what the orders handed down from the administrator specify. Men like this need practice in making the dozens of management choices a farmer faces. A cooperative has been organized among all of the colonists at Las Pataguas in hopes of providing credit, management training and technical assistance through a single organization.

Above. Pichidegua—On a fundo near Las Pataguas this inquilino irrigates corn for his landlord. In many cases inquilinos have lived on one fundo all of their lives. Even so, they lack economic incentives to produce more. They usually receive the same wage whether they work hard or, in the words of many interviewed, just "act like we are working when the *mayordomo* (field supervisor) comes around."

Above. Linares—This girl lives on a farm that is part of a Chilean government colonization project. But her father is still landless, a sharecropper for the retired school teacher who received the land as a "colonist." Since the Chilean government's colonization program was started in 1929, it has placed more than 4,000 people on small farms. Until 1962, however, these farms went to people able to pay for them and seldom to the landless. (The girl is baking bread by building a fire above and below an oven made from an old oil drum.)

Above. Linares—A cooperative has been organized on the reformed fundo San Dionisio and members are encouraged to work together on such operations as cleaning grain, shown here. This fundo will eventually support seventy-five colonist families, but in order to control managerial decisions, hold consumption expenditures within limits, and maintain certain other economies of size, it was decided to continue to operate the entire acreage as a single farm for a time. The Instituto de Promoción Agraria arranges for seeding and harvesting and takes half of the remaining crop after these costs are paid. The rest of the crop is shared by the colonists. Settlers may also rent small plots on which to grow sugar beets.

Left. Cañete—This woman is a member of one of the first Araucanian or Mapuche Indian families resettled on new farms outside the reservation by the Chilean Corporación de la Reforma Agraria (CORA). Each family gets between 100 and 225 acres. Only about 15 acres are suitable for crops; the rest are usable only for grazing. Potatoes are a staple of the diet in this region and, for the first years, this family will have little else on the table. It will get a little cash income from grazing the livestock of neighboring farmers on a share basis. These colonists are buying their land and buildings from the government. Only a few Indians have received such farms thus far.

Above. Arauco—These laborers are of Indian ancestry and are employed as harvest help by a non-Indian mediero who farms a fundo in Arauco Province. Much of the land in Arauco is owned by non-Indian "Chilenos"—although the province is usually thought of as Mapuche territory. Even within the general region occupied by Indian reservations (*reducciones*) there are large tracts of good land which are privately owned by Chileans and operated as fundos.

Abstract

THE GENERAL purpose of this study is to analyze four *fundos* (large farms) which formerly belonged to the Church in Chile and comprise the major part of the agrarian reform program of the newly established Instituto de Promoción Agraria. In addition, to put this program in perspective, the study attempts to isolate factors for the success or failure of a number of former sharecroppers or resident fundo laborers who were awarded land twelve or more years ago under the government colonization program of the Caja de Colonización Agrícola.

The study is based on the assumption that, if Chile wants development, it is doubtful whether she can afford to maintain agricultural workers in their present state of poverty and economic nonparticipation. Further, the political situation—a numerically growing and progressively more vocal lower class—makes it unlikely that Chile can stave off reform much longer. The study is predicated on the idea that when a more inclusive reform comes, technicians will be aided by studies of how small-scale reform works.

On the four recently reformed Church farms, the Instituto de

Promoción Agraria has experimented with different tenure forms: a system involving common-land farming; one involving individual family farms; and a system of sharecropping and rental which allows the fields and the irrigation system to be used without subdivision. In all cases organization of a multipurpose cooperative has been given a primary but distinct role. A detailed description of the type of farm organization used is elaborated.

This benchmark study, including the farms' first year or two under reform, shows that some new landowners will have difficulties in making their required yearly land and interest payments. Since reform on Church land is a private effort, land is charged at nearly a commercial rate. Payments are difficult to make because consumption expenditures for the families have increased markedly under reform. Operating costs have also risen, mainly because of labor hired: *campesinos* seem to mimic the system they know best—that of the Chilean fundo. Although the time period examined is short, the study concludes that colonists will have to either lower their consumption for a time or use available family labor more efficiently if necessary payments are to be met. An alternative which involves less sacrifice, however, is to raise production by more intensive farming. By comparing these farms with nearby well-managed but traditionally operated units, there is, it is demonstrated, a margin of unexploited productivity on reformed farms. It can be realized, however, only if proper technical assistance is provided to help new landowners arrive at a more optimum combination of factors.

In detailing cases, the study points out the complexity of reform from the point of view both of the campesinos who have been awarded land and of the administrators of the program. For example, many campesinos under the traditional semifeudal system have never previously had the opportunity to make agricultural decisions.

The Caja program, which awarded land to a very few who were formerly campesinos, offered very little in the way of credit, technical assistance, and even interest in the new landholders. As the years passed, Chile's economy grew slowly and few jobs were open to farmers' sons. Thus families made on-the-farm attempts to accommodate offspring who had few opportunities for alternative employment and few of the skills necessary to take outside jobs even if available. These colonists are living largely at a subsistence level today and income from the parcels has become progressively more subdivided with each passing generation.

The study concludes that land for the campesinos is not a sufficient condition for reform. Physical inputs and education are also necessary if productivity is to be increased.

A section of this monograph features a series of photographs taken in Chile by Professor Fritz Albert, University of Wisconsin, in February and March 1965.

Chile's
Experiments
In Agrarian
Reform

Chapter 1

The encomienda *and the* hacienda *built up an aristocracy which, once the government of Spain was overthrown, stepped into the place vacated by the representatives of the crown and set up a new government in harmony with the existing social order. The common people took virtually no part.*
—Benjamín Subercaseaux. *Chile: A Geographic Extravaganza (Chile: Una Loca Geografía).*

ON NOVEMBER 3, 1964, when Eduardo Frei began his term as the thirty-eighth President of Chile, he admitted, "The situation of the country cannot be more dramatic." In addition to noting that there are heavy interest payments on external debts due—and a growing rate of inflation—he stated, "The nation ought to be told that there is not a single cent in the national treasury to meet November and December payrolls." Frei's campaign was predicated on regenerating his country's stagnant economy. It was no accident that his platform gave a central role to a thorough rejuvenation of the agricultural sector.

THE STATE OF THE AGRICULTURAL SECTOR IN CHILE

There are indications that the plight of agriculture is becoming worse with each passing year. Agricultural productivity cannot keep up with demand, and the sector is contributing progressively less to gross national product even though the number of people engaged in agriculture has remained fairly constant. In 1952, 30.1 percent of

the labor force was engaged in agriculture. By 1960 this percentage
had dropped to 27.5 while, in absolute terms, almost the same number of people were employed as at the beginning of the fifties.[1] In 1952
about 18 percent of the gross national product of the country came
from agriculture. But by 1960 the sector's percentage share in the
gross national product had fallen to 12 or about 6 percent under its
1952 level.[2] Although this could indicate the usual decline in the
relative importance of agriculture in an economy in which other sectors are growing rapidly, in Chile this explanation is not sufficient.

It is extremely difficult to show how much the agricultural sector
has lagged since statistics and measurements of growth vary widely.
One of the most reliable sources of information is probably the Inter-
American Committee for Agricultural Development (CIDA) which
has cited the Ministry of Agriculture and the Corporación de Fomento de la Producción (CORFO, or Chilean Production Development
Corporation) as the source for its conclusion that "during the 15 years
from 1945 to 1959 the cumulative annual rate of growth of the agricultural sector was 1.8 percent while population growth was 2.2 percent."[3]

Assessing the five years from 1955 to 1960, the Ministry of Agriculture states, ". . . while the population of the country grew by 2.7 percent . . . agricultural production grew by 2.29 percent."[4]

During the six-year period from 1958 to 1963 gross national product
grew by an average of 3.1 percent each year,[5] indicating that GNP
is—just barely—keeping up with population increase. Agricultural
production, however, reached a peak of E° 510 million in 1960 and,
from 1960 to 1963, dropped off at an average of 2.3 percent a year,
totalling only E° 475 million in 1963. All other sectors showed a
small average rise during this period.[6]

In addition to undoubtedly adding to the country's high rate of
inflation,[7] growth in internal demand working against an inelastic
food supply adds to Chile's chronic balance of payments difficulties.
Agriculture has not shown a positive export surplus since 1939. From
1935 to 1939 annual net surplus of agricultural products in foreign
trade was US $11.8 million. From 1953 to 1957 annual net deficit of
agricultural products in foreign trade was US $67.8 million. Continu-
ing to trend upward from 1958 to 1963, this annual net deficit averaged US $82.9 million over the five years.

The drag agriculture places on the economy of Chile has been steadily growing. In 1958, 21.9 percent of all Chile's imports and only 10 percent of her exports were attributable to agricultural produce, a deficit of 11.9 percent. This percentage deficit had grown to 19 in 1963 when 25.2 percent of Chile's imports and 6.2 percent of her exports came from agricultural produce.[8]

These indicators—low and decreasing percentage of agriculture's contribution to the gross national product, recent absolute drops in the productivity of the sector, and increasing deficits of agriculture in foreign trade—show that the sector is performing inadequately, probably helping to prevent both stability and development.

IS CHILE CAPABLE OF A DYNAMIC AGRICULTURE?

Perhaps Chile has an inadequate natural resource base and for this reason is unable to produce enough food for her growing population. Although a relatively small part of the country is arable, this does not seem to be the case.

Chile extends for some 2,630 miles along the southwest coast of Latin America. It averages a width of 110 miles and at no place is its eastern frontier more than 250 miles from its western boundary at the Pacific Ocean.

The geographic framework of the country is composed of three roughly parallel units running north and south: the Andes on the east, which gradually decrease in height from north to south; the central plateau of the west; and a depression running between the two (Map I). It is this latter area which, in the middle provinces, is the agricultural heart of the nation—the region of greatest agricultural productivity and highest potential. Santiago, the country's capital, is located here, and middle Chile, between the mountain ranges, is the area of greatest population density. Of this area, Butland states:

This Mediterranean region, particularly the central valley component of it, is the most typical Chilean region. It was from the earliest days of European settlement the nucleus of the nation-to-be, enclosed in its sixteenth-century formative period by desert, ocean, mountain, and forest, fertile in its lands, and blessed with a climate familiar to its Spanish colonists, and favourable to human settlement and progress. For over three centuries this earth-region was Chile for all practical purposes, and the ribbon has only grown northward and southward in the

LEGEND

OVER 10.000 FEET.

600 TO 10.000 FEET.

UNDER 600 FEET.

100   0   200   400   600   MILES

MAP I. Relief Map of Chile.
Source. **CIDA**

last 70 years, until the expansive process has stretched well beyond the tropic and to the last habitable rocks of the continent.[9]

James comments:

The most distinctive feature of middle Chile is the climate. Between Coquimbo at latitude 30 S. and Concepción south of latitude 36 S. there is a transition between the desert of the north and the continuously rainy lands to the south. This is a climate of mild, wet winters and cool, dry summers, to which the name "mediterranean" is commonly applied.[10]

It is its Mediterranean climate—which implies little or no rainfall in the growing season—that makes irrigation an important component of Chile's agriculture (Map II). In summer, the melting snows in the Andes fill rivers which run to the sea at roughly right angles to the central basin. Water is undoubtedly as valuable as land itself. Without irrigation, most of middle Chile would be almost as barren as the mineral-rich northern desert, which is cut only occasionally by a river and contains one of the driest areas of the world.

The part of middle Chile that is not taken up with mountains and plateaus is largely usable for agriculture. Between Santiago and Concepción the intermountain basin is more or less continuous. Further north the valley of the Aconcagua River is cut off from the valley of the Mapocho, where Santiago is located, by a mountain spur. Other rises divide off rich areas of middle Chile from the main basin.

In the rainy third of the country south of the Bío-Bío River (the usual line of demarcation between middle and southern Chile), an area of crop and livestock farming gives way to hardwood forests, which are most dense at the level of the Island of Chiloé. Further south, an archipelagic zone followed by range land appears. The climate in this area becomes progressively more harsh as one nears the Straits of Magellan. Agriculture in this entire southern area is not nearly as important as it is in middle Chile.

Is the relatively small amount of farm land in Chile, usually estimated at about 38 percent of its total area, enough to support agriculture at higher than its present stagnation levels? Considering only natural resources, would it be possible to convert agriculture into a positive force for Chile's economic development? Although a precisely quantifiable response is impossible, nearly every commentator on the Chilean scene has felt that both questions should be answered affirmatively:

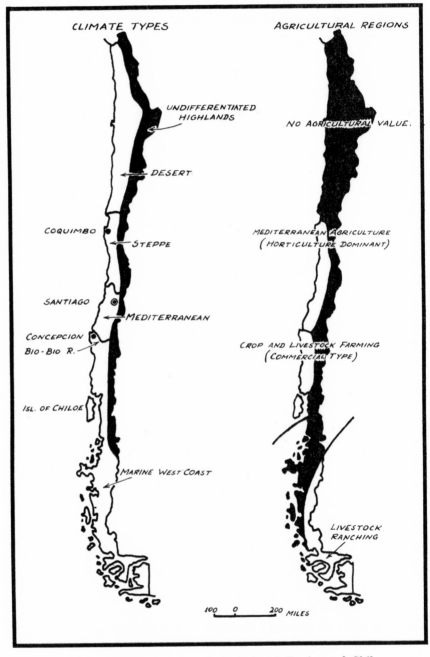

MAP II. Climate Types and Agricultural Regions of Chile.
Source. CIDA

The level of agricultural development in Chile is so low that to raise it should not be difficult. Chile has an adequate resource base in agriculture if not compared with the United States. It has an abundance of arable land per inhabitant when compared with other areas of the world including most of the western hemisphere.[11]

Bray, likewise, has concluded:

Moreover, the natural resource endowment of the country seems to be adequate to support a population much larger than the present 7.5 million and at higher levels of living.[12]

In a footnote, he continues this argument:

The United Kingdom, for example, has a comparable area of arable land of probably poorer average quality, a less advantageous climate for agriculture and yet produces about 40 percent of the food requirements of 50 million inhabitants. This would appear to be about 3 times the volume of Chilean output, without specifying the composition of product in value terms.[13]

Along the same lines, Kaldor states:

There can be little doubt that the combination of natural and human resources of the country—its climate and geology, its mineral resources as well as the potential fertility of its soil, the natural vitality and intelligence of its population derived from a combination of strains of European stock which in the similar climatic but different social environment of North America produced spectacular results—are as favorable, if not more favorable, than that of the economically most developed nations of the globe.[14]

The Corporación de Fomento de la Producción has asserted that "between 1945 and 1959 Chile imported farm and livestock products valued at US $1,220,000,000." Of this, it estimated that US $790,000,000 or about 65 percent could have been produced domestically.[15] Dorner noted that "at the 1960 level of imports, this rate of import substitution would result in an annual saving of approximately US $75,000,000. This implies an increase in production of from 15 to 20 percent."[16]

There seems to be little doubt that production rises of 15 to 20 percent are perfectly feasible in the short run. Morales calculates that productivity for an area of O'Higgins Province which he studied could be raised 30 to 40 percent.[17] CIDA concluded that in the irrigated area of the country between Santiago and Cautín, 479,536 hectares or 44.1 percent of the total number of irrigated hectares— in one of Chile's richest agricultural areas—was devoted to natural pasture. It concluded that this represented underutilization of land, "because natural pasture maintains only .5 animals per hectare per year while artificial pasture is capable of supporting from 1.5 to 2 animals."[18] This says nothing about possible uses of this acreage in intensive crops for which much of the land is admirably suited.

THE STRUCTURE OF CHILEAN AGRICULTURE

To attempt to determine reasons for agriculture's present stagnation—or even retrogression—in the face of adequate resources, we must turn to the structure of Chile's agriculture. Who owns or controls the factors of production which must be used if production is to rise? How, generally, is agriculture organized?

In Chile a small group controls a large part of the land riches of the country. Sternberg notes:

The concentration of land ownership in Chile is among the highest in the world. In 1955, 4.4 percent of Chilean landholders owned approximately 80.9 percent of the total farm land, 77.7 percent of the agricultural land, 51.5 percent of the arable land, and 43.8 percent of the irrigated land.[19]

Powelson points out that in Chile there are 3,250 farms over 1,000 hectares each, making up 75 percent of the land in the country.[20] Sternberg concludes that Chile appears to have the highest degree of land concentration among countries of the Western Hemisphere.[21] Pointing up the minifundio problem, he continues:

On the other end of the scale, 36.9 percent of the holdings contained roughly 0.3 percent of the total farm land, 0.3 percent of the agricultural land, and 2.3 percent of the irrigated land.[22]

The control over resources and the resultant control over laborers by a relatively small class in Chile is best illustrated by a description of the land tenure system implied in the above statistics. In Chile the traditional system of land tenure is still pretty much intact. The structure consists of a small number of very large farms, a large number of very small ones, and an increasing number of landless workers. Before we detail the organization of Chilean agriculture today, a brief description of the historic development of this system is in order.

Historic Development. The bulk of the land in Chile with highest productivity and greatest potential is owned as large estates which are both large properties and large enterprises.[23]

In the New World the latifundia of the twentieth century can be traced to several colonial institutions: *encomiendas,* trusts whereby the Crown granted to a conqueror the right of tributes of an Indian community in exchange for certain benefits; and *mercedes* or *estancias,* direct grants of land. Both were given by the king, usually in his name through his authorized representatives in the colonies: the governor, the town council, or the conquerors themselves. Since the Spanish colonists had no intention of farming or mining personally, land grants without Indian labor were nearly worthless. For that reason some land grants were given near the encomiendas.[24] In other cases, although it was legally prohibited, colonists moved the Indians they had been assigned nearer to their mercedes or estancias.

Relationships of the *encomendero* with Indians in his charge were largely feudal. Indians were to have the right of peaceful occupation of their land. Their obligations or tributes usually consisted of giving up a certain amount of their produce and devoting time to labor in the mines. Encomenderos, in return, had to pay taxes, maintain bridges and roads in their domain, concern themselves with the religious training of the Indians, and be prepared for military service.[25]

Although encomiendas were not meant as land grants, encomenderos came to think that they owned not only the service of the Indians, but all the land they occupied. Indians, since they were accustomed to communally held property, did not really understand the meaning of private ownership. All they wanted was the right to work the land and collect the usufruct as before. They felt the technicalities of possession of little importance.

The crown tried to rectify the inherent abuses of this system by sending a surveyor to Chile to review all land titles in 1603. Those owners holding too much territory would have to return the excesses to the Indians. The crown also attempted to govern the working conditions of the native population, which subsequently got worse as demand for labor increased. These efforts from Spain largely failed. Land was neither returned to Indians nor were working conditions improved. The authorities in Spain were too far away, and their representatives in Chile who were beneficiaries of the new system were understandably unwilling to stem the tide.

By the time the labor laws were decreed, landless laborers were already very much a part of the system. Indeed, as McBride states:

The colonists loudly proclaimed that they could not possibly occupy the land and maintain themselves there except by means of the forced labor of Indians. Chileans of the present day, although condemning the severity with which the first Chileans were treated by their conquerors, readily admit that only through some such method could settlements have been established and the country brought under exploitation. It was taken for granted then, and still is, that white men could never have done the work themselves, and could hardly have been expected to do so.[26]

In effect, the shadow of the encomienda "has remained as an implied system of territorial authority until the present day."[27]

Even so, the encomienda system did not function as smoothly in Chile as in many other Latin American countries. Although fewer in number, the Araucanian Indians (now also called "Mapuche" which is the language they speak), who occupied most of the southern part of middle Chile, were much more hostile to Spanish advances than other tribes to the north. For one hundred years after Pedro de Valdivia founded Santiago in 1541, the Spanish and the Araucanians were in constant warfare. Violent attacks broke out from time to time after that even though a treaty had been signed recognizing the Bío-Bío River, at the southern extreme of middle Chile, as the northern limit of Mapuche territory.

Supplies of natives, who were increasingly needed as labor demands grew, diminished as they fled south to avoid persecution and slavery. Furthermore, most of the tribes of middle Chile, unlike many of the Indians of northern South America, were not accustomed to dwelling in permanent farming villages.[28] They lived in temporary shelters for a time, farmed a piece of land until it was depleted, and then moved on. Problems of extracting tribute from them became increasingly great as colonization proceeded. Thus the belligerence of the Araucanians, the low initial number of Indians in the central zone, and their nomadic existence tended to frustrate the encomienda in Chile.

When in 1791 the crown finally succeeded in abolishing the encomienda in Chile, there were few of them left. The *hacienda* and its subdivision known as the fundo had already evolved from the colonial institutions.

Upon legal abolition of the encomienda, another institution served to maintain large estates: entail (*vinculación*), the most important legal doctrine of which was primogeniture (*mayorazgo*).

In Chile, as in most of Latin America, the revolution against Spain can hardly be considered a social revolution. It merely substituted creole for Spanish rule. Once independent, whether to maintain primogeniture became a major issue. The revolutionary hero Bernardo O'Higgins abolished it in 1818. This and his other attempts at reform which would have reduced the privilege of the aristocracy contributed to his downfall as leader of the new republic. Primogeniture was restored again, not to be finally done away with until laws were passed in 1852 and 1857.

Even the abolition of primogeniture did not bring about any large-scale division of land. Indeed in 1880 " . . . the concentration of land, in one sense, was at maximum, that is, fewer people owned the land of Chile than ever before or since."[29]

After 1875 and through the first third of the twentieth century, acreage used for agriculture doubled and irrigated acreage tripled in response to demands for agricultural products by expanding mining centers in northern Chile, by growing internal commercial centers, and by presently developed foreign countries which were not then self-sufficient in staples.

Felix has noted that the fundo showed a fair degree of adaptability to changing market stimuli while products demanded were "land extensive and required modest technical competence."[30] Since untilled land was available, agricultural expansion in the nineteenth century was relatively easy as the population spilled into the heretofore forested region south of the Bío-Bío and European colonists entered the area around Valdivia. These movements were facilitated after the War of the Pacific (in which Chile earned many of its mineral riches), when in 1883 soldiers were sent from the north to finally pacify the Indians in the southern region. But with few exceptions this settlement was accompanied by little increase in yield per acre.

Grain prices turned downward from 1873 to 1896 and the scope for easy extensive expansion began to disappear. Grain tended to compete with pasture land and rather than increasing per-acre yields on land already in grain, pastures were converted into cultivated fields. By the first decade of the twentieth century, the size of herds in the entire central zone had levelled off; numbers of livestock reported by the 1935–36 agricultural census were slightly below that of the 1907 census.[31] By 1964 there were only 10 percent more live-stock than in 1936. Livestock (which contributes just under about half of the agricultural output each year) was the weakest segment of the agricultural sector.[32]

The expansion of crop acreage, however, more than doubled from 1910 until the mid-1930's, when it also ceased; but the expansion was partly offset by a 20 percent decline in yields per hectare for the major grains and beans. This seems to have been the combined result of relatively constant yields on the rich valley lands and the extension of cultivation onto forested slopes in the south Central Zone—where, after a few plantings, soil leaching and erosion tended to set in.[33]

Yet until 1930, agricultural production per capita rose and net agricultural exports showed only a slight downward trend. There was some shift from livestock into dairy, but intensification through artificial pasture spread slowly. Viniculture expanded until the 1930's when vine growers established a licensing system for lands on which grapes were to be grown for wine. And mixed agriculture "made only minor inroads into the dominance of extensive grain-cattle farming."[34] Apparently the nitrate and copper booms and intermittent inflation cushioned the blow to Chilean agriculture. The burden of taxation was shunted to the mining sector and irrigation facilities for agriculture were financed out of the public coffers. This relieved landlords of many of the costs of bringing new land under the plow. But with the mineral-boom collapse, the sorry plight of agriculture was revealed. Between the mid-thirties and the mid-fifties, yield per acre increased 20 percent.[35] But this was inadequate to support the burgeoning rate of population growth and not comparable to the "yield-per-acre takeoff" in presently developed countries when expansion of agriculture onto new lands became impossible.[36] In fact, this increase in productivity merely made up for losses in the early decades of the century when agriculture was moving onto progressively more marginal lands. Thereafter, agricultural output per capita in Chile began its precipitous fall.

Meanwhile, subdivision of large estates proceeded slowly. In 1934 Cox wrote:

In respect to landholding, Chile is far from making substantial progress. In 1928 some 513 persons, less than one half of one percent of all the landholders, were reported to own 60 percent of the land in private hands; two and a half percent of all landed proprietors possessed 78 percent of the arable land.[37]

Besides the splitting of haciendas into fundos, division of holdings took another form—the most important, considering numbers involved. Small pieces of what was usually poorest quality fundo land were splintered off and sold largely to agricultural workers. Upon transfer of these properties, fundo owners assured themselves of a more or less permanent labor supply for which they would have no direct maintenance responsibilities. Largely because of this creation of minifundios, an index relating the percentage of owners to the percentage of land by size of holding shows that the concentration of land increased rather than decreased through fragmentation, at least to 1954.[38]

The Organization of Chilean Agriculture Today. In addition to the *minifundistas*[39] who serve large landholders by being a ready source of labor (their own plots are frequently too small to allow them to earn a living, especially since these holdings—or at least the incomes from them—are often subdivided with each generation), other landless groups make up the agricultural working force in Chile. Landholders and their families seldom work their farms personally without assistance. Indeed, they could not. As we have already implied, fundos are usually too large and are not "family units" in any sense of the term.

The rural laborer and the landholder are divided by great social distance and economic means. The working class in Chilean agriculture makes up about 87 percent of the active agricultural population and receives about 34 percent of the income from agriculture.[40] This is a lesser percentage than that received by working classes in Chilean cities.[41] While the bulk of the rural laboring group—especially those with no specialized training or supervisory responsibilities—live in penury and suffer from a lack of education and social services, landlords frequently live well. Many of them apply little of their skill to their property, living most of the year in town, while technical matters are left to a trusted administrator. Land, with some exceptions of course, serves them as a hedge against inflation rather than as a factor of production.

On the demand side of the market, the landlord is also criticized for contributing little to Chile's economy. Aníbal Pinto Santa Cruz, noted Chilean economist, has asserted:

. . . the demand of the landlords, like that of other upper class groups, is geared to luxury imports. . . . The market for consumers' goods is already narrow. This element [demanding luxury goods], together with the quantitative limitation of the agricultural sector [its slowness to grow] . . . puts a large barrier in the path of the growth of domestic industries.[42]

Along these lines, it was claimed by Kaldor that if the upper-income groups had the same consumption pattern as their counterparts in the more advanced countries, the savings rate could be doubled.[43] Adding evidence to this assertion, Sternberg, who studied a small group of Chilean landlords, generalized:

The largest landowners in the Central Valley—owning half of the farm land—save and invest half the percentage of their income than [sic] similar groups in the developed nations. The large landholder consumes over 60 percent of his disposable income, 75 percent of which goes for luxury consumption. Twenty-five percent or more of his consumption expenditures are for imported products.[44]

A developing economy can depend no more on those who spend their earnings out of the country and yet demand domestic items with few internal multiplier effects than on those at subsistence levels. We shall turn, briefly, to the laboring groups in Chilean agriculture.

Fundo labor is composed of *afuerinos*, laborers who do not live on the fundo; resident farm labor; and *medieros*, who may or may not live on the fundo.

Resident labor is hierarchically ranged including the *inquilinos* at the bottom of the ladder, followed by those workers with varying degrees of specialization or supervisory responsibility called *empleados*, all the way to the highest fundo empleado, the administrator.

The term inquilino, while it means "renter" in Spanish, has a unique meaning in Chile. An inquilino is a resident laborer who, in addition to a small cash wage, is given the use of a house and usually a small piece of land for growing crops of his choice. If the plot is watered, the inquilino may grow spring-planted row crops such as corn, potatoes, squash, and beans—collectively called *chacra*. The inquilino is usually also given a small piece of land near his house (most often used for growing vegetables if it is watered) called a *cerco*. He may also receive other perquisites (*regalías*) such as several loaves of bread, a plate of cooked beans at noon, the privilege to pasture a certain number of animals, firewood, etc.

In return, inquilinos usually work all day—six days a week—on the landlord's fundo.[45] They often work on their chacras or cercos on Sundays or on some specified holidays. Frequently, grown sons of inquilinos also work, receiving a higher percentage of their wage in cash. The inquilino himself is usually called the *obligado*—the obligated one. He is responsible for performing his work requirement himself or, in cases where his *patrón* (landlord) allows it, sending a substitute.

Total minimum remuneration for agricultural workers—afuerinos and resident laborers—is set each year by the government as is the percentage of the wage that must be paid in cash. There are some indications that minimum wages in agriculture have eroded recently. Expressed in 1960 Escudos, the minimum was E° .99 in 1953–54, while in 1960–61 it was E° .62.[46] It has been estimated that even if an inquilino were to spend between 70 and 80 percent of his cash income on food, he could not provide the minimum nutritional standards for himself and his family.[47]

Whether *inquilinaje* (the labor system which uses inquilinos) is a lineal descendent of the encomienda system or not is currently an open question. Gay, a mid-nineteenth-century French scholar and prolific chronicler of Chilean history, traces the inquilino to Indians who, after abolition of the encomienda, did not have the economic power to transform themselves into free agents. Preferring to work for their old masters rather than to embark on the unknown, they remained on haciendas, and inquilinaje developed.[48] Diego Barros, writing a few years later, agrees that inquilinaje is the last transformation of the encomienda. But he adds the fact that the Indians soon became "mestisized" by intermarriage with the whites.[49]

Current evidence seems to be on the side of Góngora,[50] however, who claims that former theories which linked inquilinaje to the encomienda were wrong. After an exhaustive study of early Jesuit records and the archives of the *Real Audiencia* and the *Capitania General,* as well as other documents, he traces the modern-day inquilino to a group of "poor Spaniards," itinerant Indians from the north (*yanaconas*), and others who arrived with the conquerors. Up through the conquest, this group had lived from the fruits of war. But after winning middle Chile for the Crown, the only remaining duty for soldiers who wished to continue fighting was battling the fierce Mapuche Indians in rainy and forested Arauco or Valdivia.

Since this alternative was unattractive, and since the demand for soldiers was now more limited than previously, the majority of this group was incorporated into the rural scene in middle Chile. Some became hired agricultural workers. But the majority settled on "loaned" land on the extremes of large properties. They did not need to pay a rent since land was nearly a "free good" at the time. As land values rose slightly, this settlement was encouraged since colonists could return the obligation of guarding property boundaries for the privilege of land occupancy. By the time of their establishment on the fringes of large farms, most of these people were already mestisized. Only a very few were pure Indian.

With further settlement, land became more scarce and, hence, more valuable. More work, such as assistance at rodeos, was required of renters in addition to the usual chores of vigilance. In the eighteenth century, wheat trade with Peru encouraged a more intensive cropping pattern, and from Aconcagua to Colchagua, land prices rose. Work obligations increased proportionally as more labor internal to the hacienda was needed.

At this time, collection of cash rents also became more common. Most rents were valued in pesos, but paid in kind or work. Only on northern dry-land areas where inquilinos were especially far from the center of operations did they maintain a degree of autonomy. In the central zone they became thoroughly dominated by their patrones.

During the conquest, all conquerors from servants and simple soldiers right up through the ranks were united in military camaraderie. This group considered itself to be of much higher status than the Indians who were to be conquered. But, with rising land values, agrarian aristocracy soon substituted for the *camaradería de la conquista.* And at the end of the eighteenth century the terms *"arrendatario"* and "inquilino," used interchangeably before, separated meanings. Arrendatario became any cash renter on the farm or in the city and implied a social and economic status much higher than any inquilino.

Fundos may also employ medieros. A mediero is a sharecropper working on halves who often farms a different plot on the fundo each year. In the central zone of Chile, medieros usually contribute all of the labor and half of the seeds, fertilizer, and some other operating costs. The patrón, who owns the land, may contribute the tilled soil, the remainder of the inputs, and living expenses and operating credit necessary for the mediero until the crop is harvested. Physical product is divided 50–50 so that the mediero can either sell his product elsewhere or keep it for his own use.

Management is the responsibility of the mediero even though the patrón may share in important decisions such as what crops are to be grown and quality and quantity of fertilizer. There are many variations of this system (as there are of inquilinaje) as one moves from one part of middle Chile to another and even from fundo to fundo. (In Chapter 5 we will discuss a specific case.)

The mediero who lives outside the fundo may be migratory, accepting *medias* on one fundo in one year and on another in the second.

The inquilino-mediero works under this same general system but always lives on the fundo. He usually retains all of the responsibilities of an inquilino and uses *mediería* to supplement his income and absorb the extra labor of his family. He is often given poorest fundo land for sharecropping—land that the patrón might not ordinarily use. In general, the production of the inquilino-mediero is less oriented to the market than that of the non-resident sharecropper. While the inquilino-mediero enjoys the benefits of the social security system which covers agricultural workers, the non-resident mediero is considered an entrepreneur in his own right and does not have these benefits.[51]

The fundo, because of its sheer size and high labor requirement, may be very complex in its organization. Again we admit to many possible variations, but, risking some accuracy, will concentrate on describing the general organization on a typical large fundo. While labor may be supplied by afuerinos, resident laborers (who are collectively, with the exception of the obligados, called *voluntarios*), and outside medieros, supervision and technical help is provided by a staff of empleados. The administrator may have an assistant if the farm is especially large and/or a *mayordomo mayor,* through whom his orders are transmitted. On a lower level there are usually several mayordomos in charge of crops on various sectors of the fundo. On the same supervisory level as the mayordomo is the *capataz,* in charge of the livestock, to whom the *vaqueros* (cowboys) report. Mayordomos and capataces usually supervise workers in their charge from horseback.

Fundo buildings are usually centrally located, and working out of this nucleus in the farm's granaries, machine shops, storehouses, and office may be mechanics (*mecánicos*), smiths (*herreros*), tractor drivers (*tractoristas*), warehouse or granary tenders (*bodegueros*), handimen (*maestros*), a bookkeeper-paymaster (*cajero*)—even a baker if the farm offers bread as a perquisite. The *llavero,* or key-keeper, supervises the distribution of supplies.

The service staff of the patrón also works out of the nucleus of the fundo. The patrón lives in a centrally located house frequently referred to by fundo workers deferentially in the plural—*las casas.* It is often at the end of a grove of eucalyptus or poplar trees and surrounded with a garden (called a *parque*). The patrón may hire a housekeeper, cook, gardener, and chauffeur. Of course, a separate service staff is needed if the patrón maintains another house in town.

All of the fundo *empleados,* as the *inquilinos,* are usually paid part of their salaries in kind and part in cash.

The Chilean fundo is a community in itself, perhaps a more basic social, economic, and political unit than the country village. Usually there is a school on the fundo—or on a nearby fundo. The fundo operator may pay for the school construction while the central government pays the teacher. There is often a chapel on the fundo and a priest (usually called the *capellán* or chaplain), who is paid by the patrón and who may come to say Mass once or twice a month. A few fundo operators even operate their own store called a *pulpería,* for the benefit of "their people." A doctor and maybe even a dentist may visit the fundo regularly. One commentator has noted:

The hacienda is not just an agricultural property owned by an individual. The hacienda is a society, under private auspices. It is an entire system and governs the life of those attached to it from the cradle to the grave. It encompasses economics, politics, education, social activities, and industrial development.[52]

As the "company store" becomes less common on fundos, this statement is becoming less true in Chile. But although villages are evolving, they are doing so at a slow rate since the subsistence level at which campesinos live discourages merchant and professional service investment, and in-kind payments and lack of alternative employment opportunities tie the poorly educated workers to the economy of the fundo. Landlords generally do not use services of villages but travel to cities instead.

In some cases workers have lived on the fundo all of their lives. Even so, they lack economic incentives to produce more—they usually receive the same wage whether they work hard or, in the words of many interviewed, just "act like we are working when the mayordomo comes around."

Over the years some safeguards for fundo workers have been built into the system which probably make their situation a little better than that of their counterparts in many other Latin American countries. Inquilinos were given full juridical freedom in the latter half of the nineteenth century. Debt peonage in the prerevolution Mexican sense is uncommon. In addition, a minimum wage has been established (albeit it has declined in real terms in recent years and is not always paid); a provision for paying a percentage of the inquilino's salary in cash has been instituted to make the system less "feudal" (paradoxically, however, with inflation so rampant, some preference has been expressed by inquilinos for in-kind payment);[53] and the length of time before an unsatisfactory inquilino may be discharged has risen from eight days[54] to two months.

Furthermore, farm workers are migrating to cities at roughly the rate of population increase. This appears to be due partially to city attractions and somewhat to the adoption of labor-saving machinery by a few landlords. Duty breaks and some exchange rate advantages for such importation have been granted by the government in some years. In cities, however, campesinos are frequently unable to find productive employment in the slow-growing industrial sector (in which their poor preparation hardly equips them to compete for the jobs that are available). Those who move cityward may live in slums (callampas), which belt and pepper all major cities, and find employment—usually partial—in the rapidly growing tertiary sector of the economy. There, they use their meager wages to exacerbate still further the internal demand for food.

The rural laborer, perhaps more so than his city counterpart, faces a system that discriminates against him, making the possibility that he can effectively countervail his landlord by group action difficult.

The educational system is one example. Even though the school system has expanded lately, facilities—both private and public—are nowhere near demand. The result is that access to schooling is granted to those relatively well-off, and education has not increased social mobility or performed a task of democratic equalization. Out of one hundred students who enroll in first grade, only thirty reach secondary levels and no more than 9 percent reach the university. One percent finally receive their university degree.[55]

Because public education is free and facilities inadequate, there is a strong pressure to fail students in year-end exams to help relieve congestion. Even when they could continue, families in lower classes are often not able to purchase the uniforms and books plus pay for transportation to the oftentimes distant schools. This tendency, of course, is accentuated in rural areas where schools are farther from dwellings; where incomes are, on the average, lower than in town; and where children are considered an economic resource. Yet country people value at least a modicum of education very highly. This author has visited areas of Chile where families regularly deny themselves certain meals and use resultant savings to pay the bus fare to send their children to school.

Furthermore, city private schools—primary and secondary—offer a better education than public institutions, as a general rule. Thus, those who have means (and time to capitalize on connections to convince recalcitrant administrators that their children should be enrolled) are more apt to be granted admission.

To receive their high school diploma (*bachiller*), and, hence, be granted admission to a university (publicly or Church supported and requiring very low tuition), all students, be they educated in private or public secondary institutions, must pass a state-administered, standardized examination. Those who have been educated in private institutions are less apt to fail (or when they do, have more leisure time in which to make up their failure) and are more apt to be able to take advantage of highly subsidized institutions of higher learning.

Those who receive highest scores on their *bachillerato* exam—again those who undoubtedly have been educated in private institutions—are most likely to be skimmed off by schools such as medicine, law, and engineering, professions traditionally occupied by Chile's elite. Thus the privilege of those already rich is reinforced through the school system.

Less than 2 percent of university students are of working-class origin and these are found in the less traditional fields.[56] The number of

working-class university students who come from rural areas is min-
iscule. An important part of President Frei's campaign platform
dealt with correcting these educational inequities.

Another example of discrimination is in labor organization. In
1960, about 15 percent of all laborers in Chile were members of
trade unions; under 1 percent of Chilean agricultural laborers were
organized. One reason for the difference is that while the Chilean
labor law (*Código del Trabajo*) makes industrial and professional
trade unionization difficult, it makes agricultural labor organization
well-nigh impossible.

The dual standard finds its historic roots in the election of 1920
which put Arturo Alessandri in the presidency:

With the election of 1920 . . . political power in the nation as a whole passed
from the rural landlords to the city. However, Alessandri was only allowed to
come into office as the result of a tacit agreement that the landlords be left un-
touched. This meant that there would be no attempt at agrarian reform, and
that the government would not allow the organization of agricultural workers
into unions.[57]

After a bitter congressional fight, the social laws forming the basis
of the present Código were approved on September 8, 1924. With
additions to date, the social-labor legislation was codified in 1931.[58]
As it is enacted by Congress and signed into law, labor legislation is
amended to the Código. Some stipulations of the labor law are common to all workers in Chile. But key sections of the code treat only
agricultural workers. Articles 75–82 deal mainly with agricultural
contracts and Articles 418–93 aim to control the organization of
agricultural trade unions.[59]

The major legal inhibitions against agricultural trade unions
are:[60]

(1) Violating the International Labor Organization (ILO) Convention (which Chile has signed), Article 426 states that agricultural
trade unions can be organized only if all members live on the same
farm. Article 431 specifically prevents federating several *sindicatos*.
These provisions supersede Articles 365–66 which allow workers to
unionize depending on their industry or profession. And federation
for purposes of education or mutual assistance is permitted for industrial unions (Article 386). Government and municipal workers
may not join unions, however (Article 368, Regulation 1030, Section 58).

(2) According to Article 418, the part of the statute which protects union officers from being fired without legal cause (Titles I, II, and III of Book II) does not apply to agricultural workers. This is again contrary to the ILO Convention.

(3) Article 433 states that agricultural trade unions may be organized on properties having more than twenty workers who are over eighteen years of age with more than one year of consecutive service on the same farm and who represent at least 40 percent of the workers on the fundo. At least ten workers must know how to read and write.

Twenty-five members are necessary before an industrial union can be organized (Article 384), but the higher number is not as exclusive as for smaller agricultural enterprises which may unionize only within the farm boundaries. In industrial unions 55 percent of the workers in the industry or enterprise must be represented in any union that is constituted (Article 385), but only the five officers need to be able to read and write (Article 376).

Referring to the above restriction to the organization of agricultural trade unions, one study concludes:

> . . . two-thirds of the campesinos work on fundos where there are less than 20 workers . . . in order to form a *Sindicato de Campesinos* these 20 must have more than one year of consecutive service on the same fundo. Permanent workers represent only a part of the total personnel on the fundo, so although during certain seasons more than 20 workers are actually working, it still is impossible to establish a sindicato. With this stipulation the workers eligible to belong to a union, which, as we have indicated, may be a third of all workers, is again diminished. Of the 100,000 workers who might organize themselves into sindicatos, maybe one half or 50,000 are seasonal workers.[61]

Troncoso, a Chilean labor lawyer, noted that because of the twenty-member requirement, the legal organization of labor unions is prevented on 96 percent of the fundos in the country. And provision that at least ten of the workers joining an agricultural union must be able to read and write halves the 4 percent of the farms on which unions can be organized. Even this assumes that all workers on fundos are over eighteen years of age, which they undoubtedly are not.[62]

(4) Right to strike (established in Book IV, Title II, Article 627) does not apply to agricultural workers (Article 469). One impediment to an agricultural strike is given in Article 470 which states that petitions of complaint can be presented only once a year and not during seeding or harvest season. The "time of seeding or har-

vest" is determined by zonal inspectors and cannot be less than sixty days for each. Substituting for the strike privilege given to other trade unions, Article 482 states, "If all attempts to conciliate fail, a [Special Conciliation and Arbitration] Commission will arbitrate."

Government recognition of unions is dependent on a complicated procedure which probably discourages even some of those which meet all legal requirements. Legal personality is obtained through registration and the publication of a decree signed by the Minister of Labor. This procedure has been called "one of the longest and most unnecessary procedures now operative in the Chilean Public Administration. It literally takes months to obtain official recognition."[63] The conclusion of both studies referred to is that the law be radically changed.[64]

The current Christian Democratic government has promised to "repeal or leave without effect, the present agricultural trade union law and establish legislation which promotes free regional and national unions...."[65]

It is too early to tell whether the Christian Democrats will be able to live up to their promise. But after the Presidential elections of 1964 the government made it clear that all petitions of complaint on such matters as landlords who were not paying minimum wages would be heard by the local representatives of the Minister of Labor, regardless of the state of the law. Previously, functionaries of the Ministry merely turned a deaf ear when they found that complaints were emanating from an illegal but de facto union. One of the most dramatic early effects of the Frei government was the spate of agricultural union-management disputes in 1965. Many of them seemed to be resolved in favor of the workers, even though the law had not been changed.

Factors other than the oppressive nature of the law have been responsible for campesino group movements not being effective in Chile while they seem to have been in Mexico, Bolivia, Cuba, and even Venezuela.[66] Undoubtedly the heterogeneous nature of agriculture, coupled with the stratified social structure, has been importantly responsible. It should be recognized that differing interests of laborers stem from their varied land tenure status. This fact will always make their agreement on specific agricultural policies difficult.

But if the *Código del Trabajo* were changed, at least the first step toward correcting the inequities that rural labor currently faces could be taken. As we have seen, legislation, made or substantially influenced by landlords, is calculated to reduce trade unions to "isolated bodies which represent neither an occupational force nor a weapon to defend the interests of the rural workers."[67]

Even though the patrón delegates responsibilities, it is he who holds the power in the system. This relationship, a landlord with "his people," is the epitome of paternalism. (On a national level it is manifest as "state paternalism.")[68] The patrón protects but also dominates and makes decisions. The labor supply is largely held to the fundo by lack of viable alternative opportunities, education, and tradition.

It is this system that has stamped itself indelibly upon the society of Chile, its laws, and its institutions. The new industrial and banking oligarchies have been accommodated within the upper class and even the growing socio-economic middle group in the cities seems firmly committed to a two-class society.[69] This "middle class"—salaried and white-collar workers, professionals, government workers, and sometimes even certain higher-level laboring groups—does not seem to act as if it had a common, identified interest as a class. The majority in this group seems to aspire to and identify with the upper class. As such, the middle elements do not perform the functions a similar class served in nineteenth-century Europe or North America. They have not spearheaded reforms which would tend to draw the "submerged masses"—the rural and urban lower class—into the greater society. Rather, allied with the upper class, they have favored the status quo.[70]

Pike carries this point further, asserting:

Frequently, middle groups have committed themselves more passionately than the upper to preserving the gulf between those who guide and benefit from the course of natural development, and those who are supposed to accept and suffer from it with resignation.[71]

In an article quoting some Chilean scholars, Pike and Bray note:

Jorge Gustavo Silva observes: ". . . in whatever profession they enter, middle class elements seek to obscure their humble origins and to convert themselves, even at the risk of appearing ridiculous, into aristocrats and oligarchs" ("Nuestra Evolución Político-Social," 1931, p. 100). The renowned Chilean novelist, Pedro Prado ("Un Juez Rural," "Alsino," etc.) is noted for his anti-middle class sentiments, arising from convictions that this class has turned on the humbler elements of Chilean society. Nearly every Chilean author, in fact, who has concerned himself with middle class–upper class relations has detected the same tendency.[72]

CHANGE: ANALYSIS, PREDICTIONS, AND PRECURSORS

That the structure we have briefly described must and will change has been postulated again and again. In a letter to Francisco Bilbao, Santiago Arcos said, as early as 1852:

In order to make our country prosperous, it is necessary to first improve the situation of the people by giving human status to those who now work as if they were farm tools for the powerful landlords.[73]

McBride, writing about three decades ago, saw reform as imminent:

No superficial reforms can long retard the movement. Only a fundamental modification of the hacienda-inquilino system seems capable of saving the country . . . change is inevitable.[74]

In 1945 Ellsworth added:

The chief obstacle [to agricultural development] appears to be the influence of the easy-going tradition of the hacienda, which continues to dominate farming in the most productive area of the country. This obstacle is gradually being worn down. . . . Progress, however, is very slow and it is doubtful if it can become sufficiently rapid without great changes in Chile's landholding system.[75]

Still, however, there was no basic change, and more recently Pike has noted:

Why has the situation in Chile become so critical? Basically, I think that the reason is that Chile has clung to a set of values associated with a rapidly disappearing way of life. The cardinal feature of this way of life is a socio-political structure based on paternalism and on the perpetual existence of a participating, privileged minority that is served by a non-participating, non-privileged majority.[76]

Contemporary Chilean intellectuals are not without participation in the discussion which, as Keller realizes, has political implications:

Until 1958 the fundo and hacienda workers had always voted for the candidates which their patrones had chosen for them and these workers were always considered part of the inventory of the latifundia that would assume the politics of the landowner. In 1958, however, there was a rebellion of campesinos who voted against the candidate of the patrones for the candidate of the extreme left. Because of this, the latifundia in Chile have been transformed into a political problem.[77]

In the 1964 presidential elections an even higher percentage of the voters than in 1958 opted for the extreme left. By this time, however, as we shall see in the next chapter, the entire political spectrum seems to have moved leftward. This seems to indicate that although the staying power of the privileged class in Chile has been consistently underestimated, its power may be eroding. That many have enunciated the necessity of change that has not come about seems to indicate again that reform of traditional institutions is not initially a social or economic question, but one of power. Structure will change only when the equilibrium alters sufficiently to allow it: when the force of those demanding change overrides the pressure of those holding to the status quo. As Warriner has said, reform is, in its initial stages, a political matter and not a question for experts who would "advise it into existence."[78]

In Chile pressures for reform continue to mount as egalitarian ideas, demands for new merchandise, and drives for social and economic development that take many forms penetrate to the lower class. This class in Chile is growing numerically and, despite impediments, is becoming more organized in the process. Of course, the privileged class, too, is articulating its plans for reform. But its programs, deliberately designed to move slowly, are becoming more and more unacceptable to the "non-participating, non-privileged majority." In the face of these pressures and from what we know about what happens in social revolution, one is forced to conclude that "either the system will be altered by 'relatively' orderly means (which will necessarily involve compulsion, some loss of property, and quite possibly some disorder), or the system will be changed by mass violence . . . ."[79] Hopefully the present Christian Democrat government will be able to bring about Chile's reform peacefully. If it does, this will be an event without precedent in Latin America.

The purpose of this paper, however, is not to document political forces which mold reform, but to discover some of reform's economic components. For while political power is important initially, at the moment of reform the issue is transformed into a primarily economic and social matter.

ECONOMISTS' INTEREST IN THE STRUCTURE OF CHILEAN AGRICULTURE

The general debate on agrarian reform, a subject long relegated to other social scientists, picked up more economist advocates in the decade of the fifties.[80] This discussion gathered steam after the Charter of Punta del Este in 1961 which made Alliance for Progress aid to Latin America dependent on the country in question effecting an agrarian reform program.

In Chile a substantial number of economists became interested in land reform by way of a phenomenon that has plagued that country since approximately the mid-nineteenth century—inflation. Although inflation there has long been chronic, its rises and swells have become legend. In discussing the Chilean case, Hirschman has likened inflation to a drought: when it reaches a certain degree of intensity, "a strong compulsion to do something is felt and results in a spate of decision-making."[81] To cope with these periods of special intensity a long series of foreign advisors have been called in beginning with Courcelle-Seneuil, the French economist, who advised the Chilean minister of finance from 1855 to 1863. US and UN counsel was requested in subsequent years, and when it appeared that inflation had "run away" in 1954 and 1955 (it reached 71 and 84 percent respectively), the American Klein-Saks mission was summoned. All policies recommended by these foreign counselors tended to utilize the same monetary tools—fiscal, credit, foreign exchange, wage-price, and social security measures. The entry upon the scene of the Klein-Saks group broke a deadlock between President Ibáñez and the Congress, and the legislature accepted its recommendations: a 1956 wage and salary adjustment to only 50 percent of the amount of the inflation in 1955 (rather than the customary 100 percent), tighter credit restrictions (on which inflation control policy has long rested in Chile), and a revision of the foreign exchange system.

These measures had already been recommended by Chileans, however, and the Klein-Saks group served as a device permitting the contending groups who were requesting wage and salary adjustments "to evade once again [as they had many times in the past] their responsibility to hammer out a workable compromise" among themselves to solve inflation.[82] The mission's recommendations did help curb runaway inflation as 1956–57 cost of living increases were only 38 and 17 percent respectively. But inflation was arrested only by paying a high price—the economy stagnated and per-capita income declined. As a result, the Klein-Saks mission was widely writ-

ten off as a failure, and some economists began to give more currency to other explanations for the economic malaise of the country
that had found expression—but not much support—as early as the
1940's. The resultant method of analysis, widely known as the "structuralist" school (counterposed for argumentative purposes against
the "monetarist" school), placed the blame for inflation not on impo-
tent monetary procedures, but on the land tenure system and other
monopolistic economic institutions. Furthermore, it placed economic development and not the curbing of inflation as the higher desid-
eratum. Monetary measures had their place in structuralist reasoning—but would be effective only after certain monopolistic bottlenecks were broken.

Thus land reform comes into structuralist reasoning through the
back door, not through its proven strengths, but through the already
cited defects of the present agricultural system which does not supply the growing economy with enough food and brakes economic development.

Structuralists place the blame for the inelasticity of supply of agricultural products and the perpetual upward pressure on import and
food prices on the latifundia system. Increased domestic costs set off
wage demands. Oligopolistic pricing facilitates the upward movement of prices, and a general rise of the cost-price level results.[83]
Felix and Grunwald[84] have shown this process in more detail and
both agree that although structuralist policy recommendations are
not altogether clear, price incentives and other monetary solutions
are not sufficient. At the very least, some method must be found to
revitalize the agricultural sector.

That this cannot be done without incurring costs is obvious—
there is presently no public land in Chile that can cheaply be
brought into production. The solution seems to lie in bringing un-
derutilized land into greater production by releasing it from the
grips of the hacienda system. At the same time that supply problems
are being rectified, demand for internal products should be increased and demands for foreign luxury goods reduced. Monetary
policies applied before institutions are altered may tend to reinforce
the traditional structure by adding to the incomes of those already
well-off. A succinct summary of the position of the structuralists is
presented by Hirschman:

a. The low productivity of agriculture and its lack of response to economic incentives [are] due to the latifundio pattern of ownership; as a result, industrialization and urbanization lead to rising food prices.

b. The tendency to a deterioration in the terms of trade, which derives from the fact that the demand for imports (of equipment, semi-manufactures and food) increases faster in a country like Chile as development proceeds than does foreign demand for its exports; this results in a tendency for the price of imported goods to rise, usually as a result of devaluation.

c. Sometimes, the uneven distribution of income is designated as a further structural factor. It is argued that, instead of leading to higher labor savings and investment, this distribution leads to continuous pressures against two critical shortage areas: food consumption on the part of the bulk of the population and foreign exchange demands on the part of Latin America's rich with their weak stay-or-reinvest-at-home propensities.[85]

We have shown the economic difficulties of agriculture in Chile which seem to jibe with the ills of the economy that the structuralists describe. In addition to low productivity, we have described monopoly or "uneven distribution of income elements" which characterizes Chilean agriculture.

Though some see this situation being solved without a basic alteration in institutions by relying on price incentives and other policies applicable when wealth is more evenly divided, wealth is not evenly divided in Chile. The agricultural means of production are owned by a few who also monopolize the labor supply whose bargaining power through the years has been kept weak and ineffectual. The society that this relationship has established seems to have stamped the remainder of Chile with the same mold.

Not only are pressures for change becoming stronger, but an agrarian or land reform, meaning the redistribution of economic and political power through a reordering of the rights to the use of resources, may be necessary for Chile's long-run development.[86] Realizing this, if possible (even probable) further dips in the productivity of the sector occur as the immediate result of reform, procedures must be developed to keep them to the very short run.

PLAN OF STUDY

Rather than contributing to the theoretical formulations of the structuralists or the monetarists, therefore, this paper is designed to show what happens when reform takes place, with the understanding that the probability of occurrence on a wide scale is constantly becoming greater.

While the broad outlines of traditional society in Chile remain little changed, there are some isolated but interesting experiments in land reform taking place. In this monograph we will analyze some of them to determine what problems confront the reform institutions and the new colonists who have been given land. This approach assumes that the political decision to reform has been taken —which, indeed, it has on the experiments we will describe. Even though reform is not a matter for technicians to propose and declare, technicians will have to cope with reform once it is seriously attempted. And it will fall to them to recommend and make plans. The political power capable of reform in no way guarantees its success. All the problems of creating viable new institutions to take the place of the old ones remain at the moment of reform.

Even though we will describe land reform experiments in a traditional society, we are not arguing that all the problems encountered and to be detailed might come to pass if reform should occur across the board. But neither will they all be irrelevant. The Alliance for Progress and all land reform programs in yet traditional societies in Latin America argue that reform across the board—as in the Mexican, Bolivian, and Cuban cases—is not the only way reform can happen. We also recognize that some of the projects to be described are new—and allocation of the firm's resources after several years may be quite different than it is immediately after reform. Yet a broader reform will also have its "first years" during which it is important to use resources as optimally as possible. Chile's economy can hardly afford a drop in marketable farm surplus as a result of reform—even in the short run. Taking into consideration policy shortcomings on new and small projects could conceivably avoid larger and more costly errors later.

While planned colonization on purchased fundos as a means to redistribute land has a long history as a policy of the government of Chile, dating from the creation of the Caja de Colonización Agrícola in 1928, relatively little land was given out. What land has been distributed went largely to people who could not have been classified landless laborers by any stretch of the imagination.

Lately, however, with the reorganization of the Caja into the Corporación de la Reforma Agraria (CORA) in 1962 and the subsequent victories of the Christian Democrats, more landless laborers are coming into possession of their own property. If President Frei's programs pass Congress and are effectively administered, the number will burgeon in the near future.

Also established in the early sixties was the program of redistribution of some Church-owned fundos in Chile. The agency carrying out this reform has come to be known as the Instituto de Promoción Agraria (INPROA).

This paper will study four cases of reformed fundos under the Instituto de Promoción Agraria and, later, in an attempt to gain perspective, will focus on the present living conditions of selected cases of former landless laborers who received land twelve or more years ago under the program of the Caja de Colonización Agrícola. For the present we will attempt to trace briefly the development of government colonization which came to be called "agrarian reform" after 1962.

HISTORICAL DEVELOPMENT OF GOVERNMENT COLONIZATION PROGRAMS

Planned colonization in Chile had its nominal beginning in the Constitution of 1925 which, for the first time, admitted that a proper distribution of land resources of the nation was a legitimate government concern. On December 10, 1928, Law 4496 established the Caja de Colonización Agrícola (Agricultural Colonization Bank) to carry out land redistribution activities.

The first Caja colony was settled on January 1, 1929. Forty-three German families were established on a colony near Santiago. The Caja purchased the fundo Santa Adela, divided it into small plots of about ten hectares each, and sold parcels to the immigrants on a partial-payment plan. Instead of beginning colonization with Chile's own landless, the Caja settled foreigners because, as Caja officials reasoned, "intelligent, thrifty Germans"[87] would provide models after which small farms for Chileans could be patterned. Although Chileans subsequently got land, Caja officials were reluctant to grant farms to common agricultural laborers. The general model has remained much the same through the years: the government agency buys a fundo and subdivides it into smaller units for beneficiaries of the program.

The Caja program picked up speed immediately after the enactment of Law 5,604 in 1935, largely because this legislation provided new sources of finance. In addition to funds furnished directly by the government, the law permitted the Caja to borrow from the Social Security Banks.[88]

In February 1960, the Caja was recognized by DFL (Decreto con Fuerza de Ley—"Decree with the Force of Law") 76, passed in 1959. Previous to DFL 76 there were "no fixed norms so that political influence, among other factors, played a prime role . . . ." in colonist selection.[89] The old law merely stipulated that to be eligible to acquire a parcel the colonist must not be younger than twenty-one or older than sixty, must be married, in good health, and have "good habits." These criteria, together with a new point system, were the basis for colonist selection under the 1959 legislation:

(a) For each three years of practical work in agriculture   1 point
(b) For having specialized in the type of work to which the new farms
    will be dedicated or for having worked five years consecutively on
    the farm to be colonized   1 point
(c) For having worked as a farm manager or supervisor for more than
    five years:
    1. In any part of Chile   3 points
    2. In the province where the project is located   4 points
    3. On the farm that is being colonized   5 points
(d) For college training as follows:
    1. College degree in agriculture or veterinary science from a Chilean
       university   5 points
    2. The same from a university in another country   4 points
    3. Title of *Práctico Agrícola* (high school diploma in agriculture)   2 points
    4. Enrollment in a college of agriculture or of veterinary science   2 points
(e) For each E° 400 of savings deposited in a bank, up to E° 800   1 point
(f) For each family dependent   1 point
(g) For each E° 400 saved in the Caja's bank that has been on deposit
    two years   ½ point

This system was still hardly weighted to favor farm laborers. On one of the last colonies given out under this point system,[90] Esmeralda, only three of the forty parcels were assigned to inquilinos; the remainder went mainly to higher-level fundo employees.[91]

Other important innovations of DFL 76 were:

(1) It permitted the Caja to settle colonists on *huertos* as well as parcels. These smaller lots would provide for inquilinos and fundo workers who would not qualify to receive a parcel and for those with trades—like mechanics—who, it was planned, would work for those

given parcels. Many former fundo inquilinos on Esmeralda, for example, were accommodated on huertos.

Several observers who visited Chile after the enactment of DFL 76 wrote, in a confidential report:

> . . . the system . . . now implies the continuation of a social system similar to that existing in feudal agriculture, with settlers employing hired labor on a permanent basis but with less job and income-earning security for farm workers. Family "huertos" are only apparently a solution to excess farm labor. It must lead to strong social conflicts in the long run and rural slums in the short run.

(2) The Caja was given an increased budget and was permitted to acquire capital by issuance and sale of colonization deposit certificates having an initial value of 50 Escudos, each carrying 3 percent interest. The certificates would be readjusted annually in accordance with the percentage increase in price of wheat or baled wool. Few of these were sold since returns on other investments were superior.

(3) Each annual payment due from colonists for land became subject to a yearly readjustment for inflation according to the percentage variation in the wholesale price index of soft wheat in the central zone. In the case of land allotted primarily for sheep-raising, the index used in making the adjustment may be the price of baled wool.[92]

It was no accident that DFL 76 dealt in detail with financial matters. For fourteen years the Caja had been nearly paralyzed since it was, for all intents and purposes, bankrupt. Previous to 1960, mortgages were not adjusted for inflation. Since no provision was made for deferred payment either, the Caja found itself buying farms at somewhere near market value, paying for the land immediately, and giving forty-two-year mortgages fixed in currency to parcel recipients. (DFL 397 in 1953 shortened the mortgage to 28 years.) The value of each year's pay-back diminished as Chilean currency depreciated. In the mid-1960's, making their land payments seemed to be the least of established colonists' worries: most had paid off their land in much less time than necessary and many of those who still had a land debt had to make but a nugatory payment each year.

Before the new government took over in November 1964, the vice-president of the Corporación de la Reforma Agraria (CORA), successor to the Caja, cited one case where parcel holders were paying only 210 pesos a year (in mid-1964 about US $.07) for their land.[93] One parcel holder bought and assumed the debt of E° 2 apiece on three parcels which he now rents out yearly for E° 1,000 each, the lease adjustable for inflation. By 1959 only 5.5 percent of the Caja's yearly budget was being supplied by mortgage payments from colonists.[94]

From its founding until June 30, 1962, the Caja settled 4,206 colonists on farms in 166 colonies from Arica to Magallanes. This averages 124 colonists each year for the thirty-four years of the Caja's existence. Only about 15 percent of the colonists (618) were sold land in the central nucleus (the valley areas of the ten provinces from Aconcagua to Ñuble)—the best farming area of Chile.[95]

The CIDA study estimated that "in 1960 the parcels formed by the Caja represented less than 2.5 percent of the farms in Chile and the colonists and their families represented not more than 1 percent of Chilean families engaged in agriculture."[96] We will return to a more detailed study of some colonists settled by the Caja in Chapter 6.

RECENT LAND REFORM LEGISLATION IN CHILE

Changes to existing legislation introduced in DFL 76 were further modified with the passage of the Agrarian Reform Law, effective November 26, 1962 (Law 15,020).[97] Together, these two measures constituted the agrarian reform program of the government of President Jorge Alessandri (1958–64).[98]

The acclaimed law must be recognized as an extension of existing colonization legislation now called "agrarian reform" mainly because of its incorporation of the ideas of regional agricultural planning. This focus was slightly different from the usually strictly colonizing approach of the old Caja. Indeed, the Charter of Punta del Este called for more than a colonization program and, as signatory to the document, Chile agreed:

To encourage programs of comprehensive agrarian reform leading to the effective transformation, where required, of unjust structures and systems of land tenure and use, with a view to replacing latifundia and dwarf holdings by an equitable system of land tenure so that, with the help of timely and adequate credit, technical assistance and facilities for the marketing and distribution of products, the land will become for the man who works it the basis of his economic stability, the foundation of his increasing welfare, and the guarantee of his freedom and dignity.[99]

Pursuant to her pledge, in 1961 Chile submitted a broad national plan for economic and social development. Although it began independently of the two Alliance conferences, this plan fell within the terms of the Charter of Punta del Este.

The *Yale Law Journal* traced the emergence of Law 15,020:

In early 1962, the bill, drafted by a committee composed of representatives of the three parties in the Chilean coalition, was introduced in that country's legislature. Its terms were shaped to a considerable extent by the displeasure which had been voiced with respect to the land tenure aspects of the 1961 Chilean proposal to the Alliance. The first draft provided the Executive with broad, but discretionary, special decree powers for establishing agencies, standards, and rules to bring about land reform. The parties of the left outside the coalition, however, were constantly pressing to have stronger, broader laws enacted faster. The least conservative party in the government coalition was sympathetic to this position, in part because of its need to attract popular support for the upcoming presidential election in 1964. Passage of the bill as originally introduced was blocked in the Senate, which insisted on maintaining greater legislative control of the program. A compromise was reached which resulted in the elimination of certain provisions from the law and the addition of a framework of limitations upon the Executive's power. In November, 1962, this land reform bill was finally approved.[100]

The main provisions of the 104-article law, its 8 transitory articles, and its 26 enabling amendments were:

(1) The Caja de Colonización Agrícola became the Corporación de la Reforma Agraria (CORA).[101] The Consejo de Fomento e Investigaciones Agrícolas (CONFIN) became Instituto de Desarrollo Agropecuario (INDAP). CORA will have its own credit department for new colonists[102] and INDAP will serve established colonists and other small farmers besides being in charge of government experiment stations.[103] CORA is empowered to acquire land for division, prepare it for parcelling, regroup minifundios, and establish cooperatives. It has sole responsibility for land reform in Chile. The efforts of these two organizations will be coordinated by the new twenty-one-member Consejo Superior de Fomento Agropecuario (CONSFA) which will outline priorities for agrarian reform.[104] INDAP and CORA are both responsible to CONSFA: the secretary general of CONSFA reports to the Minister of Agriculture although he is appointed by the President of the Republic.

(2) It became possible to establish regional councils which would

plan for the development of all the land in a specified area and be delegated powers accordingly.[105]

(3) Elaborate provisions are made for expropriation of land.[106] Only a cursory summary is possible here. Poorly used or abandoned land, land not used directly by its owner, currently unusable land on which improvements are possible, minifundios (for regrouping),[107] land rented out for less than six years (which has not received special permission for a shorter lease—see Article 45), land up for public sale assigned to credit institutions, and land needed to round out a regional plan may be expropriated.[108] An owner whose land is expropriated may retain a minimum of ten economic units for himself, and one unit for each child up to a maximum of twenty units (an "economic unit" is land valued at twenty times the minimum annual wage for private employees in Santiago).[109] A two-thirds vote of CORA's council is necessary prior to expropriation.[110] A special court of agrarian expropriations shall review claims against expropriation.[111]

(4) Unlike DFL 76 the point system was weighted more definitely so that former fundo residents would get first preference in obtaining land.[112] Those who have worked on the property at least three years and do not qualify for a parcel are to be paid an indemnification.[113]

(5) Parcel or huerto holders who are up to date in their land payments may get a 2 percent discount on their remaining debt for each child who finishes the sixth year of grammar school or a 4 percent discount for each child who gets a certificate as a Práctico Agrícola or finishes the third year in a college of agriculture, forestry, or veterinary medicine.[114]

(6) Those who come from outside the fundo to be colonized must make a downpayment of neither less than 3 percent nor more than 5 percent. For former fundo residents CONSFA may reduce the downpayment to 1 percent which may be paid over two years.[115] The remainder of the parcel value is payable in no more than twenty and no less than thirty years. This represents easier terms than outlined in DFL 76.

(7) According to the new law, the parcel holder must live on his parcel (not live in a residence elsewhere and maintain another on the parcel). He must not rent out his land without CORA's permission. He must work his land personally except for some occasional labor which he may hire from outside.[116] As in the Caja legislation, parcels

are indivisible. Now, however, a small landowner can have his land declared an "agricultural family property," agreeing in return for certain tax exemptions not to divide it unless certain improvements are made so that the property could support more than one family[117] (in which case the government may release it from its indivisible status). Clear title to one's land should be easier to receive under Law 15,020 than previously. Land can be divided into irrigated lots of less than fifteen hectares or non-irrigated lots of less than fifty hectares only with special permission.[118] CORA-divided parcels are exempt from this provision, however.[119]

One regional plan—that of Maule Norte—is being developed. It will be supported through studies of the Chile-California AID contract with Alliance for Progress funding. This project, located in the province of Talca, will include 199,860 hectares of which 124,000 hectares will be brought under irrigation for the first time. It should, according to its planners, also have especially favorable effects on the development of the city of Talca. They estimate that in three or four years the area should be ready to be declared an agrarian reform zone in which three or four thousand campesino families can be settled.[120] However, the priorities of the new Christian Democrat government made it appear, in late 1965, that progress on this project might be retarded considerably.

The knottiest problem which Law 15,020 faced was deferred payment for land it purchased which, in a country with as much inflation as Chile, may be tantamount to confiscation. Even readjustable payments may not return the commercial value to its owner. The new law stated:

The purchase price will be paid with a maximum of 20 percent cash payment and the balance in equal installments in not less than 10 years. The installment payments shall bear an annual interest rate of four percent which can be adjusted according to the same index which is applied to the prices of the parcels.[121]

Since the constitution provides for "inviolability of all property without distinction," the deferred-payment portion of the law in cases of expropriation was soon declared unconstitutional and could not be put into operation until a constitutional amendment was passed.

Although President Alessandri transmitted his version of an

amendment to Congress January 16, 1962, it was not passed until October 1, 1963 (Law 15,295), as section 10 of Article 10 of Chile's constitution. Its major provisions state:

> . . . If for the purpose of facilitating the suitable division of the rural property, abandoned lands, as well as those which are naturally poorly exploited and those below the adequate levels of productivity, land may be expropriated for public use, the owner must previously receive 10 percent of the indemnification and the balance in equal installments not exceeding 15 years, with the interest rate fixed by the law.
>
> This form of indemnification can only be applied in conformity with the law that permits the presentation of claims against the expropriation before a Special Tribunal whose decision is subject to appeal in the respective court of appeals, and that establishes an annual readjustment system for the balance of the indemnification, in order to maintain its value. . . .

This amendment cannot be put into effect until an enabling act is passed. Although an enabling act to set up provisions for this new amendment has been written, it was not presented to the Assembly for action before Alessandri left office. At present, CORA is restricted to lands it can purchase for immediate cash (in cases of expropriation), transfers of farms from one government agency to another (which are also cash transactions although there is usually a certain downpayment after which readjustable payments are made over a number of years), and sale agreements (in which the owner of a fundo offers his farm for sale to CORA and the two parties agree to a certain amount down and the remainder in readjustable payments over a set number of years).

The land reform law of Chile, with its enabling amendments, is an extraordinarily complicated document. At first glance, one would think that armed with it and assuming provision for deferred payment is made, the government should be able to carry on a program in which any number of formulas for land reform would be legal. It is, however, cumbersome and laden with possibilities for delay. Had the enabling act been passed, delay—through the court appeals—would have retarded the progress of its intent. Added to its inherent complications was the political make-up of the agencies during the Alessandri regime.[122] The heads of CONSFA, CORA, and INDAP belonged to different parties which constituted the tripartite government coalition.

As Carroll has commented:

Land reform laws are invariably long, complicated, and detailed. This makes their implementation very difficult. Only a fraction of the laws have actually been carried out....[123]

Hirschman dwells on a similar theme:

More generally, passage of the Land Reform may have been facilitated by the long tradition of issuing well-meaning and socially advanced laws which turn out to be ineffective because of lack of enforcement or clever obstruction. This tradition means that politicians, confident that nothing of importance is going to change, will frequently ostensibly vote in favor of "progressive" measures because of the political advantages connected with such a stand. . . .[124]

Hirschman does inject a note of a bit more optimism in his observations, however:

Yet, every once in a while, these politicians outsmart themselves by acting in this way and they find out too late they have started up a machine which they cannot control....[125]

It is beyond the scope of this chapter to analyze the political pressures that were important to passage of the law and its subsequent administration, to analyze the law in detail, or to speculate on what changes the government of Eduardo Frei will achieve. We state only parenthetically that Frei's present program calls for establishing 100,000 campesinos with land rights in the six years of his administration.[126] Half the irrigated acreage of the central zone of Chile will be "reformed" and the process, according to the government, will be declared "complete" by 1970.[127] We will devote the remainder of this chapter to a brief analysis of what Law 15,020 was able to accomplish in the first year and a half of its existence.

The 1955 agricultural census shows that there are over 300,000 landless agricultural workers in Chile. Assuming there are 175,000 minifundistas, there are more than 475,000 potential recipients of land rights in Chile, not considering population growth since 1955.[128] CORA originally planned to create 5,200 new properties in 1963 and 7,500 in 1964, assuming funds were made available.[129] Its program fell far short of that goal, however.

By July 22, 1963, no land had yet been distributed under the new law, but 99 parcels and 15 huertos were distributed to complete work begun by the Caja. Since all distribution of land was suspended between the signing of the law on November 27, 1962 and publication of decree number RRA 11, March 27, 1963, this property was actually distributed between March 27 and July 22, 1963.[130] By mid-1963 CORA had approved projects calling for the assignment of 639 parcels and 495 huertos during the balance of 1963. This modification of original plans was made partially due to the delay in passing the enabling acts to Law 15,020 and the resultant postponement of the Inter-American Development Bank funding for infrastructure which required a high degree of planning prior to completion of the loan.

The goal for 1964, announced late in 1963, provided for the establishment of 7,288 units of which 1,725 would be huertos. When the Social Progress Trust Fund Annual Report for 1963 went to press in February 1964, it reported more modest goals: "Plans for 1964 call for the formation of 4,208 parcels and 921 family garden plots...."[131]

Soon, publications began to mistake plans for progress, and, for example, the *Yale Law Review* listed the Pan-American Union and *The New York Times* as sources for its statement, "Administrators contemplate the creation of 15,000 such farms per year, a marked increase from the present rate of 5,000 per year."[132]

However, on May 3, 1964, *El Mercurio* reported: "From the promulgation of Law No. 15,020 CORA has effected 1,354 land divisions totalling 51,442.58 parcelled hectares corresponding to 885 parcels and 469 huertos."[133]

But even this last statement proves to be a bit too optimistic. In responses to a questionnaire the author administered to personnel of the Corporación de la Reforma Agraria, agency representatives revealed that up to June 30, 1964, CORA had effected land divisions on nine colonies. On these properties, 615 parcels and 313 huertos were established in 1963 and 183 parcels in 1964. Total 1963–64 land divisions to June 1964 were 1,111. However, on only a part of this land had titles actually been given out. As we have shown, the current CORA program has proceeded slowly with land division despite the optimistic goals set at the time Law No. 15,020 was passed. Leaving aside all political and bureaucratic factors which have played a very important part but are beyond the scope of this paper, a number of economic bottlenecks have been responsible for this slow progress:

(1) *Provision must be made for deferred payment in cases of expropriation.* Land transfers to CORA to date have been limited largely to land bought from another government agency or from landlords who were willing to sell on deferred-payment terms. Most of the purchases from landlords seem to have been made at a level comparable to or higher than the landlord would have gotten by selling his fundo on the open market. CORA and the landlord who wants to sell usually have arranged a mutually agreeable contract for "cash down and the remainder in readjustable payments over a specified number of years." The speed of the program has been made contingent upon funds the government of Chile allowed for land purchase purposes which, in 1964, was only about 34 percent of CORA's E° 7,700,000 budget.[134]

It is extremely unlikely that United States funds could be used to purchase land since the Social Progress Trust Fund (Inter-American Development Bank) is prevented by statute from allocating funds for land purchase.[135] Although AID funds can legally be used, objections of the United States Congress would probably be adamant.[136] Furthermore, it is doubtful that Chileans would approve of United States money being used to purchase their land regardless of the good intentions of the transaction.

Because of fiscal limitations, therefore, Chile must enact a provision providing for deferred payment in cases of expropriation. This further implies that if Chile is interested in an agrarian reform, she must enact a "quick-taking" procedure similar to that used by the government for condemned property in the United States. Property could then be pressed into use in the public interest immediately; financial arrangements could be negotiated later. (Under Law 15,020 actual taking would languish in courts—not merely discussion of terms. Investment on the property in this interim period could be expected to drop off drastically.)

Jacques Chonchol (now head of INDAP under Frei) has discussed levels of landlord remuneration for expropriated property and has called low payment one of the fundamentals of agrarian reform in Latin America:

The more paid for land the less agrarian reform can do.

. . . (1) Productivity has little to do with land values in a land market in which there is prestige to land ownership and speculation in land is rampant due to inflation, as a defense against taxation, etc. (2) Landlords will tend to use the land payments for investments outside of the country, thus aggravating balance-of-payment difficulties. (3) Commercial values are four or five times higher than the evaluation on which land owners have been paying real estate taxes. (4) Latin American countries simply do not have funds to pay for land without necessary remuneration completely halting the land reform.[137]

(2) *As currently conceived, land reform in Chile involves large expenditures for infrastructure and these funds must come largely from outside the country.* Lending agencies are anxious that these projects be well conceived and plans carefully formulated. Delays in receiving the foreign funds slow the entire effort.

It is possible that the new government will reduce the per-parcel funds necessary for infrastructure. Rafael Moreno, new vice-president of CORA, indicated that some change in CORA's policy might be in the offing:

. . . [CORA will] not give out more finished houses nor fenced-in parcels. The investment will not be more than E° 2,000 or E° 3,000 each. We will give colonists a foundation, sanitary facilities, and a roof. Then we will draw up a zonal plan and the parcel holder will receive credit for buying capital and animals and technical assistance for building his own house. As far as fences are concerned, we will establish parcel boundaries and each parcel holder will receive credits for posts and wire so that he will be able to fence in his own land.[138]

(3) *Parcelization itself will always be a costly answer to land reform in Chile.* Not only does it require developing entrepreneurial talent on a large scale, which is a long and costly process, but individual farms necessarily involve division of such resources as the irrigation system which is currently adapted to large fields. Even if social overhead capital is reduced, economic overhead capital is bound to raise the costs of a land reform parcelization program enough to slow the program considerably.

Apparently with this in mind, Moreno stated:

. . . there will be two types of properties: a family unit and cooperative property. The first will enable the agricultural family to produce and prosper without hired workers. In the second, the worker is just as much a property holder as the former, but a cooperative farming system will be used.[139]

Later interpretation of Moreno's words seemed to indicate the government's interest in establishing cooperative farming as an interim arrangement—one that would aim at preparing campesinos for the trying responsibility of being landowners and entrepreneurs.

As mentioned earlier in this chapter, however, it is too early and proposals of the new government on land reform are too vague to speculate on the specifics of the new government's plans. We must turn, rather, to analyzing operational programs—those under Church sponsorship and, later, those of the Caja de Colonización Agrícola—to attempt to discover elements that make for success and failure of an agrarian reform.

NOTES

1   The percentage of total population classified as rural in 1950 was 41.3. The comparable figure in 1960 was 34.7 percent. (Johannes L. Sadie, *Población y Mano de Obra en Chile, 1930–75,* CORFO/CELADE, Santiago, 1962, p. 17.) There were 648,000 people in the agricultural labor force in 1952; this figure was unchanged in 1960. (Ministerio de Agricultura, Departamento de Economía Agraria, *La Agricultura Chilena en el Quinquenio 1956–1960,* Santiago, 1963, Cuadro 4, p. 8.)

2   *Ibid.,* Cuadro 134, p. 174, and calculations from Corporación de Fomento de la Producción (CORFO), "Cuentas Nacionales de Chile 1958–1963" (mimeographed), Santiago, June 1964, p. 3.

3   The Inter-American Committee for Agricultural Development, called Comité Interamericano de Desarrollo Agrícola (CIDA) in Spanish, surveyed land tenure forms in selected countries of Latin America in 1962 and 1963. This project, now expanded to other countries, will soon provide the most complete description available of land tenure forms in Latin America. The effort is jointly sponsored by the Organization of American States, the Inter-American Development Bank, the Economic Commission for Latin America, the Food and Agriculture Organization of the United Nations, and the Inter-American Committee for Agricultural Sciences. Its preliminary draft report on Chile, "Estudio Sobre la Tenencia de la Tierra en Chile" (mimeographed) Santiago, 1964, will hereinafter be cited as "CIDA borrador, 'Chile'." CIDA borrador, "Chile," p. 45.

4   Ministerio de Agricultura, *op. cit.,* p. 3.

5   Corporación de Fomento de la Producción, *op. cit.,* p. 17. All figures were expressed in 1961 Escudos prior to making this calculation. GNP in 1958 was E° 4,172 million while in 1963 it had risen to E° 5,117 million.

6   *Ibid.;* these figures are also expressed in Escudos of 1961.

7   Inflation in 1964 was about 38 percent. In the decade 1950 to 1960 it averaged 36 percent with a high peak in 1954 and 1955 which levelled off later. Albert O. Hirschman, *Journeys Toward Progress,* Twentieth Century Fund, New York, 1963, p. 160.

8   Calculated from Ministerio de Agricultura, Departmento de Economía

Agraria, "Sinopsis de la Agricultura Chilena 1961–1963" (mimeographed), Santiago, August 1964, Cuadro 10, p. 23.

9 Gilbert J. Butland, *Chile: An Outline of Its Geography, Economics, and Politics,* Royal Institute of International Affairs, Oxford University Press, London and New York, 1951, p. 9.

10 Preston E. James, *Latin America,* third edition, Odyssey Press, New York, 1959, p. 245.

11 Marvin J. Sternberg, "Chilean Land Tenure and Land Reform," unpublished Ph.D. thesis, University of California, Berkeley, September 1962, p. 6.

12 James O. Bray, "Demand, and the Supply of Food in Chile," *Journal of Farm Economics,* Vol. 44, No. 4, November 1962, p. 1005.

13 *Ibid.*

14 Nicholas Kaldor, "Economic Problems of Chile," unpublished paper, Economic Commission for Latin America Library, Santiago, Chile.

15 Corporación de Fomento de la Producción, "Chile: National Economic Development Program, 1961–70" (mimeographed), Santiago, January 1961, p. 16. The program calls for a 5.5 percent growth in the agricultural sector each year.

16 Peter Dorner, "Problems in Chilean Agriculture and Land Reform," prepared for AID (mimeographed), Santiago, 1964.

17 Héctor Morales Jara, "Productividad Presente y Potencial en 96 Predios de la Provincia de O'Higgins y su Relación con el Tamaño de las Propiedades," unpublished thesis, Facultad de Agronomía, Universidad de Chile, Santiago, 1964.

18 CIDA borrador, "Chile," p. 54.

19 Sternberg, *op. cit.,* p. 34.

20 John P. Powelson, *Latin America: Today's Economic and Social Revolution,* McGraw-Hill Book Company, New York, Toronto, London, 1964, p. 36.

21 Sternberg, *op. cit.,* p. 34.

22 *Ibid.*

23 Doreen Warriner, *Land Reform and Economic Development,* Fiftieth Anniversary Commemoration Lectures, National Bank of Egypt, Cairo, 1955.

24 See Jean Borde and Mario Góngora, *Evolución de la Propiedad Rural en el Valle de Puangue,* Vol. II (of two volumes), Map I, Editorial Universitaria, Santiago, 1956.

25 James Becket, "Land Reform in Chile," *Journal of Inter-American Studies,* April 1963, pp. 178–79.

26 George McCutchen McBride, *Chile: Land and Society,* American Geographic Society, New York, 1936, pp. 78–79.

27 Andrew Pearse, "Regional Introductory Paper: Agrarian Change Trends in Latin America," paper given at the First World Congress of Rural Sociology, Dijon, France, 1964.

28 Peruvian Indians dwelt in *Ayllu* while Colombian Chibcha Indians like-

wise lived in permanent settlements. In Mexico the "Toltecs" lived in villages (*calpulli*) while the "Chichimecs" of the north were nomadic. Other large groups of nomadic Indians in Latin America occupied the River Plate area and parts of Colombia other than those occupied by the Chibchas. See Silvio Zavala, "The Frontiers of Hispanic America," in Walker D. Wyman and Clifton B. Kroeber (eds.), *The Frontier in Perspective*, University of Wisconsin Press, Madison, 1965, pp. 35–58, and Eric Wolf, *Sons of the Shaking Earth*, University of Chicago Press, Chicago, 1959 (Phoenix Edition, 1962), pp. 69–101; 117–29; 135–38.

29 Sternberg, *op. cit.,* p. 25.

30 David Felix, "Chile," in Adamantios Pepelasis, Leon Mears, and Irma Adelman, *Economic Development: Analysis and Case Studies*, Harper and Brothers, New York, 1961, p. 291. This essay (pp. 288–325) briefly summarizes the economic development of Chile.

31 *Ibid.,* p. 294.

32 Calculated from Ministerio de Agricultura, Departmento de Economía Agraria, "Sinopsis de la Agricultura Chilena 1961–1963," Cuadro No. 5, p. 11 and Merwin L. Bohen and Morton Pomeranz, *Investment in Chile: Basic Information for United States Businessmen*, United States Department of Commerce, United States Government Printing Office, Washington, D.C., 1960, pp. 68–69.

33 Felix, *op. cit.,* p. 294.

34 *Ibid.,* p. 295

35 *Ibid.*

36 Lester R. Brown, *Increasing World Food Output: Problems and Prospects*, Foreign Agricultural Economic Report No. 25, United States Department of Agriculture, Economic Research Service, Washington. D.C., April 1965.

37 Isaac Joslin Cox, "Chile," in A. Curtis Wilgus, *Argentina, Brazil, and Chile Since Independence*, Vol. III, Russel and Russel Inc., New York, 1963, pp. 401–2 (copyright 1935 by George Washington University Press).

38 Gene Ellis Martin, *La División de la Tierra en Chile Central*, Editorial Nascimento, Santiago, 1960.

39 For a description of a minifundio area see Hernán Burgos Mujica, *Análisis Económico Agrícola para un Plan de Crédito Supervisado, Comuna de Navidad, Año Agrícola 1960–61*, Investigaciones en Administración Rural No. 19, Ministerio de Agricultura, 1962.

40 Sternberg, *op. cit.,* p. 56. (These are 1954 data but they are corroborated by more recent evidence. See Universidad de Chile, Instituto de Economía, *La Economía de Chile en el Período 1950–63*, Vol. I, Santiago, 1963, p. 99.)

41 Aníbal Pinto Santa Cruz, *Chile: Un Caso de Desarrollo Frustrado*, Editorial Universitaria, Santiago, 1962, p. 87.

42 *Ibid.,* p. 88.

43 Nicholas Kaldor, "Problemas Económicos de Chile," *El Trimestre Económico*, Mexico City, No. 102, April–June 1959, pp. 170–221.

44 Sternberg, *op. cit.,* p. 151.
45 There has been a tendency lately to understate the time an inquilino is required to work on the hacienda. On the farms on which I have conducted interviews, six days a week was the most common response to questions dealing with the time worked for a landlord. (Of course, this says nothing about underemployment.) United Nations, *Progress in Land Reform* E/4020/ Add. 2, May 14, 1965, reports on page 3 that inquilinos on Chilean haciendas normally work about 150 days a year for the landlord. Perhaps this error stems from a misinterpretation of an excellent earlier study, Ministerio de Agricultura, *Aspectos Económicos y Sociales del Inquilinaje en San Vicente de Tagua Tagua,* Santiago, 1960, which, on page 5, notes an instance of a 160-day work obligation in colonial times (hereinafter referred to as "Tagua Tagua Study"). CIDA uses 270 days a year as the inquilino work requirement. CIDA borrador, "Chile," p. 116.
46 Ministerio de Agricultura, Departamento de Economía Agraria, *La Agricultura Chilena en el Quinquenio, 1956–1960,* p. 177. The part of this which must be paid in cash is also specified by law.
47 Tagua Tagua Study, p. 57.
48 Claudio Gay, *Historia Física y Política de Chile: Agricultura,* E. Thunot and Company, Paris, 1863, Vol. I, pp. 117, 120, and Chapters VIII, IX, X, XI, and XII.
49 Diego Barros, *Historia General de Chile,* Vol. VII, Santiago, 1886, pp. 32–33 and 465–67. See also McBride, *op. cit.,* p. 116; Domingo Amunátegui Solar, *Historia Social de Chile,* Editorial Nascimento, Santiago, 1932, for others who agree with this general point of view.
50 Mario Góngora, *Origen de los Inquilinos de Chile Central,* Editorial Universitaria, Santiago, 1960.
51 Legal definitions for agricultural workers covered by social security are given in Servicio de Seguro Social, *Manual de Instrucciones del SSS, 1961–62,* Unidad No. 23393 en el Registro de Propiedad Intelectual de la Biblioteca Nacional, Santiago, p. 11.
52 Frank Tannenbaum, *Ten Keys to Latin America,* Alfred A. Knopf, New York, 1962, p. 80.
53 Tagua Tagua Study, p. 20.
54 Gay, in his description of inquilinaje, notes that an inquilino may be discharged with eight days notice. Reported in Góngora, *op. cit.,* p. 14.
55 Osvaldo Sunkel, "Change and Frustration in Chile," paper presented to Conference on Obstacles to Change in Latin America, Royal Institute of International Affairs, February 1965, in Claudio Véliz (ed.), *Obstacles to Change in Latin America,* Oxford University Press, London, New York, Toronto, 1965, p. 136. Again, statistics vary. Sunkel's 9 percent for university entrants seems a little high. Sergio Molina, President Frei's Minister of Finance, thinks 2 percent more realistic, *Latin American Times,* October 4, 1965, p. 3. In a speech at the University of Wisconsin on December 9, 1965, Chile's Ambassador to the United States, Radomiro Tomic, used

the figure 1 percent. These divergent figures underline once again the difficulty of finding reliable data.

56 Sunkel, *op. cit.,* p. 138.

57 Robert J. Alexander, *Labor Relations in Argentina, Brazil, and Chile,* McGraw-Hill, Inc., New York, San Francisco, Toronto, London, 1962, p. 238.

58 For a brief summary tracing the development of labor legislation in Chile, see Moisés Poblete Troncoso, "Cuarenta Años de Legislación Social Chilena," published in *El Mercurio,* September 7, 1964, p. 5.

59 Juan Díaz Salas, *Código del Trabajo,* Vol. VII, comprende desde Febrero de 1954 hasta Marzo de 1956, Editorial Nascimento, Santiago, 1956, pp. 37–40; pp. 167–85. See also Hernán Troncoso, "Trade Union Freedom," dittoed English translation of a pamphlet originally published by Acción Sindical Chilena (ASICH), prepared for the Congreso Nacional de Abogados de Concepción, 1957, p. 1. In this publication (hereinafter referred to as "Troncoso Paper") Troncoso presents suggestions for changing the *Código del Trabajo;* Tagua Tagua Study; Economic Commission for Latin America (CEPAL), Tenth Session, Mar del Plata, Argentina, May, 1963, *Social Development of Latin America in the Post War Period,* E/CN.12/660, April 15, 1964, p. 35. The study again points out that this double standard is part of a larger phenomenon: the social security program is poorer among rural workers, school facilities are inferior, etc. The study calls this the "marginality of the rural population" (see pp. 30–45).

60 The following four points were condensed by the author from the Troncoso Paper, the Tagua Tagua Study, and the *Código del Trabajo,* all cited previously, and personal conversation with Hernán Troncoso, Chilean labor lawyer, American Embassy, Santiago.

61 Tagua Tagua Study, p. 9.

62 Troncoso Paper, p. 1.

63 *Ibid.,* p. 3. Troncoso notes, "The procedure requires the presentation of an application by the union and the checking of the applications, statutes and by-laws by the following offices: Regional Labor Inspection Office; the Provincial Labor Inspection Office (Control Divisions, Provincial Inspector, Division of Social Organizations), Direction-General of Labor (Control Division, Legal Division, Division of Social Organizations, Director-General of Labor), Ministry of Labor (Control Division, Ministerial Decree of Recognition), the Ministry of Justice (Control Division, Decree granting Legal Personality, Minister of Justice), Signature of the President of Chile, the Comptroller-General of Chile (Review of the legality of the Decrees). The return of the documents to the Unions through the same offices: Comptroller-General, Ministry of Justice, Ministry of Labor, etc. to the Regional Labor Inspection Office. The file is transmitted by regular mail throughout the process (see Regulation 1030, Article 21). What makes this procedure obsolete and superfluous is that application, statutes and by-laws are copied verbatim and sent from one

office to the other; it is impossible to explain the need for all this pro-
cedural review."

64 *Ibid.*, pp. 4–11; Tagua Tagua Study, p. 10.

65 Partido Demócrata Cristiano, *El Libro de la Tierra: Movimiento Nacional
de Liberación Campesina,* Santiago, 1964, p. 23.

66 See R. J. Penn and Jorge Schuster, "La Reforma Agraria de Venezuela,"
Revista Interamericana de Ciencias Sociales, Vol. 2, No. 1, Unión Panamericana, Washington, D.C., 1963.

67 Seventh Conference of the American States, Members of the International
Labour Organization (Buenos Aires, 1961), *Condiciones de Trabajo y de
Vida de los Trabajadores Agrícolas (Informe IV),* pp. 42–43, quoted in
Economic Commission for Latin America (CEPAL), *Social Development,*
p. 37.

68 Víctor Alba, "The Latin American Style and the New Social Forces," in
Hirschman (ed.), *Latin American Issues, Essays and Comments,* Twentieth
Century Fund, New York, 1961, pp. 43–44.

69 These points are stated tersely here because they have been documented
in Víctor Alba, *Alliance without Allies: The Mythology of Progress in
Latin America,* Frederick A. Praeger, Inc., New York, Washington and
London, 1965; George McCutchen McBride, *op. cit.*; K. H. Silvert, "An
Essay on Social Structure," American Universities Field Staff Letter, West
Coast South America Series, November 1956; T. Lynn Smith, "Values
Held by People in Latin America Which Affect Technical Cooperation,"
Rural Sociology, Vol. 21, No. 1, March 1956; Claudio Véliz, "Obstacles
to Reform in Latin America," *The World Today,* January 1963; United
Nations, *1963 Report on the World Social Situation,* E/CN.5/315/Rev.
1/ST/SOA/52, Chapter XI, "Social Development in Latin America," New
York, 1963, pp. 122–41; Sunkel, *op. cit.*; Peter Dorner and William C.
Thiesenhusen, "Relevant Research Programs to be Conducted in De-
veloping Countries," *Journal of Farm Economics,* December 1964, pp.
1095–105.

70 It does, however, seem as though agriculturists have had to compromise
with the groups in the new oligarchy for the privilege of keeping their
land and their favored tax status by accepting some government pricing
and other monetary policies which discriminate against the sector. See
Mamalakis' segment of Markos Mamalakis and Clark Winton Reynolds,
Essays on the Chilean Economy, Richard D. Irwin, Inc., Homewood, Illinois (a publication of the Economic Growth Center, Yale University),
1965, especially pp. 117–48. Mamalakis' publication arrived as this monograph was being sent to press and its arguments have not been incorporated into the text.

71 Fredrick B. Pike, *Chile and the United States, 1880–1962,* University of
Notre Dame Press, Notre Dame, Indiana, 1963, Introduction, pp. xxii–
xxiii.

72 Fredrick B. Pike and Donald W. Bray, "A Vista of Catastrophe: The

Future of United States–Chilean Relations," *Review of Politics,* Vol. XXII, No. 3, July 1960.

73 Reported in Marcelo Carvallo Drién, "Land Tenure and the Development of Chilean Agriculture," unpublished Master's thesis, University of Wisconsin, Madison, 1963, from J. D. Jobet, *Precursores del Pensamiento Social de Chile,* Editorial Universitaria, Santiago, 1955, p. 23.

74 McBride, *op. cit.,* pp. 379, 385.

75 P. T. Ellsworth, *Chile: An Economy in Transition,* The Macmillan Company, New York, 1945, p. 156.

76 Pike, *op. cit.,* Introduction, p. xxi.

77 Carlos Keller R., "Minifundios y Latifundios," *Chile: Su Futura Alimentación,* Editorial Nascimento, Santiago, 1963, pp. 14–15.

78 Doreen Warriner, *Land Reform and Development in the Middle East: A Study of Egypt, Syria, and Iraq,* Oxford University Press for the Royal Institute of International Affairs, London, 1957, p. 9.

79 Dorner and Thiesenhusen, *op. cit.,* p. 1098.

80 Kenneth H. Parsons, Raymond J. Penn, and Philip M. Raup, *Land Tenure* (Proceedings of the International Conference on Land Tenure and Related Problems in World Agriculture in 1951), University of Wisconsin Press, Madison, 1956.

81 Hirschman, *Journeys Toward Progress,* p. 161. See his chapter "Inflation in Chile," pp. 159–223.

82 *Ibid.,* p. 209.

83 Nicholas Kaldor states of Chile, "The inflation therefore was 'demand-induced' as far as agricultural prices are concerned; and it was 'cost-induced' as far as the non-agricultural sectors were concerned." Quoted in Mamalakis and Reynolds, *op. cit.,* p. 121.

84 David Felix, "An Alternative View of the 'Monetarist'-'Structuralist' Controversy" and Joseph Grunwald, "The 'Structuralist' School on Price Stabilization and Economic Development: The Chilean Case," in Albert O. Hirschman (ed.), *Latin American Issues: Essays and Comments,* pp. 81–123.

85 Hirschman, *Journeys Toward Progress,* pp. 213–14. For various views on this argument see also papers by Roberto Campos in Hirschman (ed.), *Latin American Issues,* pp. 69–79; Nicholas Kaldor, "Problemas Económicos de Chile;" Dudley Seers, "A Theory of Inflation and Growth in Underdeveloped Countries," *Oxford Economic Papers,* June 1962, pp. 173–95; and Mamalakis and Reynolds, *op. cit.*

86 Sometimes "agrarian reform" and "land reform" are given different connotations. Agrarian reform becomes, then, the more "integral" concept including credit, extension, etc., as well as a change in property rights. See Philip M. Raup, "The Role of Research in Agrarian Reform," *Agrarian Reform and Economic Growth in Developing Countries,* United States Department of Agriculture, Economic Research Service, Washington, D.C., March 1962, p. 52. In this monograph the terms will be used inter-

changeably as they are in Spanish where *reforma agraria* covers both concepts.

87 McBride, *op. cit.*, p. 272.
88 United States Department of State, Foreign Service Dispatch, "Chile: Agrarian Land Reform," No. 863 (mimeographed), June 15, 1960, p. 1. See Law 5,604 published in *Diario Oficial*, Santiago, February 16, 1935; El Reglamento de Ley 5,604, published in *Diario Oficial*, Santiago, May 27, 1935; and Decreto con Fuerza de Ley No. 397 published in *Diario Oficial*, Santiago, August 5, 1935.
89 CIDA borrador, "Chile," p. 308. An advisor to the Caja told the author the following anecdote: The Caja Council would meet, the *técnicos* carrying their briefcases full of information on deserving new colonists. The political chiefs of the Caja would go into the meeting with lists of people to whom they had promised land. The politicians, who represented different parties, would make deals with their fellow council members. "I'll vote for your four candidates for parcels if you'll help me fulfill my five promises by voting for my applicants," they would say. In the end very few of the técnicos' choices were awarded land.
90 It was replaced, as we shall note later, with a new system in 1963.
91 Caja de Colonización Agrícola, Departamento Registro de Colonos, April 4, 1962, Santiago (published in *El Mercurio*).
92 From Decreto con Fuerza de Ley No. 76, *Diario Oficial*, February 24, 1960.
93 Eduardo Silva Pizarro, "Reajuste al Valor de las Parcelas," *El Mercurio*, September 15, 1964, p. 3.
94 Joaquín Leiva and Sergio Maturana, "Documentación Sobre Aspectos Específicos de los Programas Nacionales con Enfasis en la Creación de Nuevas Unidades" (II), paper presented at the Segundo Seminario Latino-Americano sobre Problemas de la Tierra, Montevideo, November–December 1959 (mimeographed), p. 26.
95 These data have been calculated from the "Cuadro de Parcelizaciones Efectuadas por la Caja de Colonización Agrícola desde el 1° de Enero 1929 al 30 de Junio 1962," Corporación de la Reforma Agraria, unpublished, Santiago, July 1962. A few of these land divisions were actually somewhat larger than parcels and were technically called *lotes*. They were awarded to highest-level fundo employees. The number of huerteros (included in the calculations in the text) established from the passage of DFL 76 until the approval of Law 15,020 was 527. These figures do not include some subdivisions in the far southern and extensively farmed provinces of Magallanes.
96 CIDA borrador, "Chile," p. 303.
97 *Diario Oficial*, No. 25,403, November 27, 1962.
98 President Frei introduced his agrarian reform law to Congress November 22, 1965. This legislation faces a long debate in Congress. Because the bill will probably be modified by Congress before it is passed, and since its introduction corresponds to the time in which this monograph is being

sent to press, no analysis of it will be included in this volume.

99 *Charter of Punta del Este,* Title I, Sec. 6.

100 *Yale Law Journal,* "Notes and Comments, The Chilean Land Reform: A Laboratory for Alliance-for-Progress Techniques," Vol. 73, No. 2, December 1963, p. 314.

101 Law 15,020, Article 11.

102 RRA 11 Article 135. See also Hugo Ossio Sivilá, "El Crédito Agrícola Supervisado en Chile," Memoria para optar al Diploma de Graduado en Economía Agraria, Programa de Estudios Económicos Latinoamericanos para Graduados, Universidad de Chile (mimeographed), Santiago, 1964.

103 Law 15,020, Article 12.

104 *Ibid.,* Article 4; Article 5.

105 *Ibid.,* Article 5a; Article 13; Article 16.

106 *Ibid.,* Articles 15 through 33.

107 The Alessandri government apparently regarded consolidation necessary for 100,000 minifundistas. See President Alessandri's message March 3, 1962 in Boletín No. 165 of the Cámara de Diputados.

108 Law 15,020, Article 15. A law to expropriate badly used land and 30 percent of all private land improved by public funds had, however, been in existence for years.

109 *Ibid.,* Article 18.

110 *Ibid.,* Article 21.

111 *Ibid.,* Article 29.

112 *Ibid.,* Article 11c. Article 75 of RRA 11 assigns one point to each year worked on the fundo to be colonized while there was no such provision in DFL 76. It also lowers the points that can be earned by Ingenieros Agrónomos and restricts assignment of parcels to those who already have land worth over five basic yearly salaries (*sueldos vitales*) in Santiago.

113 Law 15,020, Article 67.

114 *Ibid.,* Article 66.

115 *Ibid.,* Article 11d; RRA 11, Article 63.

116 RRA 11, Article 70.

117 Law 15,020, Articles 34–36; Article 51.

118 *Ibid.,* Article 62.

119 *Ibid.,* Article 63.

120 *El Mercurio,* "Programa para el Desarrollo Regional y Reforma Agraria en la Provincia de Talca," August 28, 1964. See also "Sesión Ordinaria del H. Consejo Superior de Fomento Agropecuario" (mimeographed), April 7, 1964, pp. 13–26.

121 Law 15,020, Article 11a. The readjustment system was established in legislation after the original law and its enabling acts were passed.

122 Of course, passage of a measure providing for delayed payment in cases of expropriation that does not run the risk of delays through court obstruction is a key legislative goal of the present Christian Democrat government.

123 Thomas F. Carroll, "The Land Reform Issue in Latin America," in Albert O. Hirschman (ed.), *Latin American Issues: Essays and Comments*, p. 198.

124 Albert O. Hirschman, *Journeys Toward Progress*, pp. 156–57.

125 *Ibid.*, p. 157.

126 See mention of this in Chapter II and *El Mercurio*, "Gobierno Hará 100.000 Nuevos Propietarios en Seis Años con Aplicación de Reforma Agraria," Santiago, November 19, 1964.

127 Radomiro Tomic (see note 55 above).

128 This figure is probably too low. Although some of the 175,000 could be satisfied by regrouping on land they now own, the 1955 figure should probably be much larger since there is a yearly net increase in farm families of between 5,000 and 15,000.

129 *El Diario Ilustrado*, January 1, 1963, and CORA Press Release, "The Chilean Agrarian Reform" (in English), August 1963. As early as June 1962, *El Mercurio* published a story estimating that the government would probably plan to settle "about 5,000 settlers" annually. *El Mercurio*, Santiago, June 13, 1962.

130 RRA 11, however, was passed February 5, 1963. This was the last of RRA implementing decrees published; there were twenty-six.

131 Inter-American Development Bank, *Social Progress Trust Fund: Third Annual Report 1963*, Washington, D.C., 1964, p. 184.

132 *Yale Law Review, op. cit.*, p. 319. The publications this article cites as sources for this statement are the Pan-American Union, "The Alliance for Progress Weekly Report," No 25, February 18, 1963, p. 21 and the *New York Times*, April 21, 1963, p. 22, col. 1. The error of stating that 5,000 farmers are being settled each year under the CORA program was also repeated in James Nelson Goodsell, "Chile: Parcelling Out the Land," *Christian Science Monitor*, July 21, 1964.

133 *El Mercurio*, "Reparto de Tierras en Virtud de la Ley de Reforma Agraria," Santiago, May 3, 1964.

134 *South Pacific Mail*, Santiago, January 3, 1964; *El Mercurio*, Santiago, January 2 and 22, 1964.

135 Article 1, Section 1.04 (a) of *Social Progress Trust Fund Agreement*.

136 See 106 *Congressional Record*, 16842 (1960).

137 Jacques Chonchol, *El Desarrollo de América Latina y la Reforma Agraria*, Editorial del Pacífico, Santiago, 1964, pp. 96–98.

138 *El Mercurio*, "Reforma Agraria Se Basa en Factores de Orden Humano, Cívico, Social, y Económico," Santiago, December 15, 1964, pp. 25, 31.

139 *Ibid.*

THE INTEREST OF THE CHILEAN CHURCH IN LAND REFORM

Chapter 2

It is not enough to assert the natural character of the right of private property, but the effective distribution among all social classes is to be insisted upon.
—Pope John XXIII. *Mater et Magistra* (Official English Translation).

Our program operates on a small scale, but we believe it has already proven of great value. Through it, other private property owners have been encouraged to carry out similar programs . . . our program is assimilating training and experience that will benefit the national government—and other nations—in their plans of land use.
—Cardinal Raúl Silva Henríquez, Archbishop of Santiago.[1]

THERE WAS little doubt that in the establishment of land reform projects on three Church-owned fundos the liberals within Chilean Catholicism were having their say. The land reform project began when the Bishop of Talca, Manuel Larraín, turned over the farm Los Silos (Chapter 3) to a campesinos' cooperative on June 26, 1962, after having appointed a committee to handle all technical matters of the transfer. The Archbishop of Santiago, Cardinal Raúl Silva Henríquez, soon followed suit, announcing a reform project on two fundos his diocese owned: Las Pataguas (Chapter 4) and Alto Melipilla. He also named a Technical Committee to ready the farms for reform. On June 5, 1963, the Technical Committees appointed by the prelates merged and the Instituto de Promoción Agraria (INPROA) was born.

Those familiar with the history of Latin America will find the Church's current interest in land reform a turnabout in official attitude. The Church, with a long history as a landowner itself and with the most influential of its faithful being landed aristocrats, was, for a matter of centuries, one of the most conservative forces in Latin America.

One researcher, speaking of the Church's interest in land in Latin America, summarized the situation:

The clergy was an economically privileged class from the beginning. The members of it received large grants of land from the crown. Many monasteries, cathedrals and individual prelates were given encomiendas which had more or less the same history as those conferred upon laymen.

For the erection of churches, monasteries and residences, the royal treasury furnished half the money, the encomenderos or the Spanish population in general furnished the other half, and the Indians did the work without remuneration. Ecclesiastical capital was free from taxation—legally in early days, virtually always . . . From the outset [the Church] had an economic advantage over even the richest of the encomenderos, who had to build their own houses and provide their own working capital, and had not the resources of income that the clergy had. So with the immense prestige of the Church behind them, it is not surprising that the clergy dominated the colonial era economically and politically.[2]

One of the admitted objectives of the conquerors was to Christianize the natives they found upon coming to the New World. This, at the time, was one of the justifications for the encomienda. Later, after the evolution of the hacienda, the Church prospered best when allied with the owners of huge landed estates instead of the new capitalist classes in cities.[3]

Early Landholdings of the Church in Chile. The Jesuits, the group which dominated agriculture in colonial times, arrived in Chile in 1593. From this date they began to gather land riches about them. In colonial times the Jesuits were without a doubt the largest landholders in the country. They became owners "of all the land irrigated by the Mapocho," "of all the land through which the Santiago-Valparaíso railway passes," and "of all (or almost all) the province of Valparaíso."[4]

Besides Jesuits, the Augustinian order had considerable property in the province of Talca, and Dominicans (as well as Jesuits) owned large acreages in the province of Santiago. But the holdings of the Jesuits during colonial times were at least twice those of all other orders together.[5]

Not only were the Jesuit lands extensive, they were also rich, encompassing some of Chile's best farm land. All indications are that the Jesuits farmed well. They had sufficient tools, and controlled, at the peak of their power, large numbers of Indians. Jesuits engaged in selling livestock from some of their farms and also produced wine, wheat, *aguardiente,* and dried fruits. They hedged against middlemen by building their own warehouses at ports and by hiring their own dispatchers in Peru. Their activities substituted a new monopoly for that of agricultural merchants in Lima, even though later in the eighteenth century, the viceroy of Peru prohibited these dealings.[6]

In Chile . . . the Jesuits monopolized the meat industry, operating slaughter houses and retail stores. They even built small vessels, engaged in the manufacture of lime, pottery, and other articles, and trafficked in drugs and medicine. They possessed similar economic interests in other parts of the Americas, and their wealth increased steadily as devout followers lavished benefits upon them.[7]

Such favorable worldly status aroused jealousies and antagonisms not only with laymen, but among less favorably situated orders.

During the period that the Jesuits were enjoying such extreme privilege and their riches were being eyed enviously by others in the colony, a wave of anticlerical liberalism was sweeping Europe. Caught up in the spirit of reform, largely inspired by French liberal thought at the time, Charles III decreed the expulsion of the Jesuits from all Spanish colonies in 1767. There are no available records of Jesuit landholdings at that time in Chile, but just one of their forty-seven properties included 126,000 hectares.[8] Expulsion broke Jesuit monopoly powers since much of their land went up for sale; thereafter this land was not as rationally farmed. Indeed, "in Chile, their departure was attended by an almost complete revolution in the commercial life of the colony."[9] The Church never recovered its lost land wealth in Chile. After independence more land was confiscated from the Church during the government of Freire in

1824. Although some restitution was made in later, more conservative governments, this was made usually in specie and not in land.[10]

Even through these setbacks, the Church remained a large landowner with all the power and privilege over the affairs of state
which that implies. In describing the "República Liberal" from
1861 to 1891 McBride states:

. . . with the spirit of tolerance and the practical common sense characteristic
of many leaders of the upper-class Chileans, the dominant group itself introduced more liberal features into their government. There was always, it was
true, an obstinate inner circle, jealous of their "privilegios de la cuna" (privileges of the well-born) which opposed every measure tending toward a lessen-
ing of their grip on the affairs of state. Side by side with such ultraconservatives
always stood the hierarchy of the Church. Clerical bodies were themselves great
landlords. Some of the richest of Chilean haciendas belonged to these organizations, and the Church held mortgages on many other great properties. These
two groups constituted the most solidly united single interest in the country.[11]

While anticlericalism never went as far in Chile as it did in Mexico or in Guatemala, where the Church may own no property except
for that strictly needed for religious services, Church power was held
in check in Chile by rather strong anti-Church groups which gained
strength during the last of the nineteenth and the first quarter of the
twentieth centuries.

The New Attitude. After a long period of political controversy, a
law of Church-state separation was passed in 1925 with the approval
of the Chilean hierarchy. In this separation the Church retained its
properties and full control over its schools. "It became an independent entity within the state, which abandoned the important prerog-
ative of patronage, with its implied right to interfere in the internal
administration of the Church."[12]

Soon after the position of the Church in state affairs was weakened, attitudes internal to the Church began to change in Chile.
This "liberalization" was a trend all over Latin America at the
time:

The opening of Catholic universities . . . has been indicative of a renewed
interest in intellectual affairs on the part of the Church in Latin America. Likewise, it has helped to provide a new Catholic intelligentsia, which is beginning
to make its weight felt. . . . Many of these Catholic intellectuals are followers
of such progressive Catholic thinkers as Henri Bergson, François Mauriac, and
Jacques Maritain . . . the Church has tended to shift its emphasis from defense

of the economic, social, and political status quo and of its own privileges, toward a more critical attitude toward Latin American society to which it is ministering.[13]

What has caused this change in Chile? What prompted, for example, the Church's interest in land reform and the organization of the Instituto de Promoción Agraria? We turn now to a brief review of these matters, keeping in mind that INPROA is one of a whole series of small social action agencies now operating in the Chilean countryside.[14]

Quite basic to an understanding of social action agencies of the modern Church is the realization that the Church in Chile, as elsewhere, is not monolithic. Some churchmen would oppose—most of them tacitly—any social action program under clerical aegis. Others would argue that the Church has obligations to society but should not undermine the traditional position of the elite; their favor would probably encompass social action but certainly not social reform. Yet another group (most notably represented by some of the Christian Democrats in Chile) recommends in its public pronouncements "rejecting the old norms of social relations, as withered leaves upon dying trees" and peacefully evolving a new society which includes the masses.[15] This latter group—indeed, the latter two groups—represent new thinking since old liberal-conservative arguments within the Church were usually focused on issues like charity and not on social action and reform as such. As Pike has noted:

In the mid–twentieth century, then, the Church has had to concern itself with the masses. More and more its prelates have begun to speak out in favor of social justice. However, as has been so true in the past, the Church is divided. Social justice has divergent meanings to different Churchmen. To one group it means preserving the stratified, closed society. . . . On the other hand, numerous Catholics contend that the old social structure is doomed and that paternalism and charity will never suffice to keep the masses in line. They envision the emergence of genuine social pluralism in which all classes and functional interest groups will have the power to protect their essential rights and to compete on a basis of relative equality of opportunity for the advantages the nation has to offer.[16]

The ideological underpinnings of social action and social reform agencies supported by the Church can be traced to the end of the nineteenth century and the 1891 encyclical of Pope Leo XIII, *Rerum Novarum (On the Condition of Workers)*, to which Pope

John XXIII referred in his own *Mater et Magistra.* Pope John XXIII also lauded another of his predecessors, Pope Pius XI, who wrote *Quadragesimo Anno (Forty Years After on Reconstructing Social Order),* another liberal encyclical, in 1931.[17]

The work of Pope Pius XI and that of Pope Leo XIII strengthened the position of a group of Chilean Catholic liberal activists throughout the first third of this century. The result was the organization of numerous groups protesting against the Conservative Party (the sectarian Catholic party made up largely of landlords), like the Partido Social Sindicalista in 1932. Furthermore it caused the splintering off of the Youth of the Conservative Party (Juventud del Partido Conservador) in 1935. The roots of the Christian Democratic Party of today can be traced to these groups of liberal Catholics.[18]

In *Mater et Magistra,* Pope John said in 1961:

It is not enough to assert the natural character of the right of private property, but the effective distribution among all social classes is to be insisted upon. Rural workers should feel a sense of solidarity with one another, and should unite to form cooperatives, . . . if they are to defend their products. . . . The rural workers engaged in improving the conditions of the whole agricultural world can legitimately demand that their efforts be seconded and complemented by the public authorities. . . .[19]

The Chilean bishops had quickly followed *Mater et Magistra* with a pastoral letter of their own the Sunday after Easter 1962, in which they announced their plans on agrarian as well as other reforms:

Conscious as we are of the situation of the campesino and desirous of collaborating not only with the fundamental doctrine, but also with an example of a concrete program, we have agreed in plenary session to recommend the study of an eventual colonization of the agricultural properties that are the property and in the use of the hierarchy to a commission that would prepare legal, economic, and technical antecedents to facilitate access of the campesinos to the land.[20]

On Independence Day (September 18) of the same year the bishops added the pastoral *El Deber Social y Político* which mentioned not only agrarian structure but singled out other problems: poor housing, unemployment, low wages, illiteracy, bad diet, and government inefficiency. The bishops noted that a true Christian cannot stand in the way of change.[21] Needless to say, many Catholics on the Chilean right were rankled by these statements.

The New York Times commented:

> No sector of the Chilean community was spared from criticism as the pastoral letter ranged over a wide range of problems and attitudes.
> The letter noted that in the Chilean countryside a minority of proprietors had the greatest part of the best lands and that the majority lived in poverty.
> Despite some gains, there is general agreement here that there are gross social inequalities. But the meat of the latest message from the Church is that reforms are going entirely too slowly and that too many so-called faithful Christians in Chile are showing cold indifference to the problems of the masses that have now reached the emergency stage.
> The pastoral letter criticized those wealthy Chileans who deposited their money abroad or who "spend enormous sums on totally useless things or amusements here" while millions were in misery.[22]

The pastoral also hinted that this attitude was not completely inspired by the evolutionary development of the social doctrine of the Church even though this dogma did play a large part.[23] Surely a part of the *raison d'etre* for the organization that eventually became INPROA, for example, was the need to answer the far-left's charges that the Church was not encouraging land reform and that a Communist-Socialist government would be more conscious of the social function of land if it gained power.

On this matter, *The New York Times* continued:

> While attacking the abuses of the liberal capitalist system, the pastoral letter also declared that it was simply impossible to cooperate with the Communist movement here. The Communists are working with various democratic parties only with the idea of using them as a stepping stone to totalitarian power, the letter said.[24]

Father Albert J. Nevins has called the Communist movement in Chile "a threat to the Church's life."[25]

During the Vatican conclave in 1963 Cardinal Silva Henríquez gave an interview to *L'Osservatore della Domenica,* saying in part: "The Church in Latin America must decide and choose among the people who push for grand reforms or the people who want to conserve the current situation." He also declared that all of Latin America "can fall under Communism by the end of this century if political and social conditions are not transformed."[26]

The Church can well afford to be alarmed; the anti-Church far-left in Chile has shown accelerated growth lately.[27] The Popular Action Front (FRAP), in which the Communist Party plays a major role, polled 350,000 votes in the presidential election of 1958, losing the presidency by only 35,000 votes.[28] In the 1961 congressional elections FRAP pushed its total to over 400,000 votes, more than enough to have given it victory two years previous[29] and registered "a greater increase in voting strength than any other political organization."[30]

The Communists within FRAP seem to be becoming more ascendent. Pike notes:

... in the December 1959 election for the executive committee of the Single Center of Chilean Workers (Central Unica de Trabajadores de Chile), the principal labor confederation, Socialists lost several seats, leaving the Communists in clear control of the organization that had traditionally been led by non-communist Marxists. Even more significant, in the March 1961 national congressional elections, the communist slate was supported by 154,130 voters, while the Socialist Party gained a disappointing 147,883 ballots.[31]

The growth of the Communist Party is astounding by any measure. In 1948 it was declared illegal when President Gabriel González Videla, turning against the Communist Party which was instrumental in electing him, enacted the "Law for Permanent Defense of Democracy" with congressional approval.[32] The party was not legalized again until the closing days of Carlos Ibáñez' second term in 1958. González Videla's and Ibáñez' controls on the Communist Party were complete enough to lead K. H. Silvert, one of the most knowledgeable commentators on the Chilean scene, to observe in 1957 (the year before the party was re-legalized):

The tendencies can perhaps best be exemplified by the dwindling importance of the Communist Party and the growing influence of the Christian Socialist *Falange*. The former, who reached their heights of power in 1946 and 1947 with cabinet posts and important appointments in administrative agencies, are now an outlawed party every day falling further and further into desuetude as their ideology becomes less applicable, their primitiveness and inflexibility more obvious. As they cling ever harder to dreams of a class revolution in the United States, the "inevitability" of the self-destruction of the "capital forces" by international war, the necessity for a dictatorship of the proletariat in their own Chile, the realities of international politics and of the internal dynamics of Chile draw ever further from their unadjusted preconceptions. Concomitantly, their power of ideological persuasion, hitherto their most potent weapon, has become weak and comparatively ineffectual. At the same time, the *Falange* has moved in to conquer some of the more important persons in the universities, the trade union movement, and in many of the new and often directly or indirectly publicly sponsored industries, such as steel. This party, with its democratic political ideals, its roots in a traditional religion consistent with today's mode, and its neosocialistic economic doctrines has not grown in direct proportion as the Communists have declined, but it has demonstrated ability to fill the political needs of important policy groups and has enough popular support—even among some anti-clericals—to allow it to dream of the presidency with some justification.[33]

While being quite wrong on his forecast of the growth of the Communist Party—he did not seem to foresee its re-legalization or sense its extralegal growth under the guise of other parties—Silvert was correct in his assessment of the parallel growth of the National Falange, founded in 1937 by splintering off from the Conservative Party. (In 1957 the Falange changed its name to the Partido Demócrata Cristiano, the Christian Democratic Party.)[34]

Although Eduardo Frei Montalva, the Christian Democratic candidate, came in third in the 1958 presidential elections, he did get about one third of the total votes cast. In the March 1961 congressional elections the Christian Democratic Party won some 212,000 votes. This marked the first time it surpassed the Conservative Party which obtained about 197,000 votes.[35] As might be expected, however, the conservative wing of the Church rebelled against the Christian Democrats and, as Pike has noted, engaged the Christian Democrats "in one of the bitterest pamphlet wars in modern Chilean history."[36] The 1964 presidential election saw the Conservatives supporting the Christian Democrats after a twenty-seven-year estrangement.

By 1964 the number of voters had doubled, due to new enfranchisement, population growth, and voting procedures which made it more necessary for eligible voters to register. As the result of a strong campaign predicated on anti-Communism but left-of-center reforms, the number of votes for Frei approximately tripled in 1964. However, a comparison is more fairly made in relative terms. The combined votes for Jorge Alessandri (who won) and Frei in the 1958 elections included about 52 percent of the total vote. In 1964 the vote for Frei totalled about 55.6 percent. The March 1965 congressional elections gave Frei the mandate he requested: 8 seats above the outright majority in a total of 147 Chamber seats. Furthermore, in the 45-seat Senate, all 12 Christian Democrat candidates were elected (making a total of 13 Senate seats filled by Christian Democrats). This vote seemed to undermine those who thought Frei had won the presidency only with the aid of rightist votes. The

CD Party captured between 40 and 45 percent of the popular vote.

The Communist Party within FRAP did not lose ground, however. The percentage of the vote it captured grew from 11.0 in 1961 to 11.8 in the 1965 congressional election. In presidential elections FRAP grew from about 350,000 votes in 1958 to about 975,500 votes in 1964, more than keeping up with the doubled vote. Relatively, FRAP's share of total votes in 1958 was about 25 percent of all votes cast; in 1964 its share had grown to 38.5 percent.[37]

Although this is not the place for a detailed analysis of the Church's changes to meet these new challenges, a few generalizations are in order:

(1) The application of the social doctrine of the Church in Chile probably dates from the end of the last century. This doctrine began to be translated into concrete action programs in the countryside in the 1950's, although city Catholic action agencies had an earlier beginning. Late impetus has been provided by Pope John XXIII and, internal to Chile, by liberal Catholic clergy, foremost among them the Archbishop of Santiago, Cardinal Raúl Silva Henríquez; the Bishop of Talca, Manuel Larraín; some priests who have come from Europe to serve vacant parishes in Chile; and prominent Jesuits. Other clergy, those who are non-Jesuit and/or possibly non-Christian Democrat, also have fostered some social action programs. They often find themselves at odds with the aforementioned group. These programs, although stemming from Catholicism, are not monolithic, and intense rivalries between them are common.

(2) The recent growth of social action and social reform programs in the countryside is probably not due solely to the current popularity of the social dogma of the Church, although this body of thought is important. Other factors which have played a part, all underlaid by demands for economic progress emanating from heretofore disadvantaged classes, are:

(a) The desire for Church groups to bring back to the fold Catholics who have fallen into non-attendance at Mass, and hence non-support of the Church, by offering them more earthly rewards for their faith. Related to this point is the fact that Protestantism has shown increased growth recently—especially among lower classes.

(b) The lack of enough effective public-supported institutions of social action operating in the countryside in Chile. The Church's parish-diocese arrangement may be a more effective administrative unit for basing community action than the provincial government itself, which has been traditionally weak, power being strongly centralized in Santiago.[38] At any rate, the Church has felt it necessary to play a role not usually expected of it in developed countries with a federal system of government. The high percentage of Catholics in Chile makes the Church a logical organization to perform functions which might elsewhere be undertaken in the public sector. Its mere size makes aloofness from politics impossible and also means it may become the object of attacks by politicians.

(c) The need of the Church to respond to the growth of far-leftist political groups which promise sweeping reforms that the Church in Chile has historically opposed. The Church must adapt to its changed and ever-changing environment if it is to remain institutionally strong.

THE INSTITUTO DE PROMOCION AGRARIA (INPROA)

INPROA—whose staff and supporters are largely Christian Democrats or CD sympathizers—has become a laboratory which can test ideas on reform and counter the agrarian platform of FRAP[39] as well as illustrate the Church's interest in land reform. As the Christian Democrats assumed power in Chile after November 1964, a number of INPROA's technical people were hired away by the government land reform agency. It seems likely that via its trained personnel, rather than in any official way, INPROA will play a part in the reform program of the new government.

Press Misunderstandings Regarding Land Reform on Church Land. INPROA's own words set forth its fundamental goal:

It is INPROA's fundamental purpose to elaborate and develop an operative model of agrarian reform whose results serve to demonstrate its necessity and its urgency and thus counter many of the prejudices against agrarian reform.

Later, if INPROA receives necessary financing, it will use it to give access to the land to 1500 families.[40]

In the face of these admittedly limited and realistic objectives, reports on the Church land redistribution program began to appear in the popular press in the United States and Latin America. In general, they indicated little knowledge of the Church's stated mission and tended to overstatement and, more serious, naïveté. For example:

(1) . . . In the face of Latin poverty [the Church has] felt justified in taking drastic steps. . . . It has put together stopgap relief measures, broad-scale educational projects, political innovations, social reforms. . . .

You can see the progress of this movement best in Chile. The Church has scored tremendous gains there in the past two years.

The Church's real master strokes came last fall. *First, the Church gave, absolutely without strings, all its existing lands to those working them.*[41]

. . . the Church program is radical; *it has purely and simply handed over all its lands to the people working on them. . . .*[42]

(2) The Archdiocese of Santiago . . . has a yearly income of about $165,000. Three fourths of that amount comes from donations. The other quarter comes from property rentals—*but nearly half will be lost to the Church, which, under its own agrarian reform program, is liquidating the farms from which rentals come.*[43]

(3) Practicing what Silva Henríquez preached about agrarian reform, the Roman Catholic Church in Chile undertook its own land-distribution program, *parcelling out 13,200 of its own acres in the Andean foothills. . . .*[44]

(4) Two large estates totalling over 3,000 acres belonging to the Santiago Archdiocese were then divided. The average distribution was a section of about 23 acres, although some exceptionally capable farmers received up to 75 acres. *Since then land transfers have gone on steadily.*[45]

(5) There are already signs of success: . . . *farm families take to cooperative techniques quickly.*[46]

(6) . . . the episcopate considered it fundamental to undertake an Agrarian Reform. *They preached about it, without any ideological hesitation,* with a social criterion pervading the concept of property, reaffirmed by Christian thought. . . .[47]

Clearing up statements like these and offering a detailed description of the Church reform is one purpose of this monograph. The following paragraphs briefly treat each italicized inaccuracy cited above.

(1) The Church did not give all of its land to those working it. The amount of land given out was 7,371 acres of irrigated land and 6,120 acres of dry land. Of the dry land, much is unusable. All told, this means that a total of 13,491 acres on five properties are in various stages of being turned over to colonists. The census of 1955

and the Bureau of Internal Revenue (Dirección de Impuestos Internos) show that Church land in Chile includes about 2,065 properties —many of them merely lots—encompassing about 123,550 acres (50,000 hectares). At the time the census was taken it was estimated that half of the land was rented; half was worked directly.[48] The majority of this land is owned by Orders; a smaller part by dioceses. About 11 percent of Church land, then, is currently included in the INPROA program. Furthermore, the Church did not give the land "absolutely without strings." The general case is that land was sold to colonists over a twenty-year period with 5 percent interest.

(2) The INPROA program is not set up to lose money for the Church. A duty of the Church is to maintain the integrity of possessions which are willed to it for social action and the INPROA program is designed accordingly.

(3) Parcelization is the stated eventual goal of INPROA's present reform program, but not all of the 13,491 acres in the INPROA program have been parcelled out. In the case of Los Silos, INPROA has experimented with a system of communal farming. We shall see a different system in the case of the fundos of San Dionisio and Alto Las Cruces, designed shortly before INPROA's birth and administered by INPROA. These colonies will be described in Chapter 5. Here mediería and a rental period are gradually preparing colonists for land ownership. On the other hand, two fundos, Las Pataguas and Alto Melipilla, were parcelled out.

(4) Land transfers have been made, contingent on payment, only on the two subdivided fundos: Las Pataguas and Alto Melipilla. Land is legally owned by the cooperative on Los Silos and a deed is in the hands of INPROA in the cases of San Dionisio and Alto Las Cruces. The land transfer program is frozen at its present level for the time being. No new fundos were added to the program during the 1963–64 or 1964–65 crop years.

(5) Farm families have not taken to cooperative techniques easily. Cooperatives everywhere in the world have their peculiar difficulties and our case studies of Los Silos, Las Pataguas, San Dionisio, and Alto Las Cruces will attempt to detail the particular problems of these cases. Cooperatives are not impossible, but their difficulties must be taken into account in any land reform program to which they are central.

(6) Any statement which presents the episcopate as being unhesitatingly and universally liberal on the issue of agrarian reform is certainly inaccurate. The author of this statement forgets about the right wing of the Chilean Church that even branded Bishop Manuel Larraín as a "red bishop" for his part in Los Silos (see Chapter 3). He further minimizes the heritage of years of Church conservatism which the present liberals of Catholicism in Chile must counter.

The INPROA *Organization.* The program executed by the Technical Committee appointed by the Bishop of Talca espoused a cooperative farming plan with built-in incentives. Aside from cooperatively worked land, each colonist would be given a small plot to farm. Cooperative members might or might not elect eventually to opt for private property. The cooperative would be made up of as many of the old fundo inquilinos as would accept cooperative principles. If replacements had to be made, the cooperative itself would decide on new colonists. Much of the intellectual guidance for this committee had come from the Jesuit-oriented Instituto de Desarrollo in Chile and its Latin American counterpart. Agricultural technicians of the Food and Agriculture Organization of the United Nations (FAO) cooperated closely with this committee.

The Technical Committee of the Archbishop of Santiago, on the other hand, espoused a plan similar to that used by the government land reform agency, Corporación de la Reforma Agraria (CORA). Under this system land would go directly into the hands of campesinos selected on the basis of a point system. A cooperative would be organized later. The Technical Committee of the Archbishop relied a great deal on the Instituto de Educación Rural (IER) and several fundo owners and agricultural businessmen, generally more conservative elements within the Church framework.

At INPROA's organization, after the Technical Committees had operated one crop year (1962–63), the Archbishop's Committee requested that INPROA confine its activities to economics and leave the social aspects to the IER. The Bishop's Committee, on the other hand, wanted INPROA to be a land reform agency dealing with all aspects—social and economic—of the reform. In the end the ideas of the Bishop's Committee seemed to take ascendency, but this does not mean that an interesting meld of ideas from the two Committees was not developed.

From the first year of experience with Los Silos and Las Pataguas, INPROA concluded:

> In almost all cases a certain amount of time is necessary to prepare land for subdivision and rational exploitation. The condition of natural resources available indicates a direct access to property by new owners is necessary. But it is also necessary to allow for a transitional period during which the campesino can adjust to his new farm. During this time, the campesino must be converted into a responsible person who can occupy a definite and responsible position in the community. There seems to be a certain conflict between access to property and the necessity that land fulfill a social function, that is, to be maximally productive. This situation is not permanent; it is a transitory condition and only lasts while the campesino is developing into a responsible business person.[49]

According to initial plans, this transitional process would take the following general form:

(1) INPROA would receive the land from the Church with the understanding that it had irrevocable right to: (a) sell, alienate, rent in usufruct or for cash; collect and set the prices or rents, (b) manage the farm; contract necessary services, technicians, assistants, and professionals, (c) contract loans and credits, (d) encumber the price of land in whatever form necessary, (e) effectuate necessary investments, and (f) perform studies on the property.

(2) Colonists must pay for land in a maximum of twenty years according to its commercial value; this value will correspond to productivity.

(3) During the first year of occupancy the colonist or his cooperative needs only to pay interest. Entering the third year, principal payments begin.

(4) The colonist must pay INPROA 10 percent of the value of his land as a downpayment upon parcelization.

(5) The sum INPROA spends on the property for investments will be paid back in the first amortization quotas.

(6) In the first year of operation the land is administered by INPROA and a campesino cooperative is organized. Production will be the basis for parcelization. During this time the number of families the farm can support will be determined.

(7) After the first year, if the cooperative chooses, the colonist-community begins cash-renting its land from INPROA. Except for unforeseen difficulties, those who enter this stage are given an option to buy.

(8) Selection of final colonist families is made by the cooperative itself.

(9) In a third step parcels will be sold to the campesinos.[50]

These were the guide lines INPROA set down as the result of the Technical Committees' experiences on Los Silos, Alto Melipilla, and Las Pataguas, to be applied to San Dionisio and Alto Las Cruces and other fundos which might come into its program.

The geographic dispersion of INPROA's current land reform program is shown in Map I. The first INPROA organization plan is shown in Diagram I. Four departments were involved in the administration of the program: Promotion, Technical, Accounting, and Marketing and Credit. The purposes of the Promotion Department were to aid in establishing cooperatives and to educate the colonists on the merits and techniques of cooperation.[51]

The Technical Department was designed as INPROA's extension division. It was responsible for advising the remainder of the INPROA organization on technical matters on the fundos, including such matters as irrigation, planning for crop rotation, division of lands, construction, etc. This department was designed to be directly responsible for the administration of the fundos prior to their parcelization. After parcelization, its purpose would be to advise on matters of technical agriculture the cooperative officials who would, in turn, pass the information along to members of the cooperative. In preparation for parcelization it was expected that this department would do all necessary land division studies and advise the remainder of the INPROA organization as to the number and kind of technicians necessary on each individual fundo. The Technical Department would be expected to map out parcelization schemes and detail necessary infrastructure with its proper cost.

The Accounting Department was assigned the duties of keeping an account of all the expenditures of INPROA and advising the fundos in the INPROA program on bookkeeping. All tax functions also fell to this department to administer.

The Marketing and Credit Department was responsible for purchasing all inputs and consumption goods necessary for the cooperatives. It also was to sell the colonists' production, collect the marketing fees, and obtain credit for colonists.

During its first year the INPROA organization grew substantially. Dia-

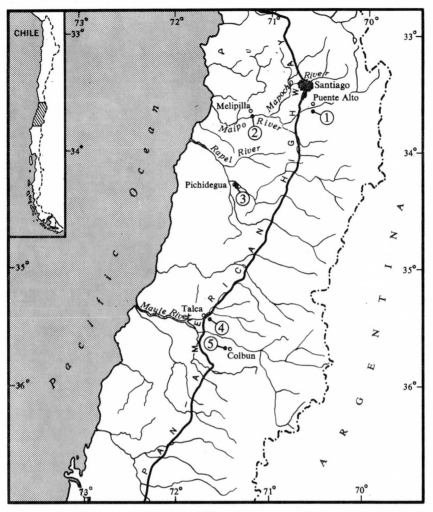

MAP I

INSTITUTO DE PROMOCION AGRARIA (INPROA)

Reformed Fundos

1 Los Silos (1962)   182.13 irrigated hectares
2 Alto Melipilla (1962)   164.47 irrigated hectares

3 Las Pataguas (1962)   1,485.50 total
                             ‾‾‾‾‾‾‾‾
                             1,213.40 irrigated hectares
                               272.10 dry hectares

4 Alto las Cruces (1963)   342.73 total
                             ‾‾‾‾‾‾‾
                               295.11 irrigated hectares
                                47.62 hectares not rehabilitated

5 San Dionisio (1963)   3,284.80 total
                             ‾‾‾‾‾‾‾‾
                             1,127.60 irrigated hectares
                               257.20 dry hectares
                             1,900.00 mountainland hectares (approx.)

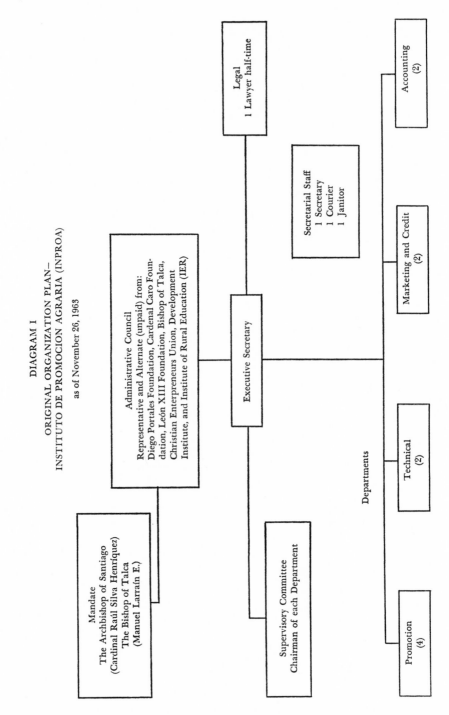

DIAGRAM I
ORIGINAL ORGANIZATION PLAN—
INSTITUTO DE PROMOCION AGRARIA (INPROA)

as of November 26, 1963

Mandate
The Archbishop of Santiago
(Cardinal Raúl Silva Henríquez)
The Bishop of Talca
(Manuel Larraín E.)

Administrative Council
Representative and Alternate (unpaid) from:
Diego Portales Foundation, Cardenal Caro Foundation, León XIII Foundation, Bishop of Talca, Christian Enterpreneurs Union, Development Institute, and Institute of Rural Education (IER)

Supervisory Committee
Chairman of each Department

Executive Secretary

Legal
1 Lawyer halftime

Secretarial Staff
1 Secretary
1 Courier
1 Janitor

Departments

Promotion
(4)

Technical
(2)

Marketing and Credit
(2)

Accounting
(2)

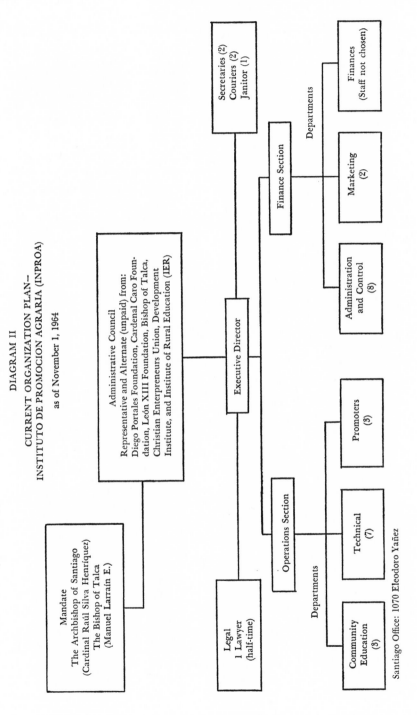

DIAGRAM II

CURRENT ORGANIZATION PLAN—
INSTITUTO DE PROMOCION AGRARIA (INPROA)

as of November 1, 1964

Mandate
The Archbishop of Santiago
(Cardinal Raúl Silva Henríquez)
The Bishop of Talca
(Manuel Larraín E.)

Administrative Council
Representative and Alternate (unpaid) from:
Diego Portales Foundation, Cardenal Caro Foundation, León XIII Foundation, Bishop of Talca,
Christian Enterpreneurs Union, Development
Institute, and Institute of Rural Education (IER)

Executive Director

Secretaries (2)
Couriers (2)
Janitor (1)

Finance Section

Departments

Administration
and Control
(8)

Marketing
(2)

Finances
(Staff not chosen)

Legal
1 Lawyer
(half-time)

Operations Section

Departments

Community
Education
(8)

Technical
(7)

Promoters
(8)

Santiago Office: 1070 Eleodoro Yañez

gram I shows that INPROA employed fourteen full-time people and one half-time person as of November 26, 1963. By November 1, 1964, as shown in Diagram II, this number had grown to thirty-one full-time people and one half-time person. The more-than-doubled staff called for the new operational structure to be put into effect in June 1964. The Office of Executive Secretary disappeared in this new plan. To make administration of the larger staff more flexible, INPROA was divided into two sections: operations and finance.

A staff member of the Development Institute, who had served as its representative on the INPROA board of directors, was brought in to serve as executive director of INPROA. The four departments became six as the promoters and the Department of Education and Cooperative Organization were created from the original Promotion and Technical Departments. While the Technical Department kept its planning functions, it gave extension duties to this new organism. The promoters are those staff members who live on the fundos and help the members of the cooperative with day-to-day problems of their organization. Each is responsible for a different fundo. The Department of Education and Cooperative Organization is set up to teach colonists cooperative techniques, civic organization, doctrinal-social orientation, technical agriculture, farm bookkeeping, diet and sanitation, reading, writing, and basic mathematics.

With the reorganization, the Credit Division was also separated from the former Marketing and Credit Department and combined with other duties relative to INPROA's new sources of outside financing (to be covered in the following section). Seven of the present staff (November 1964) are *Ingenieros Agrónomos* (holders of the highest agriculture degree granted by a Chilean university, roughly equivalent to a Bachelor of Science in Agriculture).

INPROA's operating expenses during the first seven months of its existence (June–December 1963) averaged about E° 8,500 a month. This includes all staff salaries and expenses of the Santiago office but no short- or long-term credit or infrastructural investments at the fundo level. This figure averaged E° 12,500 a month in January and February and by August was averaging E° 16,500. The total amount spent for these purposes for the first year of INPROA's existence (June 1–May 31) was E° 156,000, averaging E° 13,000 a month.

Prior to the time amortization payments begin, the Church collects 5 percent of the commercial value of the land under reform each year from INPROA as its rental. Original capital for INPROA, E° 100,000, was put up by two prelates. The statutes specify that the Archbishop of Santiago was to donate E° 66,667 and the Bishop of Talca E° 33,333 at the time INPROA received official legal status. This status was received November 12, 1963 and was approved by government Supreme Decree No. 3,272 on November 27, 1963. An organization of German bishops, MISEROER, donated the first funds—$110,000[52]—to be used for office expenses (and specified that this grant not be used for loan purposes). In 1964 they donated another $100,000 for the same purpose through government channels (Zentral Stelle) and have promised another $100,000 in 1965. A request by INPROA for a $700,000 revolving fund was made to Zentral Stelle but was not granted. A religious group in France, the Taizé Community, has donated $35,000 and the Inter-American Development Bank, late in 1963, granted $40,000. Of this latter sum, given expressly so that INPROA could do parcelization studies, $11,300 came from Social Progress Trust Fund sources which the bank administers as part of the Alliance for Progress.[53] During 1963–64 short-term credits of about E° 600,000 were obtained from various Chilean banking sources. INPROA re-loaned these funds to its colonists.

INPROA also applied for a $1.5 million loan from the Inter-American Development Bank expressly for land reform—building infrastructure and giving short-, medium-, and long-term credit. As the September 1964 elections approached, the loan had been approved by the bank, but blocked by the office of the President of the Republic. Had INPROA received this loan, it probably would have proceeded directly to enlarge its land reform efforts to other fundos. Aside from the five fundos already mentioned, INPROA had planned to expand its program to four more properties, thus giving it a total of 5,200 hectares of irrigated land. According to an early estimate, INPROA felt that an expenditure of $2,000,000 would be necessary for infrastructural and operating expenditures on all of the nine fundos in question. This included houses, all installations, agricultural machinery, draft animals, etc. This expenditure would be made in 1964–65. The infrastructure would be recoupable at the end of ten years and the operating expenses at the end of each crop year.[54] The election now past, INPROA hopes to receive this funding soon.[55]

Other funding possibilities largely closed to it, INPROA requested and received a grant of $325,000 from AID-Chile on June 30, 1964. The $325,000 grant, signed June 30, 1964, from USAID will run until June 30, 1967.[56] The grant provides for capital equipment and construction for land projects totalling $115,395.[57] Besides, it sets up a revolving fund aiding the fundos under reform (through their cooperatives) to purchase inputs such as seed, fertilizer, weed killer, disinfectants, insecticides, sacks, gasoline, oil, and grease. It also will permit purchase of similar inputs by a small number of non-land reform campesino cooperatives (also part of the INPROA program but beyond the scope of this monograph) made up of groups of small property holders. The revolving fund totals about $159,500[58] and includes an amount of direct technical help to the cooperatives "necessary to obtain success of the enterprise."[59]

Yearly, the loans will be paid back to the revolving fund by each cooperator with 12 percent interest. INPROA will collect an additional 1 percent for its lending service. (INPROA charged 15.6 percent for funds it lent to cooperatives in 1963–64.)

As the cooperatives repay the $115,395 for construction and equipment, this money, too, will be added to the revolving fund. The first and second year no payment will be required of the cooperatives for the machinery. Between the third and sixth years 40 percent will be recouped at 10 percent each year and between the seventh and tenth years the remaining 60 percent will be recouped at 15 percent each year.

A planning technician budgeted at $25,000 is also called for under this loan. He will assist in planning programs, cooperatives, and the business aspects of the operation. After he is hired, INPROA will be able to hire other technical assistance totalling $25,000.

As part of its responsibility INPROA must contribute E°300,000 to the program in cash or in kind "from its own resources and/or from donations received from Chilean or other non-US government sources."[60] In addition INPROA must develop a project to be presented to AID for PL 480, Title II goods.[61]

ALTO MELIPILLA

Alto Melipilla (164.47 irrigated hectares) will not be covered in this analysis except for this passing reference since many of the twenty-six parcels went to people basically able to pay, and not to the landless poor who must form the basis of a true agrarian reform. A required 30 percent downpayment was the discriminating factor making it difficult for inquilinos, medieros, or even lower-level fundo employees to purchase parcels. Consequently, this colony is mainly made up of people who formerly were higher-salaried fundo employees, with only a few inquilinos.

Furthermore, the parcels in Alto Melipilla are small. (They average around five hectares.) Yet some of the parcel holders already have acquired their own inquilinos, indicating that the project represents no real break in the traditional social system in the area. The cooperative is especially weak here. Most colonists apparently feel too independent and too different in background to make it work effectively. Finally, few of INPROA's resources are channelled into this project. After the land division was made, it was INPROA's decision to spend more time and money on other more needy projects.

NOTES

1 Ben F. Meyer, "Monseñor Raúl Silva Henríquez . . . ," AP dispatch, *El Mercurio*, Santiago, July 11, 1963, p. 29. From an interview in Washington after the Archbishop attended the Vatican Conclave in Rome.

2 Helen Phipps, *Some Aspects of the Agrarian Question in Mexico*, University of Texas, Austin, 1925, quoted in Robert J. Alexander, *Today's Latin America*, Anchor Books, Doubleday and Company, Inc., Garden City, New York, 1962, p. 221.

3 Fredrick B. Pike (ed.), *The Conflict Between Church and State in Latin America*, Alfred A. Knopf, New York, 1965, p. 20. The introduction to this book is an excellent statement summarizing the Church's changing role in Latin America.

4 Benjamín Vicuña Mackenna, *Historia de Santiago*, Vol. II, Santiago, 1869, p. 80 (second edition, Editorial Nascimento, Santiago, 1924).

5 Files of CIDA.

6 Juan Carlos Collarte, G. A. Palacios, P. P. Pinto, "Desarrollo Histórico de la Agricultura Chilena—Período Prehispánico—1830," Seminario en Economía Agraria, Facultad de Agronomía, Universidad de Chile, Santiago, unpublished, 1961. See also Diego Barros Arana, *Riquezas de los Antiguos Jesuitas de Chile*, Editorial Ercilla, Santiago, 1932; Carlos Silva Cotapos, *Historia Eclesiástica de Chile*, Imprenta San José, Santiago, 1925; P. Francisco Enrich, *Historia de la Compañía de Jesús en Chile*, Barcelona, 1891. These last three references are not very specific on landholdings of the Jesuits, however.

7   Donald E. Worcester and Wendall G. Shaeffer, *The Growth and Culture of Latin America,* Oxford University Press, London and New York, 1956, p. 285.

8   CIDA borrador, "Chile," p. 74.

9   Worcester and Schaeffer, *op. cit.,* p. 350.

10 Files of CIDA.

11 George McCutchen McBride, *Chile: Land and Society,* American Geographic Society, New York, 1936, pp. 202–3.

12 William Lytle Schurz, *Latin America,* E. P. Dutton and Co., Inc., New York, 1963, pp. 331–32.

13 Alexander, *op. cit.,* pp. 225–26.

14 These organizations, with direct or indirect Church support, may be classified as educational institutions and labor movements. Educational organizations are the Instituto de Educación Rural, Acción Católica Rural, and Fundaciones de Vida Rural. Labor movements include Unión de Campesinos Cristianos de Chile, Movimiento Independiente Campesino, Movimiento Nacional de Liberación Campesina, Asociación Nacional de Organizaciones Campesinas, and Instituto de Capacitación Sindical y Social. These organizations are described in William C. Thiesenhusen, "Experimental Programs of Land Reform in Chile," unpublished Ph.D. thesis, University of Wisconsin, Madison, 1965. Of course, there is also a parallel group of social action agencies under Church aegis which operates in cities.

15 Eduardo Frei Montalva, "Catholic Social Justice, Democracy, and Pluralism," in Pike, *op. cit.,* p. 211.

16 *Ibid.,* p. 22.

17 ". . . to carry on its affairs community life requires varied aptitudes and diverse services, and to perform these services men are impelled most by differences in individual property holdings" (*Rerum Novarum*), in *Two Basic Social Encyclicals: On the Condition of Workers, Leo XIII, and Forty Years After on Reconstructing Social Order, Pius XI,* New York, 1943, p. 21; quoted in *Great Political Thinkers, Plato to the Present* by William Ebenstein, Rinehart and Company, Inc., New York, 1951, p. 833.

18 One must be careful of mistaking the evolution of ideas such as these for liberal pragmatism. Fredrick Pike, *Chile and the United States, 1880–1962,* University of Notre Dame Press, Notre Dame, Indiana, 1963, traces the interest in labor groups by the Church to early ideas expressed by Padre Alberto Hurtado, known as the "labor priest," and some of his classmates in the early thirties. He notes ". . . like today's Christian Democrats in Chile, Hurtado felt that social justice based on merely pragmatic considerations and lacking in theological roots was bound to be inadequate. . . . [Intellectuals'] suspicions of the United States social system [are] occasioned by their spiritually motivated distrust of pragmatism. Chilean intellectuals in general demand an overall, total philosophical position as the foundation for their attitudes toward life. United States lack of concern with broad,

philosophical speculation and its dedication to pragmatism stand as imposing obstacles in the way of any attempt to justify its position among a people demanding philosophical-theological ultimates," p. 421. Pike lists sources for this conclusion also in note 23, pp. 420–21.

19 Pope John XXIII, *Mater et Magistra*, English translation, *Mother and Teacher*, in *Social Action Digest*, Vol. 4, pp. 8–9.

20 Quoted from *Vea*, 5–VII–1962, p. 4.

21 The Bishops of Chile, *El Deber Social y Político*, Secretariado General del Episcopado de Chile, Santiago, 1962, especially pp. 9–18.

22 Edward C. Burks, *The New York Times*, November 4, 1962, p. 32.

23 Helpful sources on the social doctrine of the Church are Johannes Messner, *La Cuestión Social*, Ediciones Rialp, Madrid, 1960; C. von Gestel, *La Doctrina Social de la Iglesia*, Editorial Herder, Barcelona, 1961; and Jean Villain, S.J., *L'Enseignement Social de l'Eglise*, Spes-Paris, 1953. See also writings of Roger Vekemens like "Análisis Básico-Social de la Situación Prerevolucionaria de América Latina," *Mensaje*, No. 115, special number, third edition, Santiago, 1963.

24 Burks, *op. cit.*

25 Rev. Albert Nevins, "Chile: Nation on a Tightrope," *South Pacific Mail*, Santiago, Feb. 21, 1964, p. 6, reprinted from *Our Sunday Visitor; The National Catholic Action Weekly*.

26 *El Mercurio*, "El Cardenal Silva Henríquez Advierte Sobre Peligro del Comunismo en América Latina," carried on AP wire from *L'Osservatore della Domenica*.

27 In the following analysis the reader may want to keep in mind the following information: In a general right-to-left arrangement, the current array of the major Chilean political parties becomes: Conservative, Liberal, Radical, Christian Democrat, Socialist, and Communist. Socialists and Communists are currently allied in FRAP, the Frente de Acción Popular (Popular Action Front). Early in the Presidential campaign of 1964 the Conservatives, Liberals, and Radicals made up the Frente Democrático—The Democratic Front—but Julio Durán, their candidate, a Radical, resigned and the Conservatives and Liberals somewhat reluctantly switched their official support to Eduardo Frei, the Christian Democrat. When Durán re-entered the race, only the most loyal of Radicals continued to support him. The majority seem to have thought their vote for Durán, whose support outside the Radical Party was now nearly nil, would merely redound to the benefit of Salvador Allende, the FRAP candidate. To complicate matters, the traditional anticlericalism of the party switched a number of other Radical votes to Allende, since they were loathe to see a Christian Democrat in power. These within-party splits make the Radical Party difficult to place on a spectrum such as the one above. Another problem with the above scheme is the location of center. Some say that the Christian Democrats, previously regarded as left-of-center, are now right-of-center since they accepted the support of the Conservatives and the Liberals dur-

ing the presidential race. This question remains to be answered by an ex post facto examination of policies now being enacted by the Frei government. The reader interested in exploring Chile's political system further should read Ernst Halperin, *Nationalism and Communism in Chile,* Massachusetts Institute of Technology Press, Cambridge, 1965, a reference not available to the present author when he was writing this chapter.

28 Fredrick Pike, *Chile and the United States, 1880–1962.* p. 264.

29 Nevins, *op. cit.*

30 Pike, *Chile and the United States, 1880–1962,* p. 265.

31 *Ibid.,* p. 263.

32 *Ibid.,* p. 264.

33 K. H. Silvert, "A Political Sketch of Chilean History from 1879," American Universities Field Staff Letter, West Coast South America Series, New York, January 1957, p. 4.

34 On the Christian Democratic Party, which has certainly also been aided by the growth of the European Social Christian parties (although their political philosophy is generally more conservative) and the dropping out of rival Christian Parties within Chile, see such sources as Luis Vitale, *Esencia y Apariencia de la Democracia Cristiana,* Arancibia Hnos., Santiago, 1964; Ricardo Boizard B., *La Democracia Cristiana en Chile,* Editorial Orbe, Santiago, 1963; *Congresos Internacionales Demócrata-Cristianos,* Editorial del Pacífico, Santiago, 1958; Jaime Castillo V., *Las Fuentes de la Democracia Cristiana,* Editorial del Pacífico, Santiago, 1963.

35 *El Mercurio,* March 8, 1961, reported in Pike, *Chile and the United States, 1880–1962,* p. 260.

36 *Ibid.* See also note 19, p. 422 for a listing of some of these publications.

37 The right saw their Chamber position weakened in 1965. The Liberals and Conservatives held 45 seats in the last House, but only 21 in the new. Radicals dropped also, from 38 seats in the previous Chamber to 20 in the new.

38 This argument is weakened because there are many Latin parishes without priests. See François Houtart and Emile Pin, *The Church and the Latin American Revolution* (translated from the French by Gilbert Barth), Sheed and Ward, New York, 1965.

39 The Agrarian Platform of FRAP is outlined in *La Política Agropecuaria del Gobierno Popular,* Imprenta Horizonte, Santiago, 1964.

40 Instituto de Promoción Agraria (INPROA),"Informe de INPROA" (mimeographed), Santiago, 1963, p. 31.

41 Ed Heister, "The New Revolution in Latin America, a Rearmed Church Battles the Reds," *Parade,* July 7, 1963. Italics in this and the next quotations are the author's and are made to point up inaccuracies which will be discussed later.

42 *The Atlantic Monthly,* "Chile," October 1962, p. 23.

43 Leonard Gross, "The Catholic Church in Latin America," *Look,* October 9, 1962, p. 28.

44 *Time,* August 23, 1963, p. 16.

45 Nevins, *op. cit.,* p. 6.

46 *Peruvian Times,* "Chilean Farm Workers Get More Land," Lima, May 3, 1963, reprinted from *The Catholic Herald of London,* February 15, 1963.

47 Otto Morales Benítez, from a manuscript prepared for publication in *El Tiempo,* Bogotá, received by the International Development Foundation, Inc., October 8, 1963.

48 CIDA borrador, "Chile," Part II, p. 401.

49 INPROA, *op. cit.,* pp. 15–16.

50 *Ibid.,* pp. 16–19 (these points were condensed).

51 Note that the use of "promotion" here is different from the usual English usage of the word: to further, urge forward, push on, raise, or elevate an already existing organization in the sense of advertising it or propagandizing for it. Here the concept includes the organization of the cooperative and the basic education in cooperative techniques which must accompany such organization.

52 Henceforth "$" in this study signifies US$.

53 Inter-American Development Bank, "BID Otorga Asistencia Técnica para Facilitar la Parcelización de Tierras de la Iglesia Católica en Chile," Press Release CP–14–64, Washington, D.C., February 20, 1964. See also Inter-American Development Bank (BID), *Social Progress Trust Fund: Third Annual Report,* Washington, D.C., 1963, p. 56.

54 Alfonso Rochac and Casto Ferragut, "Informe Preliminar Sobre Reforma Agraria de la Iglesia Católica en Chile" (mimeographed), Washington, D.C., 1964.

55 As this was being sent to press, the author received notice that the loan had been made. "The Inter-American Development Bank today announced the approval of a loan equivalent to $1.5 million from the Social Progress Trust Fund to help finance a land subdivision plan which will benefit about 600 low income families. . . . The loan was extended for a term of 20 years at an interest rate of 1¼ percent annually. A service charge of ¾ percent, payable in dollars, also will be charged on principal amounts outstanding. The loan will be repaid in 39 semiannual installments the first of which will be paid one year after the date of the loan contract." Inter-American Development Bank, "Inter-American Bank Lends $1.5 Million to Aid Church-Sponsored Agrarian Reform in Chile," Press Release, NR-59/65, Washington, D.C., November 8, 1965.

56 United States Department of State, USAID, "Rural Cooperative Development Institute, INPROA," Project Number 513–13–140–159, Agreement Number INP–I–64, Pro-Ag (dittoed), Santiago, June 30, 1964.

57 Gonzalo Puga and Hugo Jordán, INPROA, "Plan de Trabajo e Inversiones," transmitted to Mr. John Robinson, AID Director (mimeographed), Santiago, July 13, 1964, pp. 2–6 and p. 9. There will be some minor changes in the figures noted above as negotiations on specifics of the projects continue.

58 *Ibid.,* pp. 11–13.

59 *Ibid.,* p. 14.

60 United States Department of State, USAID, *op. cit.,* Section D, 6.

61 *Ibid.,* Section D, 8.

THE COMMUNAL EXPERIMENT:
LOS SILOS   Chapter 3

You are the patrones of Los Silos. You have the responsibility for the fundo. It is a great satisfaction for me to bring it to you. But very sincerely, I have also brought you increased responsibility.
—Msgr. Manuel Larraín, Bishop of Talca (from his speech to members of the new cooperative). *Ercilla,* July 4, 1962, p. 17.

Bishop Manuel Larraín "gave" us the land, but only in words. . . . This "Agrarian Reform" . . . has cut off our water supply and our fences, and is pressuring us to leave.
—Report of small group of former Los Silos inquilinos who chose not to participate in the reform. *El Siglo,* November 8, 1963, p. 6.

THE CHURCH-OWNED farm of Los Silos was turned over to a campesino cooperative in July 1962. Its curious organization today (not really private property, not a collective, not even a cooperative in the conventional sense of the word) and its accessibility (about 30 kilometers southeast of Santiago near Puente Alto) have kept it an object of attention among those concerned with alternative land tenure structures in Chile.

The issues involved in land reform are often framed in terms of political and economic power: landlords who refuse to permit a major change in the fabric of an anachronistic society are faced by pressures from the left which demand all or most of that power. If this were all that reform involved—change of the locus of power—there would be little place for economic analysis. However, economists who approach land reform often ignore power and the social questions it involves. Their studies and resultant policy proposals may center about the use of tax policy to achieve reform. Or perhaps in dealing with expropriation of land, a politically charged issue, they are specific only on what they view as economic matters, such as the means, amount and type of payment, and inflationary adjustments. Some analyses center about justifications for different types of organization—family farms, cooperatives, collectives—but draw most of their data from countries which have already gone through agrarian reform.

A central theme of this monograph is that although these studies are often useful, frequently it would be more helpful in practical terms to have studies of actual reform efforts in the very country where wider restructuralization is to take place. The ancient land tenure structure in Chile is largely intact. However, on a few private properties, like the fundos to be analyzed in this study and some properties purchased by the state, the "political decision" to implement reform has been made. But at the moment of reform, all of the basic problems of creating new, economically and socially viable institutions which are subject—especially in their youth—to a wide variety of internal and external pressures remain to be resolved.

THE SETTING

That there are pressures and difficulties—and also successes—in the course of land reform can be illustrated in the case of Los Silos, located in the commune of Pirque. Pirque, encompassing 460 square kilometers, is composed mainly of latifundia—six proprietors hold 90 percent of the land in the commune.[1]

Msgr. Manuel Larraín, Bishop of Talca, bought Los Silos, a 182 hectare fundo (all of which was irrigable), in 1952 to help support the Seminario Conciliar of San Pelayo, which depends on his diocese for its funds.[2] When the Bishop acquired the property, he immediately leased it. In the late 1950's the original renter left and the Bishop let his fundo again. Since the last renter spent very little time at the fundo, he left management to his son who lived there and served as administrator. In addition, he employed eighteen resident workers, about equally divided between inquilinos and empleados.

In mid-1961 the renter's inquilinos were paid less than ten cents a day in cash. Additionally they were given perquisites of a little over one irrigated hectare to be farmed individually, grazing privileges for two animals, and some bread each day. To protest their low income (which was well below the legal minimum for agricultural workers that year) one of the Socialist aldermen in nearby Puente Alto, in his capacity as an officer of the Federación Campesina, organized a strike among seven of the eighteen fundo workers.

On November 12, 1961, a formal protest was made to the local work inspector. An agreement was signed a week later providing workers with a 16 percent salary increase and a few more perquisites. When the renter did not fulfill the agreement, seven of the fundo's employees remained on strike, losing the harvest on their individual plots and their grazing rights. When the inquilinos notified the provincial governor of the situation through the Federación Campesina, he recommended that they leave the fundo quietly and promised to get jobs for them. Meanwhile, hoping to solve the problem, the work inspector called the Bishop's renter to his office several times, apparently to try to persuade him to comply with the agreement. But the renter neither went nor paid the fine levied on him. The renter later contacted the work inspector, but only to threaten to have him transferred because of his attitude in favor of the "insurrectionists."[3]

It was at this time of unrest—after seven months of workers' strikes—that the Bishop decided to put a reform experiment into effect. The rental contract, up for renewal on May 1, 1962, was cancelled. Plans for the fundo's operation under reform had already been drawn up, because a group of Chilean land reform technicians had tried previously to get the Bishop's cooperation in the effort.

The Bishop, belonging to the most liberal wing of the Church and already widely known for his pointed sermons on social issues,[4] had begun to get some support for his positions from Rome.[5] But when he turned Los Silos over to the campesino cooperative on June 26, 1962, he was called "a demagogue and a fool"—even by some active Catholics.[6] Besides, he risked an assured rental check each six months for less certain mortgage amortization payments. Larraín is, it should be noted, one of the poorest bishops in Chile. The income for his diocese is about US $13,750 a year and its expenses, which must be made up in donations, are twice that. His own salary is

US $40.00 a month.[7] More importantly, his Church office makes him responsible for the financial integrity of the possessions of his diocese.

Since he felt a staff of clergymen unprepared to handle the details of a reform, the Bishop appointed a committee to handle technical matters of the land transfer. A short time later, but also in time for the 1962–63 planting season, the Archbishop of Santiago proceeded with the subdivision of Las Pataguas (see Chapter 4) and Alto Melipilla.

The first crop year, the Bishop's Technical Committee put a former fundo administrator in charge of Los Silos' day-to-day operation. Save for a small piece of land each colonist would farm individually, land was to be farmed by the cooperative. The cooperative would eventually hold title to all the real estate, and all credit and technical aid from INPROA would be channelled through it. Each operator was expected to work to his capacity on cooperative as well as on individually managed land.

THE COOPERATIVE'S ORGANIZATION

All previous workers on Los Silos had the opportunity to join the cooperative and become landholders. Unlike the Chilean government land reform program, Los Silos had no point system by which parcel holders were chosen. "Whether or not they were good workers as inquilinos is not of much help in deciding whether they will be able to make decisions about their own piece of land," stated the Technical Committee.[8] But agreement with the principles of the cooperative is absolutely necessary and non-acceptance reason enough for exclusion. The colonists themselves in general session will determine whether the communal system of farming will continue.

The direction of the cooperative is in the hands of its campesino members. It is governed by an administrative council (Consejo de Administración). Chilean law requires that there be at least twenty members to organize a cooperative. Since there were not enough colonists and sons over eighteen to meet the requirement when the cooperative was founded, some wives had to join. There were twenty-six members in 1963–64. The council is elected by the colonists in general session. These councilmen are also chairmen of committees

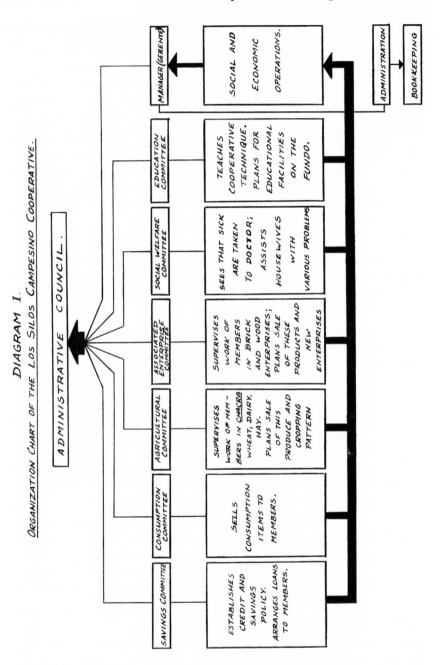

DIAGRAM I.

ORGANIZATION CHART OF THE LOS SILOS CAMPESINO COOPERATIVE.

(see Diagram I for official organization chart). *The Savings Committee* is in charge of managing and distributing funds of the cooperative, repairing installations, etc. *The Consumption Committee* sells consumption items to cooperative members. (This committee is not currently functioning.) *The Agricultural Committee* plans work, attends to current agricultural problems and gives technical assistance. *The Associated Enterprise Committee* decides upon possible methods of intensifying the cooperative's pattern of enterprises. There is currently a small enterprise for making and selling bricks; some wood grown on the fundo is also sold. *The Social Welfare Committee* sees that the sick are taken to a doctor. Medical attention is at the cooperative's expense. According to INPROA, this committee is rather ineffective at present. *The Educational Committee* plans to contract a teacher for Los Silos. Now most children in Los Silos attend school on a neighboring fundo which the owner himself admits is not very adequate. Few who go there have ever passed the necessary exams to get into secondary school.

The strong point of this organization is that it helps to develop leadership in a group in which individuals are just learning to make their own decisions. However, INPROA technicians were concentrating on raising production on the fundo in 1964–65 and did not have enough time to devote to leadership training in all committees. Those committees not directly related with production were developing slowest. The Consumption and Social Welfare Committees were at a near standstill at the end of 1965.

A problem with this organizational plan is that council members simply do not have time to do a good job as committee chairmen and do necessary farm work too. There is discussion about changing this aspect of the organization. Yet changing it implies that even more leadership ability must be developed and close coordination between the council and the committees might be lost.

THE COOPERATIVE IN 1962–63

The cooperative evolved gradually from the time the Bishop turned the land over to the colonists. At one of their first meetings the new colonists fixed a daily advance for each member with land rights and a slightly higher rate for each eighteen-year-old son who wanted to work. The first year the cooperative decided that perquisites similar to those of inquilinos would be available to cooperators with land rights. Extra profits at the end of the year would be divided or used to pay off outstanding debts for the cooperative's operating capital.

At a public sale, the cooperative purchased some of the former renter's equipment and animals. Credit was obtained from a private lending institution and the Bishop signed the necessary loans.

As INPROA took over the general administration of Los Silos, land price was set at E° 78,000 and buildings at E° 72,000, to be paid in twenty years with 5 percent interest each year. Originally, the principal was to be paid off in equal installments, adjusted for inflation by the percentage increase in the price of wheat during the year. The original amount, about E° 1,200 a hectare, was publicized by INPROA as being "65 percent of the commercial value."[9] The Church did not regard this reduction as a gift, but as a just evaluation to compensate cooperators for the low salaries they received as workers on the fundo.

It is difficult to determine commercial value: tracts of land this size in the area seldom come onto the market. Tax value often runs a fourth or less of what properties sell for. Recently, a group of small plots and another fundo in the area with a smaller amount of infrastructure brought about E° 2,000 a hectare. There is little reason to doubt that the selling price of Los Silos was substantially below commercial value. (In 1965 a re-evaluation of all property in Chile for tax purposes was completed, however.)

The adjustment for inflation may be less severe beginning in 1964–65, because it is based on whichever standard is more favorable to the colonist: the wheat index (wheat price is fixed by the government each year) or the index of a list of selected wholesale product prices (not fixed by the government). Two and one-half percent interest a year will be paid on the adjusted debt and two and one-half percent on the non-adjusted debt.

CURRENT SOCIO-POLITICAL DIFFICULTIES

What follows is an account detailing a few socio-political difficulties which have developed on Los Silos in its first years under reform. The

purpose of analyzing this situation is not to be unfairly critical of the
parties involved or to discourage reformers, but to cite examples of the
kinds of disputes reform may bring. A festering social problem would
detract from the most economically successful reform.

This section attempts to show how complicated reform may become and what skills are necessary to administer such an experiment
—however small—in a traditional society. (There is no assurance
that these problems are limited to traditional societies, but it is dangerous to extrapolate too widely from this one experience. One generalization is immediately obvious, however: whether reform takes
place in a traditional or in a rapidly changing society, it is a complex
process bringing with it unique problems which its participants will
have had little or no experience in solving.)

External Dissent and Internal Repercussions. Technicians decided
that the capacity of Los Silos would be sixteen families. Two of the
eighteen original resident workers of the fundo left soon before and
two left soon after the Bishop's turnover of land—all four of their
own volition. Two more were later expelled by the cooperative's
vote. Replacements were brought in for four of these.

Another four of the original eighteen families never joined the
resulting cooperative. Still under the influence of the Socialist alderman who had helped them during the strike, they argue that the
Bishop's words the day he turned over Los Silos to the cooperative
("You are the patrones of Los Silos.") meant that each would get title
to his own individual piece of land. They claim, even now, that they
do not understand the cooperative and its organization. Nor did
they ever accept the eight outsiders who were taken as replacements
for those who left and who came to be cooperators with land rights.
They claim the Bishop explicitly turned the fundo over to its former
residents.

The Bishop's idea, although he seems not to have communicated
it clearly enough, was that these organizational details would be left
to the Technical Committee. And he allowed the committee to
function more or less autonomously.

The Technical Committee felt that much more study would have
had to go into the fundo if it were to be divided into small farms.
There was a great deal of overhead capital represented in the barns

and the silos. Moreover, some expense (for which no funds were immediately available) would need to be incurred to change the irrigation system from one that served the fundo's large fields to one that watered parcels. Further, the Committee was anxious to experiment with cooperative farming. Los Silos would be one of the only communally farmed fundos in Chile's history.

Since it simply was not possible to continue a cooperative organization if the four dissident families were given their parcels to farm as individuals, and since the dissenting families refused to join, the cooperative voted to expel them. Subsequently, the cooperative voted four new families in to take their place. But the four old families insisted upon remaining in the homes they felt were rightfully theirs. Since there were no houses in which the four replacement families could live, two remained in their family homes in nearby Puente Alto, one lived in a room in the old patrón's house, and the fourth took up residence in the fundo's school. They waited anxiously for the old families to move so they could have their houses. And the cooperative members continued sending their children to school on the neighboring farm.

At first the old residents of the fundo who elected to participate in the reform were divided in their sympathies between the four dissident families, with whom they had worked for years, and their new, struggling cooperative. For the most part they swung to the side of the cooperative, however, and a feeling against the four families became a rallying point which seems to have drawn the entire cooperative closer together during its first year. But the problem also absorbed a great deal of the energy of the young organization which certainly might have been better used to strengthen its institutional framework in other ways. Detailing the complicated efforts to expel the dissidents makes this clearer.

On March 1, 1963, the four families were given formal notice and asked to leave in two months (the traditional procedure in Chile—a patrón gives the same sort of notice to inquilinos he fires, as we have noted earlier). The four families were offered E° 495 apiece to leave and buy land elsewhere, and the agreement was signed by the work inspector of Puente Alto. Until May 1, 1963, their light and water would be paid by the cooperative.

By May they had not moved. Since the title of the land had not formally passed to the cooperative, the Bishop refused to give the cooperative support on its move to expel the four. In April 1963 some of the dissenters began to keep their lights burning all night and left water running. The cooperative cut their electricity in October and later denied them use of the cooperative's running water. The four families still refused to leave.

The situation moved from bad to worse, and late in 1963 there was a strong move by the cooperative to take matters into its own hands, expelling the families by force. This move, however, has been quieted by legal proceedings in process since March 1964 which would force the families to leave. Aside from being firm in their decision to remain (they have no place to move to), the families now argue that the severance pay originally offered them is too small since inflation has severely devalued it.

The cooperative, until title to the property moved definitely into its hands, had no right to remove the four families. As soon as it received clear title in early 1964, the lawyer it engaged had a *Comodato Precario* issued on the families. This legal expedient indicated that the cooperative had, for a time, allowed the four families a temporary privilege to use the land they occupied but now these rights had expired. This was a less complicated legal method of expelling the families than proving they had no title, since even members of the cooperative had not been issued individual titles. The local judge in Puente Alto requested titles or other information proving ownership and later set a date for appearance of witnesses for both the cooperative and the dissenting families. Proceedings were delayed by the presidential elections in Chile, but by late September 1964 the cooperative had presented its title and two days were set aside by the local judge to hear witnesses' testimony. No one appeared for the four families. Five witnesses pled the cooperative's case. By not sending representatives to the hearing on the days set aside for this purpose, the four families have lost the right to appear.

By mid-1965 the local judge had not made a decision. When a ruling is handed down, the case may be appealed to the court in Santiago. If this is done, the case may not be finally decided for months more. If the four families lose and still refuse to move, the judge may request the governor of the Department of Puente Alto (or the *intendente* of Santiago if the case is appealed) to order the local police to expel the families.[10]

The Problem of Leadership. As institutions are being built and taking root, internal representative leadership must be developed to carry the organization forward and to draw all members into participation. Los Silos' Technical Committee was quick to recognize that this meant putting campesinos themselves—many of whom never had decision-making experience previously—into positions of responsibility in the cooperative. Unfortunately, during the time of the workers' strike, the renter lost his most capable inquilinos to neighboring farms which treated resident workers better, and Los Silos became a harbor for some of the poorest laborers in the zone.

To help fill this leadership void, the hired administrator brought Luis Pérez,[11] an employee of a fundo some 50 kilometers distant, to Los Silos. Pérez had begun his career in farming as a *reemplazante,* a substitute for an inquilino, one of the lowest positions in Chilean agriculture. Gradually, he had risen to inquilino status and by the time he came to Los Silos he had attended several short leadership courses and was employed as one of the caretakers of his former patrón's dairy herd. Still, he was very much a campesino and remained ever concerned with the campesinos' lot and enthusiastically anxious to help better it. Los Silos was a natural outlet for his talent and he was voted some leadership responsibilities soon after his arrival at planting time in 1962.

Meanwhile, the Technical Committee's appointed administrator had the responsibility of guiding the cooperative through its first year. It was the committee's original idea that the administrator would live in the old patrón's house and become a cooperative member and landholder himself. The administrator proved efficient. The cooperative showed a healthy profit as the first year under reform closed. But one of his problems was that he became very active in the local Christian Democratic Party during his tenure. At a preelection time when the Technical Committee—and later INPROA—was anxious to show its political and religious impartiality, this proved a tactical error. More serious, however, the social distance between him and the campesino cooperative members widened as he assumed more and more a paternal role. His past duties as an administrator of a large, traditional fundo had taught him all too well the relationship that exists between administrator and laborers in Chile. Members generally liked and respected him, but tended to turn to him not as a fellow cooperative worker whose technical abilities were known, but as a source of explicit direction on "what to do next." Anxious to build more self-determination into the cooperative, INPROA returned the administrator to its Santiago office as the 1963–64 crop year began.

When the hired administrator left, Pérez was elected cooperative president and named chairman of the Agricultural Committee. As such, he made many of the day-to-day management decisions of the cooperative during 1963–64, a fact important to our later economic analysis. Pérez impresses any visitor with his personal grasp of the meaning of Los Silos and his missionary-like zeal in its behalf.

His message to many visitors is a chalk talk, which he begins by drawing two large circles on the blackboard one above the other with a series of parallel lines in each. "This represents the way things are in Chile," he explains. "There are two classes with a wall between them." Referring to the lower circle, he continues, " . . . before our cooperative, we could rise in this circle if we worked hard, but we could never break through the wall and become landowners. Under this new system if we work hard the land can be ours and the wall can crumble."

The fact that two of the new colonists were Pérez' brothers-in-law has been a source of no small concern to the original residents of the fundo and to the four dissenting families. Some seem convinced that Pérez is trying to take over the fundo for the personal profit of his family. Further, some colonists believe that Pérez himself is getting rich at the expense of the other cooperators. In the face of evidence, both of these charges seem groundless. Nonetheless, they underline the difficulty of finding adequate leadership for a reform effort. A leader must not only have natural abilities to direct his fellows, but he must also be worthy of their trust. Yet he must know their lot and perform his functions without developing into a demagogue himself. One need only remember the high rate of illiteracy, the miserable poverty, and the centuries of paternalism in Chile to recognize the difficulty of locating a campesino leader who asks no special favors in return for his position.

Feelings against Pérez grew within the cooperative during 1963–64. He did almost no physical work himself, devoting himself mainly to supervision. As we shall show later, the cooperative slipped economically. He was not re-elected president or named to the Agricultural Committee at the regular election in November 1964, although he was returned to a position on the council.

Miscellaneous Complaints. Some dissenters and a few cooperative members feel the Bishop should also have let the cooperative buy the small sand pit on one extreme of the farm. This enterprise had not been successfully exploited for some time, but under the management of the Technical Committee's administrator in 1962–63 it became quite profitable and the net income from it helped pay some of the Bishop's expenses which were formerly paid by the fundo rent. The Technical Committee felt that it was not wise or proper for this income to go to the cooperative, primarily because only if Los Silos was used solely for agricultural purposes could the feasibility of reform on a broader scale be proven. They felt that profits from selling sand would only underwrite any losses the farm as an agricultural unit might show and colonists would come to rely on it to bail them out of agricultural difficulties.

A television set became another sore point. The first year the cooperative operated, it decided to buy a receiver on which cooperators and their inquilino neighbors from other fundos could watch soccer. Since it was the year of the world championship in which Chile was a participant, any means of seeing the game could be expected to draw a large crowd; some members reasoned that at any accompanying social gathering, neighboring campesinos might be convinced of the feasibility of a plan like that of Los Silos. So the cooperative in general session was asked to approve the TV purchase. A new large-screen model which the cooperative still uses was ultimately selected. "We never approved of buying that television set," one cooperator told us. "What do we want with television when we're hungry?"

Complaints like these cannot help but sound petty. Yet to a struggling new institution they take on more importance than when an organization has reached a certain maturity. One issue—disposition of the sand pit—was necessarily resolved by a decision of the reform agency. Yet careful communication of the rationale behind this decision to the members was lacking. The other, the purchase of the TV on which the cooperative voted, was simply not accepted by some members in the losing minority.

Part of the success of reform, it would seem, rests on the campesino's conception of the organizations serving him and of those of which he is a part. The two kinds of institutions are quite different in character and function. The cooperative gives its members a direct voice through their vote and their ability to sway others to their point of view. But the vote of the majority is to be accepted.

The other type of institution concerned with Los Silos, now INPROA, also has certain policies influenced by cooperative vote. But INPROA can use its veto power over the cooperative's action in other matters. Issues concerning technical agriculture, we will argue later, probably should fit into this category more than they did in 1963–64. Policy matters, such as the sand pit decision, belong in this category too.

Beneficiaries must understand the power structure involved in reform. As this understanding is made clearer, one of the sources of resistance to structural change is reduced. Even acceptance of the majority opinion is a new experience for some cooperative members. In view of this, making a multipurpose cooperative like Los Silos function well is an immense task. And the time necessarily spent simply in organization—even leaving aside all the technical matters which involve production—must not be underestimated.

Pressures Against Reform in a Traditional Society. Reform across-the-board may not be the only way reform can occur. The Alliance for Progress, for example, argues that reform can take place in piecemeal fashion within a traditional society. This is also the position taken by most land reform agencies. However, bit-by-bit restructuralization within a traditional society seems to present certain problems that would not be relevant if reforms were to take place across-the-board. This helps to explain some pressures countering even small experiments like Los Silos. For example, Los Silos is opposed—sometimes only tacitly—by various individuals and groups who stand to lose from its success.

We have pointed out that Pirque is a commune in which the dominant tenure pattern is the latifundia. The neighboring fundo operator, an extremely good farm manager, is sensitive to changes on Los Silos. About the same time Los Silos was founded, he initiated a "profit-sharing" scheme on his fundo. The four dissenting families at Los Silos were forced into a closer association with him as soon as their water source and electricity were cut and advanced salaries cancelled. Although this fundo owner is extremely paternalistic, his inquilinos are treated well—among the best in the zone. Workers' houses neighboring those of the four dissident families are well kept up and neat and have electricity and running water nearby. Since the Los Silos cooperative was founded, they have been painted. The patrón now provides work for some of the rebel families and gives them drinking water. He senses Los Silos' current problems and gladly describes its difficulties as he sees them. But in a more reflective moment he said, "You know, we have to do better than they." This spirit of competition is, to a degree, advantageous to both parties.

Perhaps more dangerous to the cooperative's future is the contact the four dissenting families have retained with the leader of the former workers' strike. Since the strike, the neighboring alderman had come to rely on Los Silos as a source of popular political issues. Even though, short of expulsion, the Bishop could do nothing about his renter, the fact that unsatisfactory working conditions existed on property the Church owned could easily be connected in the public mind with the Christian Democratic Party, the Socialist official's political archenemy. Since the cooperative farming plan was initiated on the fundo and a Communist intellectual had attempted to help the Technical Committee solve its problems with the four families, the Socialist saw Los Silos as a local Communist-Christian Democrat Alliance.[12]

Paradoxically for those accustomed automatically to attributing collectivistic ideas to Socialists, he said: "Our campesinos have a mentality shaped by the landholders. They are excessively individualistic. It is hard for them to understand cooperative and collective systems when they concern farming. . . ."[13]

As the year wore on, he aided the dissenting families from time to time in their struggle against the cooperative. It also became more and more obvious that he was acting alone—to maintain his own political position—and not within the rubric of any political party or organization.

Many of these events seem to represent a lack of understanding of one new institution by another. Others may mean a simple misuse of power vis-à-vis a youthful organization which has not yet equipped itself with all necessary institutional defenses. The two are probably interrelated at some levels.

From this experience, we can draw the following generalizations: (1) In a reform effort which relies on an organizational structure similar to the one adopted by Los Silos, it is crucial to develop leadership which truly breaks the master-serf relationship existing in the remainder of Chilean agriculture. (2) In the multipurpose organization for reform which Los Silos has adopted, much effort must be placed on institution building—and on teaching campesinos to understand the organizational structure through which they must vocalize their complaints and through which services to them will be channelled. The "rules of the game" for both the cooperative and the reform agency must be known by all. (3) Difficulties the agencies in question have had with communication (i.e., the four families, the administrator, the sand pit decision) may be a reflection of two agencies which do not fully understand one another.

Great effort must be expended in maximizing feedback between the cooperative and INPROA. It may be that the superior-inferior relationship inherited from the paternal structure of Chilean agriculture tends to block communications insofar as INPROA's dealings with the cooperative—or even within the cooperative itself (i.e., Pérez and his problems)—are concerned. Are the cooperative's desires similar to the wishes of INPROA for it? Much intercommunication is necessary if INPROA is to identify the wishes of the cooperative and constantly readjust its policies according to them. Likewise, the cooperative must learn to recognize that INPROA's veto power over some matters is useful and necessary.

THE ECONOMIC ORGANIZATION OF LOS SILOS IN 1963–64

As the 1963–64 year began, eight of the families at Los Silos had been brought in from the outside; eight were former residents who remained, one of them preferring to serve as an inquilino to the cooperative. The economic situation of these colonists in 1963–64 is our concern here. Our analysis will focus on the following questions: (1) Can the fifteen colonists meet their debt payments on land and capital? (2) How does present income of colonists differ from that in their position before the reform? (3) What is the production potential on Los Silos?

What follows is an evaluation of one year's experience, and we cannot generalize on the basis of such a short period of time. However, aside from heavy rainfall in 1963–64, there were no unusual weather or marketing circumstances which could influence the economic performance detailed below. The analysis attempts to indicate what colonists must do if they are to meet their future debt payments. Although Los Silos is a mixture of individual and cooperative enterprises, the analysis in this section will treat the cooperative as the basic business and accounting unit.

Input Enterprises. It will be convenient to describe the tenure system on Los Silos in terms of its cropping pattern in 1963–64.

Wheat made up about 32 percent of the farm's acreage and alfalfa accounted for another 35 percent. Both were grown on the common land, and the income was designated for overhead expenses: water, electricity, machinery costs, land and interest payments. In addition, the costs of fertilizer and seed and the other direct expenses incurred in growing wheat and alfalfa were paid from this income.

Individual chacras (corn, potatoes, and beans) were planted on another 19 percent of the land. Members drew lots for the plots averaging about two hectares. These are individual enterprises in that members have the major responsibility for planting, tending, and harvesting their own chacras. Income above direct expenses (for fertilizer, seed, etc.) accrues to the individual provided that the income from the common land is sufficient to cover all other expenses and principal payments. If income from the common-land enterprises is not sufficient, this individual income can be diverted to cover any outstanding cooperative expense.

In 1963–64 Los Silos had about fifty head of dairy cattle with an average of sixteen in milk. Although most members own only two or three dairy animals, they could, in 1963–64, pasture up to six full-grown animals free of charge on the cooperative's common-land alfalfa pasture. (Animals under one year of age are not counted.) A small rental fee was to be charged for the seventh through tenth animals and no member could pasture more than ten. A small building-brick enterprise and the harvest of wood for sale are operated communally. This income is, likewise, available for meeting overhead expenses.

Labor Use and Management. In 1963–64 the manager of the cooperative (Pérez) assigned and supervised labor on the common land and in the brick and wood enterprises. In addition, if a member were occupied on one of the common projects, the manager would send another cooperator or hired laborer to work on the chacra of the member so employed. The tractor drivers, mechanics, and other members with specialized functions relied heavily on other members or hired labor to irrigate and weed their plots.

All members are obligated to work on the common land and carry out other tasks for the cooperative. However, there is no clear-cut economic incentive for members to work to capacity on these enterprises. Aside from cooperative censure and personal prodding by the manager, a member's major motivation is his knowledge that income from his individual enterprises will be used to meet overhead expenses if the common enterprises do not yield enough to meet these obligations. On the surface, this would appear to be a strong enough incentive. Yet an individual can always rationalize that the common enterprises will be well operated even if he, one individual in a group, shirks his duty at times.

Members' Income Determination. Since cooperative members needed a flow of income to provide for their families while awaiting the harvest, the cooperative made a living expense advance of E° 1.1 a day. This income was to be repaid from the individual's sales of produce, all of which was to be marketed through the cooperative. The cooperative was responsible for repaying INPROA, the original lender.

Heads of families in 1963–64 were paid this advance each day they worked as well as on days when they were ill. Illustrating the problem of incentives, as harvest approached, the cooperative reported cases of malingering. Withholding advances in cases of imagined or feigned illness might create some incentives if the family is completely dependent on advances. However, in the absence of medical evaluation, state of health is difficult to determine.

Cooperators' sons who are older than eighteen can become *socios,* that is, members without land rights. In 1963–64 there were four *socios* working for the cooperative with advances of E° 1.1 a day. They are also entitled to some share in the profits as determined by a year-end accounting.[14] Two sons of cooperators under eighteen also worked for the cooperative in 1963–64, receiving E° 1.1 a day without any additional claims to profits.

All members with dependents received a governmental family allowance (under the Chilean Social Security laws called *asignación familiar*), while some members with special skills received a cash bonus in addition to some extra grazing rights. In 1963–64, then, members' cash income was expected to accrue from four sources: (1) the family allowance from the government; (2) payments from the cooperative in reward for work requiring special skills; (3) individual income above direct costs as determined by separate accounting on members' enterprises after payment of all operating expenses, land and capital amortization, short-term production credit, income advances, and marketing charges to INPROA;[15] and (4) if all expenses and obligations could be met from the common enterprises without drawing on "income above direct costs" from individual enterprises, a division of any cooperative profits among members at the end of the year according to days worked.

INPROA provided technical assistance, accounting services, short-term production credit, and income advances. In return for its services, it charged a 2 percent marketing fee plus interest of 1.3 percent per month on its loans.

Can New Colonists Meet Their Debt Payment? In analyzing the cooperative as the basic business unit to arrive at debt-paying capacity, we must assume that all income from produce sold, whether it accrues to individual members ultimately or whether it remains in the cooperative account, forms part of the gross income of the cooperative. Individual sales not channelled through the cooperative are also included in gross income. Thus data on sales from the common enterprises were obtained from the cooperative records, whereas individual sales were obtained through the questionnaires administered to members. This procedure was necessary since the cooperative did not have records of the individual sales made through channels other than the cooperative.

The analysis is limited to cash transactions during the agricultural year 1963–64. This is justified because most of the crops and livestock products were sold within the year they were produced. There was no accrual of inputs such as fuel, fertilizer, etc. We assume that cash sales of livestock plus depreciation of the milking cows are offset by the increased value of growing animals. No major purchases of animals were made during the year. The hay stored for the following year was about equivalent to that stored and held over from the year before.

We have included the government family allowances (asignación familiar) as an income item of the cooperative. This is justified because individual members are responsible for debts incurred by their cooperative. Under extreme circumstances, families might have to draw on them to meet cooperative commitments. Furthermore, one of the expense items for the cooperative is paying into the government program so that members become eligible for this family allowance. Since the expense is unavoidable for the cooperative we include the income from this source in cooperative accounts.

Including all income from individual enterprises, common land, the cooperatively operated brick and wood enterprises, and the government family allowances, the cooperative, had a gross cash income in 1963–64 of E° 63,405.80.[16]

Operating expenses of the cooperative, considered as a unit, totalled E° 47,640.44. Thus the gross income for the year (E° 63,405.80) less the operating expenses (E° 47,640.44) leaves a net cash income of E° 15,765.36. Against this must be charged cash income retained by member families and amortization payments due on capital and land. To complete the picture, therefore, we must turn to an analysis of individual accounts. What was the magnitude of cash income actually retained by members? Aside from the short-term credit, charged as an operating expense, INPROA had loaned the cooperative E° 7,628.50 for family expenses (E° 1.1 a day—referred to earlier).

According to information supplied by the cooperative and confirmed by INPROA, the cooperative was not able to recover these family living advances. This means that the fifteen members and the four socios retained this cash. Also, the asignación familiar went directly to members, a total of E° 3,602. Total income from individual enterprises amounted to E° 20,733, but the cooperative did withhold about 50 percent of the chacra harvest to cover expenses (a total of E° 5,765), leaving net cash to members from their individual enterprises of E° 14,968 (E° 20,733 minus E° 5,765). Thus the total cash income accruing to members was E° 26,198.50 (the sum of E° 7,628.50 plus E° 3,602 plus E° 14,968).

Returning now to an earlier calculation, we noted that the cooperative had a net cash income of E° 15,765.36. But analyzing the individual accounts, we see that members retained E° 26,198.50 in cash. Adding this figure of E° 26,198.50 to the E° 18,200 in amortization payments due in that year (E° 10,500 for land and E° 7,700 for machinery)[17] yields a total of E° 44,398.50. Setting net cash income of the cooperative against this we have:

Cash income retained by individual members plus
   amortization payments due in 1963–64 ....E° 44,398.50
Net cash income available to the cooperative to
   meet these payments 15,765.36
                                       —————
Cooperative deficit for the year ....E° 28,633.14

One interesting question that remains is the extent to which the members used their cash income for consumption as against saving and investment. The members with land rights were asked to estimate their living expenses according to the following categories: "What are your cash food expenses for a week?" "What are your cash expenses for clothing for a month?" "What other consumption expenditures do you have?"

An itemization of these self-estimates totals E° 21,080. Since family living advances and the asignación familiar totalled only E° 11,230.50 for the fifteen members, it seemed from these estimates that their consumption was not restricted to this amount. This surmise was verified later.

This points up a general condition to be taken into account in a reform program. The pressures for increased consumption on the part of those who have long lived in dire poverty are strong. In addition to lacking technical and managerial skill on the production side, the cooperative lacked the power and perhaps the will to restrict consumption even to levels somewhat higher than those of most agricultural workers. In the case of milk, for example, the cooperative paid members monthly without deducting expenses due the cooperative. The weakness of the cooperative is also seen in its inability to prevent some of the produce from being marketed outside the cooperative channels.

Cash income available to the fifteen members (E° 26,198.50) compared to self-estimates on cash consumption expenditures (E° 21,080), would indicate a net savings of E° 5,118.50. Our data do not permit us to estimate whether this was actually invested in production goods or whether the self-estimates of consumption were low.

In answer to the first major question posed, whether or not new colonists can meet their debt payments on land and capital, the conclusion is negative for 1963–64. A generalization on this point must be withheld until the other questions are analyzed.

How Does Present Income of Colonists Differ from that Before the Reform? The year before the cooperative was founded, the average income (cash plus evaluated perquisites) of all of the fifteen cooperative members was E° 1,156.51.[18] Cash income by itself may be a better measure of participation in the market economy. The year before the cooperative was founded the average cash income of all fifteen cooperators was E° 749.

Under the conditions existing on Los Silos in 1963–64, cash income of the fifteen averaged E° 1,640, an increase of E° 891 over the former situation. Total income, including home consumption and perquisites averages E° 2,158 or E° 1,002 more under the reform.

The legal minimum wage for inquilinos in Santiago Province for 1963–64 was E° 1.354 daily (cash plus perquisites), or about E° 494 annually. Asignación familiar for a husband with four dependents would total about E° 236, bringing the legal minimum to about E° 730. The average for colonists on Los Silos was about three times this amount.

On a well-operated neighboring fundo, a profit-sharing plan has been put into effect. While it does not break with the traditional system as the Los Silos plan does, it gives the best workers an opportunity to earn more than the poorer ones. These are among the best paid inquilinos in the zone. Yet, in 1963–64 they averaged E° 563 less than the colonists on Los Silos.

This again raises the question of whether it might be possible to limit the income accruing to cooperative members. Of course, poorly paid workers—such as those on Los Silos before the reform—must experience higher incomes and improved living conditions as the result of reform. Moreover, if their individual cash incomes had been reduced to zero it would not have solved the financial problem of

1963–64. But this is not to deny that incomes of individual members could be substantially reduced and still leave the colonists much better off than before the reform. Once the debt burden is reduced and interest payments decline, further increases in individual incomes will be possible.

What Is the Production Potential on Los Silos? Our previous analysis has shown that Los Silos showed a deficit of about E° 28,633 in 1963–64. Could Los Silos have increased its gross income by this amount? This would imply a gross of E° 92,039 (E° 63,406 plus E° 28,633). In other words, does the potential exist to maintain individual income at the 1963–64 levels and also meet repayment commitments? Let us assume for the moment an increase in gross to cover this deficit of E° 28,633 without raising cash expenses. Later, we will show how present expenses might be reallocated to make this possible.

Data from a study describing Los Silos in 1947–48[19] supply physical yields of wheat, corn, potatoes, hay, and eggs. The physical data when multiplied by current prices show that comparable gross income in 1947–48 was probably very close to the equivalent of E° 90,000.

Comparable gross income the first year under reform (1962-63—when the Technical Committee's technician was in charge of management on Los Silos) was about E° 83,000, not counting that produce sold outside the cooperative marketing channels.[20]

A third measure of potential is obtained by comparing Los Silos to the well-managed neighboring fundo referred to previously. According to maps of the Photogrammetric Project in Chile,[21] soils on this neighboring farm are very similar to those on Los Silos. Water for irrigation is plentiful, in both cases coming from the nearby Maipo River.

There are some difficulties in this comparison since the cropping pattern is different. The neighboring farm does have a peach orchard and a small vineyard to which it devotes 5 percent of its acreage. The latter enterprise would not be open to everyone who wants to produce grapes, since it is dependent on a hard-to-get license issued by the central government if grapes are to be grown for wine.

Gross income per hectare on the neighboring farm was E° 549 as compared to E° 327 on Los Silos (excluding now, the asignación familiar formerly included in gross income). This is a difference of E° 222 per hectare or slightly over 40 percent. A 40 percent increase in Los Silos in 1963–64 would have brought gross income near E° 89,000.

Data from these three comparisons seem to indicate a production potential of gross income of somewhat more than E° 87,000. This is still about E° 5,000 less than was needed to meet 1963–64 obligations. In other words, potential seems to come fairly close to the requirements we have set up.

Earlier in this section we mentioned the possibility of increasing gross income without raising expenses—that is, by a reallocation of present inputs. For example, one major means of yield increases in crop production is to increase the application of commercial fertilizer. The neighboring farm uses about 30 percent more fertilizer per hectare than Los Silos.

What are the prospects of cutting some other expenses to permit this increased expenditure on fertilizer? Our analysis shows that Los Silos in 1963–64 spent E° 5,196 on wages for hired labor. All indications are that this figure could be reduced. For example, the neighboring farm uses 30.6 man-days per hectare while Los Silos uses 59.6.[22] Although it is difficult to make a meaningful comparison with respect to labor-substituting capital on these two farms, it must be emphasized that the cropping pattern on the neighboring farm is more labor intensive. The average value of labor-saving machinery per hectare on the farms was similar in 1963–64.

A recent university-government study based on 2,766 interviews established the average number of man-days per hectare of various crops for each province of Chile under different conditions of farm size and mechanization.[23] Although this study does not provide estimates for livestock enterprises, it indicates that Los Silos should have required about 4,000 man-days for its crop production (using the coefficients most nearly fitting the case of Los Silos). Since 6,600 man-days of labor are available within the cooperative (including members and their six sons working in 1963–64), it seems likely that the labor available is sufficient to handle all crop production as well as the dairy operations. Actually, 10,120 man-days were used on Los Silos in 1963–64. The difference between labor available and labor used represents labor hired. Although these comparative measures are crude and do not take into account peak labor loads when additional help may need to be hired even though the permanent work force is unemployed during other seasons, it does seem clear that some expenses could be shifted—from present labor costs to other productive inputs.

A serious objection could be raised to this point, however. While it is true that Los Silos could benefit from reducing its hired-labor costs and investing in other inputs (thus implying that present members would have to work more), this is not a solution when the agrarian problem is considered nation-wide. Employing labor from outside Los Silos was, in fact, spreading the effects of reform to a larger number of people than its own colonists.

Looked at in another way, we need not necessarily conceive of fertilizer and labor costs as being directly competitive. Given the productivity potential that appears to exist (in comparison to yields and returns on a neighboring farm with similar soil type and irrigation possibilities), more fertilizer certainly appears profitable. The problem, then, is not so much one of direct competition between labor hired and fertilizer purchased. It is a matter of credit availability and a knowledge of input-output relations in production that will provide the incentive to use it.

Over several years, given sufficient time for establishment of higher yield levels and more livestock, it may indeed be possible to achieve the higher income levels expected by colonists while also utilizing additional labor from outside, thus spreading the benefits of reform to a wider group of workers.

FUTURE PLANS

It is important to point out that in view of the difficulties of any reform of this kind and the importance of the experiments, this analysis is not intended as criticism of INPROA. INPROA and the cooperative leadership on Los Silos recognize the weaknesses of the 1963–64 operation.

Some changes have already been introduced. In the 1964–65 year no labor from outside was hired during the planting season, and a 2 percent marketing charge for all milk sold through the cooperative is being collected monthly by INPROA. Funds from sale of milk are not being returned to members (as they were in 1963–64) until final accounting time. Rental fees for each animal grazed on the common pasture are being charged to redress some of the inequalities of the previous arrangement and to capture more of the costs incurred by INPROA. Each cooperator knows his total debt, since it was prorated among all members early in the 1964–65 crop year.

All these modifications are minor, however, in comparison to the requirements for success at Los Silos. The assignment of debt to individuals may merely result in frustration unless plans for increasing production are effected. But plans have been made, and in some cases are well advanced, for making Los Silos a going concern.

In October 1964, Los Silos received a E° 55,000 loan from the Chilean development agency (Corporación de Fomento de la Producción), to purchase one hundred good-quality cows. These will be sold to members and the loan is to be repaid in five years with interest at 18 percent. Some poorer animals in the present herd will be used to pay off part of the principal. The new stock will allow all members to own at least six good-quality dairy animals. The farm has sufficient stable space and pasture-producing capacity to support this herd.

As this enterprise is expanded, another of the cooperative's plans may become feasible. With more sons of members reaching adulthood and joining the potential labor force, additional employment will be required. The dairy cattle operation in itself will require more labor. Also, the hope of establishing some dairy-processing functions (butter and cheese making) may become a reality. And a proposed feeder-pig project may one day be realized.

The feasibility and success of all these plans will depend on the capacity of management and the ability to train and establish discipline among cooperative members. In addition to management problems in 1963–64, accounts were not well kept, and it was not until the agricultural year was well along that the cooperative and INPROA realized their financial difficulties.

This again points to a broader generalization. Since reform implies liberation from domination by the patrón, the technicians should not make all the decisions that need to be made. Members must participate. The administrator during the first year (1962–63) left Los Silos partly because he was being turned to as a patrón even though he made Los Silos an economically successful concern.

Technical help in a reform effort must combine a high degree of agricultural and management skill with a knowledge of how to teach cooperative members to make their own decisions. This also implies careful vigilance over the farm accounts and attention to institution-building. If Los Silos is to be parcelled into individually owned small farms, which is also part of the future plans, sixteen entrepreneurs (the inquilino became a cooperative member in 1964–65) must be prepared to make management decisions. For the intermediate period between inquilinaje and individual proprietorship, all evidence seems to indicate that technical help must be coercive enough so that high production, very necessary for a successful reform, is maintained. This makes it doubtful whether the cooperative leader and the technician can be the same person—at least initially —as they were in 1963–64 on Los Silos. A good manager must be hired for Los Silos—preferably one who will live on the fundo and who will assist cooperators in decision-making.

Further neglect of the entrepreneurial function will continue to result in costly losses for Los Silos. And "allowing cooperators to make their own mistakes" will not hasten the day when cooperators become rational decision-makers in their own right. To expect a person untrained in farm management who is suddenly given access to the land to become an entrepreneur overnight—simply because the traditional system has been broken—is folly.

It is planned that the new manager will not work with individuals, but through the cooperative. A farming program will be drawn up with his help, and credit will be given in conformity to how closely the cooperative complies with plans. Credit, in other words, will be strictly supervised, and if members elect to diverge from plans, INPROA funds will be withdrawn. This system will be continued even if Los Silos is subdivided into smaller farms.

SUMMARY: LOS SILOS

(1) Los Silos illustrates that a reform effort which truly changes the existing social structure is a complicated process. Problems which arise center about hard-to-solve social and political—in addition to economic—problems with which few of the participants in the reform have had experience: (a) Replacing the patrón with leadership by participants in the reform effort means that effective campesino leadership must be developed. (b) A great effort must be placed on institution-building within the campesino organization

and within the reform agency. Communications internal to both (i.e., leader with member) and between the two agencies must involve a maximum of feedback for optimal performance. Functions of each institution must be clearly understood by all parties to the reform.

(2) The experiment has released the colonists from the traditional system and given them the opportunity to be landowners if they are able to pay. It has also created a cooperative institution through which they are able to make their needs known and through which help can be given.

(3) Although the first year under reform was quite successful, allowing the cooperative to meet some of its debts, in 1963–64 production was not sufficient to allow its colonists to pay off their land and machinery debts and finance their increased consumption.

(4) Average income for colonists on Los Silos in 1963–64 was about three times the zonal minimum for inquilinos and also above the income for best inquilinos on the neighboring well-managed farm which has established a profit-sharing scheme for its inquilinos.

(5) Los Silos has the potential to produce more than in 1963–64 and could produce nearly enough gross income to meet its current obligations, assuming these obligations remain about as they were in 1963–64. This conclusion is based on a study done in 1948 detailing Los Silos' farming program at that time, the data on production on Los Silos the first year after reform, and estimates of income per hectare on the well-managed neighboring farm.

(6) Income accruing to individual colonists might be lowered slightly during years of heavy debt repayment and still leave them with much more income than before the reform and better off than workers on the neighboring fundo. This, coupled with increased productivity and more or less constant expenses, would leave little doubt that the reform would be economically successful.

(7) Operating expenses on Los Silos could probably be reallocated so that less is spent on labor and more on yield-increasing capital, costs still remaining about constant.

(8) Los Silos is taking steps to intensify its operation in 1964–65. Other steps are being taken to strengthen the cooperative institution.

(9) Technical managerial help seems vital to an experiment of this nature. Whatever system is used, it must help teach members to

make their own rational decisions on their cropping pattern and use of inputs besides helping the cooperative keep accurate accounting records. The cooperative leader and the technician probably cannot be the same person—at least initially.

(10) It seems likely that the cooperative farming phases of this experiment will end in several years and each colonist will receive his own plot of land, thus underlining the necessity of developing individual entrepreneurs.

NOTES

1   The commune (*comuna*) is the smallest political subdivision within provinces in Chile.
2   Two descriptions of the fundo previous to its transfer to the Bishop have been written. Both describe the farming programs of the fundo during one crop year. Jacques Chonchol, "Informe Pericial, Tasación y Cálculo de Rentabilidad del Fundo 'Los Silos'," unpublished, Facultad de Agronomía, Universidad de Chile, Santiago, 1948 and Helmut Seeger Stein, "Informe Pericial, Tasación y Cálculo de Rentabilidad del Fundo 'Los Silos de Pirque'," unpublished, Facultad de Agronomía, Universidad de Chile, Santiago, 1952.
3   *Ultima Hora,* December 18, 1961.
4   *Look,* October 9, 1962, p. 32.
5   See Chapter 2.
6   Personal conversation with the author, February 14, 1964.
7   *Ibid.; Look, op. cit.*
8   From the files of CIDA.
9   CIDA borrador, "Chile," p. 474. One rate of exchange will be used throughout this monograph: US$1 = E⁰ 3.25.
10 This explains the delay because of the Chilean presidential election. The governors and intendentes are direct representatives of the president in departments and provinces respectively and are appointed by him. Should they have been forced to take action before the elections, the situation might easily have been used in political propaganda.
11 This name is fictitious.
12 Personal interview, October 20, 1964.
13 *Ibid.*
14 Since, as we demonstrate later, there were no profits to divide in 1963–64, the nature of this sharing has not been clarified. The advances for socios in 1963–64 really became "wages" in the absence of profit.
15 We are, of course, omitting income in kind in the form of produce consumed, house rental value, etc. These will be included in later comparisons. We are also excluding the concept of equity which could accrue to individuals from two sources: (a) from an increase in their individual

livestock inventories, and (b) from an increase in inventories held by the cooperative and from the land and capital amortization payments made by the cooperative. As we shall see in the analysis that follows, (a) is relatively unimportant and (b) is irrelevant given the nature of the outcome in 1963–64.

16 Since these data are excerpted from the author's thesis, no effort will be made to round off figures. Tabular support may be found in William C. Thiesenhusen, "Experimental Programs of Land Reform in Chile," unpublished Ph.D. thesis, University of Wisconsin, Madison, 1965.

17 Whether Los Silos should have contracted such a large debt for labor-saving machinery when labor is such an abundant factor of production is surely doubtful.

18 All figures are expressed in 1964 Escudos.

19 Chonchol, op. cit.

20 Los Silos, "Memoria Anual, 1962–63."

21 This recent mapping project details land use capacity, ownership, and irrigation sources. It covers most of Chile and its immediate use will be for tax purposes. In this case map 3330–7030C was used.

22 This assumes they all work the same number of hours a day. This is slightly incorrect as workers on the neighboring farm work about ten hours while on Los Silos they work eight. But most Los Silos workers said they work harder now than before the reform. Another factor may be more important: according to INPROA, neighboring farm workers are very highly selected from the best in the zone. It has already been noted that Los Silos before the reform was a haven for poor workers. But in this comparison we are assuming that the eight colonists who came to Los Silos from outside the fundo up-graded the average, so this comparison is more or less valid.

23 Corporación de Fomento de la Producción, Ministerio de Agricultura, Universidad de Chile, *Insumos en la Agricultura, Año 1961–62,* Santiago, 1964.

THE INDIVIDUALISTIC EXPERIMENT: LAS PATAGUAS DE PICHIDEGUA

Chapter 4

We liked our patrón very much. He was a good worker. Now we work more, we have more worries, the system involves more sacrifices, and we need to take better care of things. We wouldn't move now, however. We're settled here.

The former system was "prettier." There was lots of machinery then. Now there's almost none. But I don't think anybody really wants to go back to the old system.

The old patrón was good. When I needed something, I got it. But it was the system that was bad.

Now I'm more interested in my work. Before I just put in hours.

—Las Pataguas Colonists.

COLONISTS ON the Las Pataguas land reform experiment exhibit varying degrees of enthusiasm in the success of its first two years, but it is difficult to find one who would be willing to turn back to the days of inquilinaje.

Unlike those of Los Silos, each of the seventy-six colonists on Las Pataguas (a 1,485.5 hectare property with 1,162 irrigated hectares) has his own piece of land. The majority (those who have made the downpayment on their land or a good percentage of it) were given a provisional title at the beginning of the 1963–64 crop year.

Colonists manage their land individually, thus giving the cooperative more limited functions than on Los Silos. On Las Pataguas no land is communally farmed. The cooperative, which acts as an intermediary for distribution of seeds, fertilizer, and other credit coming from INPROA, supplies bookkeeping and other services, acts as care-taker for the fundo's overhead investments, and markets colonists' harvest. Colonists also operate a consumers' cooperative at which members can purchase some standard food items—flour, sugar, tea, etc.—cheaper than in the neighboring villages, Pataguas Cerro and Pataguas Orilla. The cooperative "committee" structure, however, is similar to that on Los Silos (Diagram I, Chapter 3).

Since the fundo is about forty miles from the Pan-American high-way (in O'Higgins Province) and reachable only by unpaved roads, marketing farm products and buying consumption goods in the area have always been a problem. Numerous middlemen, on both the selling and buying sides of the market, claim considerable profits for nominal intermediary functions and for trucking merchandise in and out. Shops in the area, therefore, must charge relatively high prices for merchandise. Numerous stores serving a relatively sparse population contribute to high retail price levels, because they try to compensate for low-volume sales by high mark-up.

When buying from farmers, too, middlemen may demand inordi-nate margins. Since there are few competitive buyers, the farmer is at their mercy. Thus an effective marketing and consumers' coopera-tive in this relatively isolated area is even more important than at Los Silos, which has ready access by good roads to the more organ-ized markets of Santiago. Later in this chapter we shall refer to the cooperative's accomplishments and problems since its founding.

The latifundia is the predominant system of land tenure in O'Higgins Province. At the same time, a great number of minifun-distas or landless workers live in or near the small towns and make the bulk of their living working on fundos. Although farms of over 500 hectares comprise but 1.9 percent of the total number of hold-ings, they make up to 82.9 percent of the entire area of the province, 73.9 percent of the total agricultural area, and 48.2 percent of the total irrigated area. Farms of less than one hectare—minifundios—represent 55.8 percent of the holdings, but only .2 percent of the total agricultural area and .8 percent of the irrigated land.[1]

TECHNICAL COMMITTEE'S PLAN FOR LAS PATAGUAS

Las Pataguas was willed to the diocese of Santiago in July 1941. From then until May 1, 1962, the Archbishop of Santiago leased it to three successive renters, the last time for eighteen years. In September 1961, Cardinal Raúl Silva Henríquez designated a Technical Committee to plan for the reform experiment on Las Pataguas. At planting time in 1962 the renter had left and the Committee's scheme was ready to be effected.

The plan provided for the division of all the land into small farms save the small amount needed for maintaining the overhead investments: central buildings to be held by the cooperative, roads, and irrigation canals. Much of the 266 hectares of dry land was also parcelled out since it could be used by individuals for pasturing their sheep, although 142 hectares were reserved for cooperative purposes. The Technical Committee also decided to reserve 122.6 hectares including a 42.3 hectare flood plain which was rented out in 1962–63 and again in 1963–64.

Three different size-categories of plots were distributed: huertos (defined here as 1 irrigated hectare); *parcelas* (parcels averaging about 16.7 irrigated hectares); and *hijuelas* (farms of 35–86 irrigated hectares).

Again unlike Los Silos, which accepted all former residents of the fundo who agreed to the cooperative's principles, Las Pataguas awarded land only to persons who: (1) had worked in agriculture for at least five years, (2) belonged to a well-established home, (3) promised to farm the property personally, and (4) did not own another agricultural property which was bigger than or comparable to the one for which they were applying. For applicants meeting these criteria, a point system (Table I) was devised as the basis of final selection.

TABLE I—Point System—Las Pataguas

Qualification	Points
1. For each dependent	4
2. For being specialized in intensive cultivation of crops or for successful fulfillment of a position of responsibility, or for being renter or share-cropper for more than three years, up to	10
3. For each five years of work on the fundo	3
4. For being active in the Instituto de Educación Rural or a similar organization for more than a year	5
5. For maintaining a savings or checking account in the State Bank or for each three years of active membership in a cooperative	2
6. For each 10 percent of the downpayment (in addition to the down-payment) possessed, up to	2

After it was decided who would receive a huerto, parcela, or hijuela, accumulated points determined the order within each classification in which each applicant could choose his piece of land.

Of the 60 former fundo workers, 8 chose to leave; 3 were expelled by the Technical Committee. These 3 were given a severance pay for each year of service on the fundo. The capacity of the fundo was increased by 16 families (about 21 percent) by the reform. This means that 49 colonists out of 76, or about 64 percent of the present number of settlers, lived on Las Pataguas prior to the colonization. Fifty-three or 69.8 percent of the 76 Las Pataguas colonists had been either voluntarios, medieros, or inquilinos previous to the reform.

Four former Las Pataguas workers who had specific crafts—a baker, two mechanics, and a smith—were located on huertos so that they could be hired from time to time to supply work for or services to the owners of the larger properties. Aside from those with trades, huertos were given to eight applicants with the poorest work records on the fundo—those who, in the judgment of the Committee, would probably not be successful working larger plots. According to INPROA, size of the huertos was determined arbitrarily at one hectare so that they would be large enough to permit "the cultivation of fruit trees, vegetables, chicken production, etc., for the consumption of the family."[2]

Thirty-one former fundo inquilinos or medieros and four fundo employees who had some supervisory responsibilities previously, remained to get a parcel. Twenty-four neighboring minifundio operators or workers on other fundos who applied were also selected to get parcels. The dimensions of the parcels were "based on special studies of income and family capacity to work."[3] Five others (two of them former Las Pataguas empleados) were awarded larger plots, or hijuelas. One of these was sold to an Ingeniero Agrónomo who, according to the plan of the Archbishop's Committee, would serve as a technician for the project. Hijuelas were awarded to "those who [were] more able technically and economically."[4] All told, twelve huertos, fifty-nine parcels, and five hijuelas were distributed.

Awarding plots in differing size-categories defined a social class structure in the Las Pataguas community. Although one purpose of the reform was to break the rigid social system, reformers in this case perpetuated several important features of the archaic class structure existing in Chilean agriculture. The five hijuela owners quickly began to dominate the cooperative and, in fact, are now being encouraged by INPROA to withdraw their membership. Withdrawal is not being made without complaint and dissension.

The Ingeniero Agrónomo, who owned an hijuela, soon had a falling-out with the Technical Committee and later with INPROA. He tried to assume a paternal role on Las Pataguas. His technical experience was, in any formal sense, lost to other members of the cooperative since he concentrated only on making a living on his hijuela, which he then sold in 1964.

At the other end of the spectrum, huerto operators now live almost as poorly as they did formerly. Among their problems is the fact that most paid employment available to them is with parcel and hijuela owners, who often lack ready Escudos, pay a lower daily wage, and offer work more irregularly than was the case under the patronal system. Furthermore, parcel holders are more reluctant than fundo operators to make necessary payments to the Social Security Service, and huerto operators seem to worry more now than before about having their benefits lapse.

INPROA's plan is to distribute much of the cooperative reserve—along with the hijuela sold by the Ingeniero Agrónomo—to whichever huerto operators want to enlarge their holdings. This should even out the economic base of the cooperative in coming years, giving it a more homogeneous membership.

PARCELIZATION: ITS COSTS

The few fundo buildings—transferred to the cooperative at the time of the reform—have been left pretty much intact. A wing of the former patrón's house is now used for the community teacher and his family, a boarding house (*pensión*) for visitors, and a dwelling for a parcel holder whose family runs the pensión. There is also one large multipurpose building of which various rooms are used as a granary, cooperative meeting place, office, and cooperative store. The cooperative also owns a workshop and a three-classroom school.

The value of the portion of the fundo planned for division—including the former inquilinos' houses and land (on which the price was fixed after an extensive soil-typing study)—is E° 885,356.[5] The real estate to be permanently reserved for the cooperative is valued at E° 33,332, setting the total value of the fundo before costs of parcelization at E° 918,688. Costs for improvements and other infra-structure—irrigation adjustment, houses, roads, etc.—were added later.

While Los Silos used overhead capital already available on the fundo, including the inquilinos' houses, and planned to rely on the farm's profit to make improvements, the Committee planning Las Pataguas made an effort to give out complete parcels with overhead capital already intact. Part of this was a matter of necessity: some of the forty-seven adobe-brick inquilino houses at Las Pataguas were in decidedly poorer shape than any dwellings on Los Silos. Settlers built a dozen prefabricated two-room houses to serve while a cooper-ative committee[6] approved plans for more permanent ones and pre-pared to accept the corresponding financial obligation. The prefab-ricated houses accommodated people moving in from outside the fundo.

All but five of the original houses are located in a *villorrio* or large hamlet[7] along the two public roads which lead to the property. In some cases this location places houses on the land; in most, dwell-ings are quite far from farms, necessitating daily travel to and from the property. Through villorrio settlement, the Technical Commit-tee hopes to: use social overhead capital optimally; provide for ser-vices such as drinking water and sewage system; develop a sense of community among the future landowners; offer parcel holders the services of mechanics, the smith, etc., who receive lots in the villo-rrio; and give children of parcel holders the opportunity to attend school a short distance from their homes.[8]

Although the former location of most of the inquilino homes makes a villorrio a very feasible arrangement, one colonist showed such a preference for living on his land that he has built a grass and reed *"ranchito"* and refuses to move from it unless the cooperative forces him to do so. He maintains that although his house is farther from services and from installations of electricity and water and is decidedly poorer in quality, he prefers to live on his land—he says he is afraid of having his harvest robbed if there is no one to main-tain vigilance. This kind of concern is not unusual and represents one bottleneck to planning for colonization programs. An Economic Commission for Latin America publication asserts, "Instances have been reported in which beneficiaries of agrarian reform have refused to occupy houses built for them or inherited from a previous hacienda nucleus, preferring to build huts on their own land."[9] Dominguez also warns against a settlement which separates the peasant from his land.[10] The Las Pataguas cooperative has now voted to construct as many new houses as possible on parcels.

All infrastructure has not been installed on Las Pataguas although the majority of it is complete. Parcelization involves building twenty-five new houses and repairing fifteen old ones in the villorrio. The remainder of the houses are usable as they are. Fences, gates, drinking water, and an installation of a more adequate electrical system were also added. Furthermore, an 8,800 meter-long access road has been built to a rather remote section of the fundo.

Adjusting the irrigation system to the new parcels involved quite a revision of the maze of ditches which had carried water to the farm's previous thirty-eight fields. The irrigation system installed on Las Pataguas is based on a system of measured water gates (*marcos partidores*) which allow a precise amount of water into canals serving each parcel. A colonist can use all the water in his canal any time he chooses. This differs from a cheaper and more common system of "shifts" or "turns" (*turnos*) in which a colonist uses all water in the canal during a predefined time period. This provides a greater amount of water at a time than in the marcos partidores system.

Cost of parcelization, including all necessary studies that needed to be made prior to division, totalled:

Miscellaneous infrastructure (new houses, repairing houses, fences, gates, electricity, drinking water)	E° 139,305.00
Building access road	30,258.10
Irrigation adjustments	62,402.39
Total infrastructure necessary	E° 231,965.49

In summary, cost of the fundo, with all infrastructural additions, totals:

Value of fundo real estate	E° 918,688.00
Costs of parcelization	231,965.00
	E° 1,150,653.00

In total, infrastructure represents about 20 percent of the cost of the reform. Average cost of parcelization per settler was E° 3,052; average per-settler cost for a complete property was E° 15,140.

Infrastructural costs for each farm were added to the land bill of each colonist. The colonist was given twenty years to pay at 6 percent interest. The interest rate was reduced to 5 percent in 1964–65 with conditions of repayment and adjustment for inflation the same as for those described for Los Silos.

One problem of this prebilling system is that actual infrastructural costs are running higher than estimated costs. Since the colonists were given their bills before all improvements were made, INPROA found it impossible to revalue their debt based on the real costs without losing the confidence of the settlers. This means that INPROA will not be able to recoup its total investment.

A comment is in order about the magnitude of expenditures for infrastructure. Only the irrigation expenses, temporary housing facilities, and installation of drinking water represented expenditures absolutely essential during the first several years of reform. These made, each parcel holder could have lived on and farmed his own land satisfactorily. Probably building of the access road, and certainly permanent housing, fences, and even electricity might have waited until later. It is also doubtful that all adjustments on the irrigation system had to be completed immediately although, admittedly, they probably avoided certain infighting that might have developed had the water been too badly distributed. A cheaper type of irrigation system based on "turnos" rather than marcos partidores could have been established, however. Immediate costs of infrastructure could have been reduced at least 50 percent, with the lacking infrastructure being provided from the initiative of each colonist working through the cooperative. This would have saved INPROA the immediate expense, lowered the total debt to each proprietor, reduced the annual cost for interest in the critical developmental period, and given each landholder a sense of participation in the development and improvement of his own farm.

FIRST YEAR OF REFORM

The first year of the reform experiment on Las Pataguas, 1962–63, the Archbishop's Committee gave each colonist "contracts of rent and sharecropping." To build more incentives into the usual system of mediería (see Chapter 1), however, the Church program allowed the usual 50–50 income split if production of wheat was

only 40 quintals per cuadra (a cuadra is 4 acres or 1.56 hectares), but
if production was between 40 and 50 quintals the mediero would receive 60 percent of the income and if production was over 50 quintals the mediero would receive 70 percent. On other crops the division was 50–50. Operating expenses were split in the traditional
manner in all cases. Wheat in 1962–63 averaged 65 quintals a cuadra,
giving a 70–30 split in favor of the medieros.

Assessing the early accomplishments on Las Pataguas, a spokesman
for the Technical Committee said:

> . . . although the process is not complete yet . . . the number of permanent
> workers that the fundo had has risen from 60 to 97.[11] Of 65 seasonal campesinos
> that worked 80 days a year, today they work 120 days. This represents more work
> and indicates that the land can receive more people [after reform]. This in-
> creased intensification in agriculture can circumvent campesino movement to the
> cities.[12]

All evidence indicates that total production on Las Pataguas has
risen over production on the same fundo under the rental system in
1961–62, but it is impossible to determine by how much. The pre-
reform renters used an extensive farming program. They included
other agricultural investments in the same accounting, making it
impossible to make confident statements about the fundo's production now as compared with the traditional system. We can, however,
attempt to answer the following questions: What is the colonist's
ability to pay his new debts? Have the parcel holders' levels of living
risen? Then, by comparing production in 1963–64 with production
on a similar acreage on a well-managed fundo with similar irrigation
problems and soil type, we try, as in the case of Los Silos, to determine whether there is a margin of unexploited productivity or
whether operating expenses can be reallocated. Again the reader
must bear in mind that this analysis is based on but one year's experience.

Unlike Los Silos, where the cooperative was the basic accounting
unit, we have seen that on Las Pataguas the cooperative does not
play as central a role. Economic decisions were largely made by individual farmers. Therefore, to measure the economic success of the
Las Pataguas project, we were forced to turn to colonists' accounts.

We drew a random sample, stratified according to type of holding
(hijuela, parcela, huerto). We decided upon a 25 percent random
sample of parcel holders: fifteen cases out of fifty-nine. After draw-

ing fifteen cases, we plotted them on a map of the fundo to assure ourselves of geographic dispersion. We also drew two cases each from the *hijueleros* and *huerteros*; however, since hijueleros were being removed from the cooperative and most huerteros' plots will be increased next year, our analysis concentrates on parcel holders.

CAN COLONISTS PAY THEIR DEBTS?

Most income for parcel holders accrued through the marketing of crops. Cash income earned through the sale of animals or animal products was negligible. Unlike the colonists at Los Silos, the parcel holders are considered self-employed and thus get no part of their incomes from asignación familiar. Other possibilities of income during the year might have occurred through increase in the colonists' own inventories or from that of the cooperative (since parcel holders are cooperative members and must pay toward machinery it purchases for common use). Given the income situation of each cooperator to be described, the former possibility is minor and the latter payments were not collected until the end of the year. Colonists received their income with the harvest, and during the year their living expenses came mainly from several lump-sum advances from INPROA made through the cooperative, from savings they may have had from the previous year, and from cash sales of produce outside cooperative channels during the year.

We have presented the year's income and operating expenses for one colonist in Table II. His cropping pattern and yields are fairly typical for colonists on Las Pataguas, and the data for his enterprise will give a somewhat representative picture of what other colonists have done. He kept out all of his potatoes and corn and part of his wheat and beans for home consumption purposes. As in the case of Los Silos we will not include home consumption of crop and animal products in our estimate of gross cash income. Subtracting home consumption (E° 1,142) from total produce (E° 4,487) we arrive at a gross cash income of E° 3,345. The bulk of his cash income came from the sale of wheat. This colonist's largest operating expense this year was land interest at E° 948.84 (6 percent of his remaining adjusted land debt of E° 15,814).

Labor expenses during wheat and chacra harvest, together with the cost of outside labor utilized during the time of chacra weeding, and the meals which the laborers ate, totalled E° 220.07.

TABLE II—CALCULATION OF NET CASH INCOME

Former Inquilino-Tractor Driver on Las Pataguas;
Present Owner of Parcel 22 (9 Hectares)

Gross Income 1963–64

Item	Quantity		Price	Total
A—Wheat	160	quintals	E° 17.5	E° 2,800
B—Beans (Variety: *Tórtola*)	17.6	"	31	545
C—Beans (Variety: Tórtola) (C)	4.8	"	31	149
D—Corn (C)	24	"	19	456
E—Potatoes (C)	25	sacks	10	250
F—Wheat (C)	2.4	quintals	17.5	42
G—Animal income (C)				245

Total.................................. E° 4,487
Total crop consumed   (C)   (Minus)........ 1,142

Gross cash income...................... E° 3,345

Operating Expenses 1963–64

Item	Total
A—Interest on land debt (set at 6% of total remaining debt of E° 15,814) E°	948.84
B—Outside labor hired:	
Harvest of wheat...	35.00
Weeding of chacra..	70.00
Harvest of chacra..	100.00
Meals for outside laborers................................	15.07
C—Interest on E° 565 in advances............................	67.87
D—2% of crops marketed (paid to INPROA) (2% of E° 3,345).........	66.90
E—Prorated share of total land tax..........................	60.90
F—Share of weed killer (applied with airplane)....................	34.71
G—Combining of wheat (paid 12 quintals of wheat plus gasoline for tractor)..	221.70
H—Tilling land...	52.40
I—Seeds: wheat, corn, potatoes, beans	187.98
J—Fertilizer:	
12 sacks of *salitre* (E° 8/sack).............................	96.00
2 sacks of superphosphate (E° 15.84/sack)...................	31.68
K—Horseshoeing	78.00
L—Animal feed purchased	100.00
M—Share of administrative expenses of cooperative.................	107.14

Total expenses... E° 2,274.19

Gross cash income   E° 3,345.00
Operating expenses   2,274.00
Net cash income   1,071.00

INPROA collected about E° 67.87 on the advances of E° 565 loaned to the colonist on several occasions during the year. Although INPROA charged a higher rate (1.3 percent a month for the number of months of the loan) we have applied a standard 12 percent, which seems to be a reasonable average. A 2 percent marketing fee was also paid to INPROA on the E° 3,345 gross cash income marketed through its channels. Land tax on the fundo was prorated to members depending upon their acreage. The amount corresponding to this case was E° 60.90. Weed killer was applied by airplane to the wheat, and the colonist's prorated share for this service was E° 34.71. Rental of the combine is usually set at a certain number of quintals of wheat plus gasoline for a hectare or cuadra. Expressed in Escudos, he paid E° 221.70 for this expense and, at the time of seeding, he rented a tractor to disc three cuadras at a charge of E° 52.40. Seed expenses totalled E° 187.98 and fertilizer E° 127.68. Shoeing his team cost him E°78 and the feed he purchased for his animals was valued at about E° 100.

Each member of the cooperative had to contribute to the administrative costs of the cooperative on a prorated basis. Paying for the manager's salary, office supplies, irrigation rights, etc., averaged about E° 107.14. Total operating expense for this colonist was E° 2,274.19. Net cash income was E° 1,071.00 (E° 3,345 minus E° 2,274).

Income for our sample of Las Pataguas colonists is calculated in precisely this same manner; we need not repeat any more individual cases.

INCOME AND SURPLUS AMONG LAS PATAGUAS COLONISTS, 1963–64

In this section we will determine consumption and, subtracting it from net income, arrive at debt repayment capacity. Subtracting capital payments due, we will determine surplus or deficit for our sample of colonists. Table III shows these calculations. The case we described in the former section appears as A-10. After calculating net income (column 1) we asked each colonist to estimate his cash living expenses on the basis of the following categories: "What are your food expenses for the week?" "What are your clothing expenses for the month?" "What are your other expenses?" Results are displayed in column 2. A figure for calculated consumption expenses

TABLE III—Surplus or Deficit among a Selected Sample of Las Pataguas Colonists 1963–64

Case	Net cash income (1)	Self-estimated family consumption expenses (2)	Calculated family consumption expenses (3)*	Debt repayment capacity (Col. 1 −Col. 2) (4)	Capital payments due in 1963–64 (5)	Deficit or surplus for 1963–64 (Col. 4 −Col. 5) (6)	Amount to be paid in 1964–65 for land (7)	Surplus or deficit assuming a land payment (Col. 6 −Col. 7) (8)
A-1	E° 8,651	E° 2,465	E° 2,668	E° 6,186	E° 293	E° 5,893	E° 752	E° 5,141
A-2	3,428	2,546	1,940	882	43	839	890	− 51
A-3	1,777	1,966	2,182	− 189	43	− 232	710	− 942
A-4	3,663	1,242	1,697	2,421	43	2,378	801	1,577
A-5	3,734	2,686	3,628	1,048	43	1,005	750	255
A-6	1,303	1,188	1,940	115	571	− 456	713	−1,169
A-7	2,023	1,197	2,668	826	43	783	760	23
A-8	756	1,825	2,425	−1,069	1,303	−2,372	840	−3,212
A-9	1,837	4,936	3,868	−3,099	43	−3,142	750	−3,892
A-10	1,071	2,245	1,697	−1,174	743	−1,917	837	−2,754
A-11	864	1,474	2,425	− 610	43	− 653	718	−1,371

Parcel Holders

Hijueleros	Total	36,854	29,293	35,975	7,561	3,383	4,178	11,768	−7,590
	Average	2,457	1,953	2,398	504	225	279	785	− 506
	A-16	17,574	4,566	2,425	13,008	4,457**	8,551	—	8,551
	A-17	9,110	2,000	1,697	7,110	7,000**	110	—	110
	Total	26,684	6,566	4,122	20,118	11,457	8,661	—	8,661
	Average	13,342	3,283	2,061	10,059	5,728	4,331	—	4,331
Huerteros	A-18	443	556	728	− 113	30	− 143	115	− 258
	A-19	406	995	1,697	− 589	43	− 632	169	− 801
	Total	849	1,551	2,425	− 702	73	− 775	284	−1,059
	Average	425	776	1,213	− 351	36	− 387	142	− 529

* Calculated on the basis of number of persons in the family from the study by H. Burgos Mujica, *Análisis Económico Agrícola para un Plan de Crédito Supervisado: Comuna de Navidad, Año Agrícola 1960–61*, Min. de Agricultura, Depto. de Economía Agraria, Sección de Admin. Rural, No. 19, p. 23. Based on theses by Elvira Matte de Cruchaga (1938) and Violeta Sivori A. (1950), Escuela de Servicio Social, Universidad Católica de Chile and norms established by the Servicio Nacional de Salud.

** Hijueleros were required to make a land payment in 1963–64.

based on number of dependents and minimum standards set up by the National Health Service is found in column 3. Regardless of individual variations, the grand totals of columns 2 and 3 are quite close: E° 37,410 for estimated consumption and E° 42,522 for calculated consumption. We take this to mean that on the average colonists are probably able to give a fairly accurate estimate of their expenses for consumption. Subtracting self-estimated family consumption expenses from net cash income (Col. 1 minus Col. 2), we arrive at debt repayment capacity in column 4. In nine cases this number is negative.

The Las Pataguas cooperative has a total machinery inventory of E° 10,000 on which it paid E° 4,000 in 1962–63. Since it has two more years to pay off the remaining E° 6,000, the 1963–64 portion of the machinery debt for each colonist is approximately E° 43.

Land interest payments (at 6 percent—included in operating expenses) will be required of each cooperator this year, but amortization payments are not due until 1964–65 except in the case of the hijuela operators, who must make land plus interest payments this year.[13] Some cooperators have other outstanding debts they must pay back this year (since A-18, a huertero, is not yet a member of the cooperative, he need not pay a portion of the machinery debt). We have called all of these debts—machinery, land amortization (for hijueleros), and miscellaneous loans due—capital payments and have displayed them in column 5.

Surplus or deficit for the year is reported in column 6. Eight parcel holders and the two huerteros in our sample show deficits for 1963–64.

Assuming, for the moment, that a land amortization payment was necessary this year, how many could pay it?[14]

Before calculating, a word of explanation is necessary. An adjustment for inflation plus various improvements was added to the value of each parcel. Then each calculation was expressed in quintals of wheat and the amount was written into each cooperator's provisional title. For example, A-1 paid a E° 750 downpayment last year when the farm was under a sharecropping system. Early this year he received his provisional title which notes that he has 776.4 quintals yet to pay. This will be paid in eighteen years, beginning in 1964–65. It represents an amortization payment of about 43 quintals a year or

E° 752 due next year expressed in 1964 Escudos (that is, 43 times the 1964 price of wheat which was E° 17.50 a quintal).[15]

Making a similar calculation for each of the parcel holders we interviewed results in column 7. Subtracting land payment to be made next year from deficit or surplus (column 6) and displaying the difference in column 8 results in an enumeration of the parcel holders who could pay their land debt this year. Under this assumption, two more parcel holders as well as the two huerteros would show deficits.

The average parcel holder on Las Pataguas made a net cash income of E° 2,457 in 1963–64. He spent E° 1,953 for family consumption and E° 225 for debt payments and had a surplus of E° 279. If a land payment had been required in 1963–64, he would not have been able to pay it entirely since, upon subtracting the E° 785 land amortization payment from the surplus of E° 279, a E° 506 deficit appears.[16]

Hijueleros will probably have no trouble meeting their consumption expenses, capital payments, and land amortization. The two we interviewed averaged a surplus of E° 4,331 after they had met all these payments.

Huerteros, it would seem, will have difficulty even with the relatively low payments required of them in 1963–64. The two showed an average net income of only E° 425. With consumption and capital payments of E° 812, this left them with an average E° 387 deficit.

All colonists who showed deficits were presented with statements of their debt at the end of the crop year. It is mandatory that they make them up. Although no definite time limit has been set since each crop year presents different weather problems, settlers understand that their debts must be paid as soon as possible if they are to remain as colonists.

HAVE COLONISTS' LEVELS OF LIVING RISEN?

Another measure of success of the reform experiment is found in a comparison of income before the reform and income in 1963–64. It is to that situation that we will turn next.

Before the colony was founded, the colonists who were interviewed had incomes (cash plus perquisites) averaging E° 1,032.[17] Av-

TABLE IV—COMPARATIVE INCOME BEFORE AND AFTER THE REFORM: LAS PATAGUAS

	Case	Income: last year of work before becoming a Las Pataguas colonist** (1)	Under the Reform 1963–64			Rise in income after reform (Col. 4 minus Col. 1) (5)
			Net cash income* (2)	Home consumption and "perquisites" (3)**	Total comparable income (Col. 2 plus Col. 3) (4)	
Parcel Holders	A-1	E° 1,216	E° 8,651	E° 1,183	E° 9,834	E° 8,618
	A-2	1,604	3,428	1,765	5,193	3,589
	A-3	570	1,777	1,537	3,314	2,744
	A-4	623	3,663	1,454	5,117	4,494
	A-5	913	3,734	1,885	5,619	4,706
	A-6	980	1,303	249	1,552	572
	A-7	807	2,023	1,498	3,521	2,714
	A-8	1,000	756	869	1,625	625
	A-9	1,176	1,837	1,624	3,461	2,285
	A-10	1,437	1,071	1,251	2,322	885
	A-11	1,149	864	1,486	2,350	1,201
	A-12	926	760	962	1,722	796
	A-13	3,146	1,487	1,068	2,555	− 591
	A-14	616	1,052	1,674	2,726	2,110
	A-15	1,265	4,448	1,956	6,404	5,139
	Total	17,428	36,854	20,461	57,315	39,887
	Average	1,162	2,457	1,364	3,821	2,659
Hijueleros	A-16	−2,000***	17,574	1,484	19,058	21,058
	A-17	2,561	9,110	2,432	11,542	8,981
	Total	561	26,684	3,916	30,600	30,039
	Average	281	13,342	1,958	15,300	15,019
Huerteros	A-18	647	443	595	1,038	391
	A-19	953	406	562	968	15
	Total	1,600	849	1,157	2,006	406
	Average	800	425	579	1,004	204

* Using net income presented in Table III.

** Perquisites are valued by a schedule issued by the Dirección General del Trabajo (Ministerio del Trabajo) in 1963–64 prices. Wages are expressed in 1963–64 Escudos.

*** He was a renter previously.

erage total income the last year before reform for all colonists who are now parcel holders was E° 1,162, while their average cash income was E° 705.

To compare income available to the colonists now with income available to them before the reform we must add to the net cash farm income arrived at in Table III the amount of consumption in kind and "perquisites"[18] from the parcel (Table IV). To calculate in-kind consumption, we added a value for the harvest the colonist stored for family use or consumed during the growing season, and the value of animal products,[19] house rental, electricity, and garden production.

Table IV indicates that income increased for fourteen of the fifteen parcel holders after the reform. On the average, their income was E° 3,821—an increase of E° 2,659 (about 300 percent of the pre-reform situation). Average cash income for parcel holders was E° 2,457, E° 1,752 above that in their pre-reform situation, representing an increase in cash income of about three and one-half times.

Table III shows that a cash average of E° 1,953 was probably spent for each *parcelero* family's consumption expenses in 1963–64. In addition, products and perquisites valued at E° 1,364 were used for home-consumption purposes. This means that an average of E° 3,317 in cash, products, and perquisites was used by parcel holders for family consumption (E° 1,953 plus E° 1,364).

Table III indicates that, on the average, E° 225 per colonist was spent on cooperative and individual investments. About E° 279 surplus or saving is available at the end of the year for the average colonist to use for other investments or for consumption. Had a land payment been required in 1963–64, colonists would have shown an average deficit of E° 506. Yet family consumption of the average parcel-holding colonist has risen from E° 1,162 to E° 3,317—just under three times. Interviews on a neighboring fundo show that an inquilino family of nine (the average family size among parcel holders on Las Pataguas) was about E° 1,300. As on Los Silos, we must conclude that consumption by colonists could be reduced, still leaving them better off than other zonal inquilinos and than they themselves were formerly, so that they could meet their land payments.

As a less painful alternative it may be possible to raise production, or at least lower operating expenses.

A Measurement of Production Potential. Again using the Photogrammetric Project (as we did in Chapter 3), we selected for comparison with Las Pataguas a neighboring well-managed fundo which has a similar water supply and soil type.[20]

On Las Pataguas, of the 284.7 hectares operated by the nineteen colonists in our sample, 225 hectares or 79 percent were devoted to annual crops: rice, potatoes, beans, sunflowers, corn, and wheat. On the neighboring fundo of 630 hectares, 403 hectares or 63 percent of the farm were devoted to annual crops: corn, potatoes, and wheat. The other 227 hectares were pasture for fattening feeder cattle.

Wheat production on the neighboring farm was 33 percent higher per acre than wheat production on our sample at Las Pataguas. Corn production on the neighbor's farm was 87 percent over corn production on our sample on Las Pataguas, while potato production was 155 percent higher.

This evidence seems to indicate that given the proper combination of inputs, production on Las Pataguas could be raised in the short run. Commercial fertilizer per fertilized hectare on the neighboring farm was well over two times greater than for our sample on Las Pataguas, despite the fact that the neighbor's fundo was able to take advantage of well-manured pasture land which is constantly being brought into the rotation. This seems to indicate that if Las Pataguas colonists hope to increase their production, at the very least they will have to raise fertilizer inputs.

Cutting Expenses. In our description of Los Silos we hypothesized that labor inputs could be cut so that this saving might be allocated to yield-increasing inputs. We qualified our analysis in a number of ways and will not repeat our qualifications here.

On the 284.7 hectares of our Las Pataguas sample, 20,170 man-days or about 71 man-days per hectare were used. Of this, about 8,809 man-days of hired labor were used at a total cost to the colonists in our sample of about E° 15,922. Thus about 44 percent of the labor used on our sample of Las Pataguas in 1963–64 was hired.

Three pieces of evidence lead us to the conclusion that this amount of labor is excessive and could be pared back.

First: Calculations from data given to us by the neighboring fundo operator, whose production we referred to above, reveal that the number of man-days of work on his fundo each year is about 27,000 or 43 man-days per hectare. One may well argue that the neighboring fundo operator uses more laborsaving capital and so does not need as much labor as Las Pataguas. The next two pieces of evidence will attempt to show that this is not necessarily an important objection.

Second: Our information on the crops grown on Las Pataguas and the neighboring fundo was held up against the labor coefficients for the same combination of crops arrived at in the Ministry of Agriculture study referred to in Chapter 3,[21] this time for O'Higgins Province, to indicate whether labor use on Las Pataguas is really extravagant. Calculated man-day requirements on our sample of Las Pataguas equals 10,780 or approximately 38 man-days per hectare. This figure is about half of the figure actually used—20,170 (approximately 71 man-days per hectare). On the other hand, the calculation on the neighboring fundo equals 20,808 while, as we have shown, it actually uses 27,000 man-days of labor. Considering that this fundo supports a herd of feeder cattle for which labor coefficients are not available, this seems to indicate that the amount of labor used is a realistic amount—an average for the zone considering the pattern of cultivation. The calculated figure for Las Pataguas undoubtedly understates the labor need. The Ministry study sample is weighted toward large farms. Some animals are raised on Las Pataguas. And small parcels need a certain labor flexibility during rush seasons which probably shows up as redundant labor in a gross calculation such as the one above. Also, the input study sample undoubtedly includes farms which have more labor-saving machinery to substitute for hand labor. Yet the fact that Las Pataguas uses nearly double the average amount of labor for the zone seems to indicate that the labor force could be reduced.

Third: Morales' data[22] again support the conclusion that labor use could be cut back. He uses a stratified sample of 96 selected farms in O'Higgins Province. Average labor use in the first stratum studied (11 farms of from 10 to 19.9 irrigated hectares) was 45 man-days per hectare. In his second stratum (31 farms of from 20 to 49.9 irrigated hectares), labor use was 37 man-days of work per hectare. Most of Las Pataguas' farms fall into the smaller of these two size-categories.

The three indicators we have used show that from 38 to 45 man-days per hectare is probably average for the cropping pattern on Las Pataguas.

Perhaps by proposing that labor use be cut back, however, we appear to be concluding that the fundo does not have the capacity to support colonist families already living there. This is not true. Potentially available labor on Las Pataguas, considering each male colonist-family resident over 16 years living on the fundo, is 172 man-years. Boys under sixteen should probably also be figured as part of the work force, but we will assume that there is a counter overcalculation of those too old to work. Considering a man-year as 300 days, the above calculation indicates a labor force of 51,600 days (300 days × 172) on Las Pataguas' 1,162 irrigated hectares—44 man-days per irrigated hectare.

The 44 man-days of labor per irrigated hectare already available on Las Pataguas falls within the 38 to 45 man-day range set up by the evidence we have presented and seems to indicate that employing 71 man-days of labor per hectare represents an unnecessarily lavish expenditure and means underemployment of some labor resources.

Considering that our sample represents about one fourth of the acreage of the fundo and the colonists we studied spent E° 15,922 on hired labor, all settlers on the fundo probably spent four times that amount or over E° 60,000 in 1963–64 contracting labor.

Not all of the approximately E° 60,000 spent for hired outside labor could be saved, but certainly a major part might be reallocated —perhaps to yield-increasing capital—or these savings might simply push down expenses, thus yielding a greater net income.

Fertilizer: A Necessary Expense. Las Pataguas may need to spend even more for fertilizer per hectare than the amount spent on the neighboring farm (E° 54 per fertilized hectare). At any rate, we can say that the approximately E° 20 spent on fertilizer per hectare on

Las Pataguas is too low. With a larger percentage of his farm in legumes than Las Pataguas and much of the farm used for pasture, the neighbor's rotation is long. His soil is constantly being renewed from manure and from the pasture itself. Therefore, it is entirely possible that even if an expenditure of E° 54 an irrigated hectare were optimal on the farm next door, colonists would need to use even more for comparable yields. A longer rotation for soil renewal, followed on the neighboring farm, is impractical on smaller plots like those on Las Pataguas.

We conclude our economic analysis of Las Pataguas by noting that the deficits that would be recorded by average colonists if they had to make a land payment in 1964 could have been made up by some combination of the following: (a) Keeping consumption a little lower (still maintaining colonists' income above their former situation and that of zonal inquilinos). (b) Realizing the production potential that exists on the fundo. By using better management and applying more yield-increasing inputs, production can be increased. This involves the job of persuading colonists that yield-increasing inputs pay. (c) Reallocating expenses so that fewer resources are devoted to hiring labor.

Certainly the success of individual members will depend to a great extent on the success of their cooperative.

PROBLEMS AND PROGRESS OF THE COOPERATIVE: 1963–64

Cooperative organization has proven difficult on Las Pataguas. Landholders moved from the patronal system directly to the status of nearly independent landholders. As these settlers received land they felt less need for a cooperative organization than did colonists on Los Silos, for whom the cooperative was involved in every facet of their lives—even to working the land. Ironically, some of the colonists who did best economically at Las Pataguas in 1963–64 were those who sold some of their produce outside cooperative channels, thus reinforcing their independence. There must be clear incentives for selling through the cooperative if it is to be developed into an effective marketing agency.

The problem of an early spirit of independence was compounded by difficulties in incorporating the three definable social strata on

Las Pataguas into the cooperative. The hijueleros were in a class by themselves, having little contact with parcel holders and huerteros. Their relationship to the rest of the cooperative tended to be similar to that between a patrón and his people. Other colonists resented hijuelero domination of the cooperative in its early days. Hijueleros were vastly better off economically, had had some farm management experience prior to their establishment, and seemed, considering their background and interests, to have very little in common with their less-favored neighbors. Probably the only solution to the problem is the one chosen—to remove them from the cooperative. Apportioning more land to the huerteros should, in years to come, give the cooperative an important base it seems to need to be effective: a more or less homogeneous membership.

A campesino leader of the Asociación Nacional de Organizaciones Campesinas, a Church-supported labor organization, lives on Las Pataguas and began in early 1964, at the colonists' request, to devote himself part time to cooperative organization on Las Pataguas. Of course, if colonists do not see some material advantage to belonging to the cooperative, it is unlikely that this kind of encouragement will be very helpful.

INPROA's general policy of working only with the cooperative and of having its officers and committees, in turn, work with members may strengthen the cooperative. Indeed, unless the cooperative members follow the farm plan drawn up for each colonist for 1964–65, credit assistance in kind and in cash will be denied. This will require colonists to rely more on their cooperative organization. Still, it is not clear whether technical information can be entirely channelled through the cooperative without direct technician-colonist contact, considering the immense job of training to be done in such matters as labor use, fertilizer use, etc.

Channelling in-kind inputs through the cooperative means making a certain amount of fertilizer and seed, for example, available to each member, depending on the plan for his parcel. This involves careful attention to specific instructions, and care must be taken so that each colonist knows why certain inputs are being used.

Without much doubt, the farming plan in use in 1964–65 was needed. But considering the magnitude of the educational job and the imperfections that creep into any farm-management plan upon execution, a resident technical agricultural person must be available full time to assist Las Pataguas with day-to-day management problems, at least in its first years. However, the case of the Ingeniero Agrónomo who was awarded an hijuela, but left Las Pataguas in 1964, illustrates again that a technician who assumes a paternal role simply cannot make a reform effort succeed. In addition to being highly trained himself, a technical person hired to assist in reform must be able to teach colonists gradually to make many of their own rational decisions. Merely following a plan in order to receive credit has its own shortcomings. If not carefully—and pragmatically—administered, a farming plan may develop into a rigidly dogmatic substitute for a patrón which demands unquestioning obedience and fosters little or no comprehension.

Las Pataguas' cooperative has had three managers (*gerentes*) in its past two years as a colony, the last of whom was relieved of his duties by cooperative vote at the end of the 1963–64 crop year. The gerente until this date had rarely gotten into the fields. In fact, the one just removed was not trained in agriculture and admitted he knew little about farming. Numerous parcel holders informally attested to his lack of knowledge in these matters. Consequently, he did little else than keep the books for the cooperative.

Unfortunately, this shifting of gerentes has meant that even the accounts were not kept well. There was a rather long delay at the end of the harvest while the accounts of members of the cooperative were figured. Most colonists had little idea of how they were doing until they finally received the tardy year-end statement and were surprised and disillusioned to find expenses higher than they had imagined possible. It will be necessary in coming years for the cooperative to adopt a better bookkeeping system so landholders will be able to see their standing as the year progresses. Some colonists, not used to making management decisions, hired labor to the extent of their resources and did not take into account that interest would be charged on the fertilizer and seeds received in kind as well as on the cash advances. Few knew the extent of interest charges when we interviewed them. To be confronted with a debt rather than a profit at the close of the first year of proprietorship came as a blow and embittered some colonists and again illustrates the necessity for clearer communications between INPROA and the cooperative.

It is still too early to tell whether presentation of a bill showing deficits will encourage colonists to produce more next year or will merely foster a defeatist attitude.

SUMMARY: LAS PATAGUAS

(1) About 64 percent of the colonists making up the Las Pataguas experiment lived on the fundo at some time prior to the reform. Reform increased the resident capacity of the fundo by sixteen families, or 21 percent.

(2) The reform defined three social classes based on the size of the plot received. The cooperative is in the process of reversing itself and is encouraging hijueleros to leave the cooperative and will make it possible for huerteros to purchase additional land.

(3) A point system determined who would get land on Las Pataguas.

(4) Infrastructural costs added 20 percent to the cost of reform on Las Pataguas. It would seem that this figure could have been reduced considerably if more thought had been given to investment priorities. Then the parcel holders could have added less-necessary infrastructure at a later date, utilizing profits from their own farm. This would have also given colonists more of a sense of participation in the reform.

(5) About half of our sample will probably default on some payments this year, although the average parcel holder will show a slight surplus. If a land payment had been required, the number of colonists defaulting from our sample would probably have risen to a little more than half and the average parcel holder would have shown a deficit.

(6) Income for each parcel holder has been raised considerably by the reform—probably at least three times. Some of this increased income has gone into paying for land interest and other cooperatively or individually owned capital. But consumption by families has at least doubled under the reform. If consumption could be held down slightly (admittedly a painful alternative), colonists would probably still be better off than they were before the reform (and better off than average inquilinos in the zone) and would be able to meet more of their debts. This will be especially important when a land amortization payment is required.

(7) A neighboring farm under good management and with similar soil type and irrigation possibilities registered yields that are higher than on Las Pataguas. This seems to indicate that Las Pataguas has an unexploited margin of productivity.

(8) Three standards used for comparison seem to indicate that too much labor was hired on Las Pataguas in 1963–64. Operating expenses could be lowered if more efficient use were made of family labor and less outside labor were hired.

(9) Fertilizer expenditures will undoubtedly have to be raised on Las Pataguas in order to raise production.

(10) Although a supervised credit program is being used on Las Pataguas, and a planned farming program has been initiated in 1964–65, a resident technician is also necessary due to the mammoth teaching job which remains.

NOTES

1 Ministerio de Agricultura, *Third National Agricultural-Livestock Census,* 1955, and Departamento de Conservación y Administración de Recursos Agrícolas y Forestales, Ministerio de Agricultura, *Agricultura Técnica,* Anexo XVIII, No. 2, December, 1958.

2 Instituto de Promoción Agraria (INPROA), "Estudio de Parcelización Hacienda 'Las Pataguas' " (mimeographed), Santiago, 1963, p. 19; hereinafter cited as INPROA, 1963.

3 *Ibid.,* p. 20.

4 *La Voz,* August 5, 1962, Number 261.

5 We will continue to use 1963–64 Escudos. Further elaboration and breakdown of statistical materials given in this chapter may be found in William C. Thiesenhusen, "Experimental Programs of Land Reform in Chile," unpublished Ph.D. thesis, University of Wisconsin, 1965.

6 The cooperative was founded after colonists were settled on their parcels. Gradually, the Technical Committee and INPROA, when it took over, called upon more settlers—through their cooperative—to help in decision-making.

7 United Nations, Economic Commission for Latin America (CEPAL), "Rural Settlement Patterns and Social Change in Latin America," *Economic Bulletin for Latin America,* Vol. 10, No. 1, 1965, pp. 6–7: "The villorrio is usually smaller than the *aldea,* but the important distinction is not so much in the size as in the relative importance of specialized administrative and economic functions and the more rudimentary class stratification. The population of the typical villorrio consists almost entirely of small cultivators and agricultural wage workers . . . it is a sprawling

agglomeration of houses without a center—for more specialized services the villorrio must depend on a nearby pueblo."

8   Instituto de Promoción Agraria, "Proyecto Específico 'Las Pataguas' " (request to Inter-American Development Bank—mimeographed), Santiago, April 27, 1964, p. 27; hereinafter cited as INPROA, 1964.

9   United Nations, *op. cit.*, p. 50.

10   Oscar Domínguez, *El Condicionamiento de la Reforma Agraria: Estudio de los Factores Económicos, Demográficos y Sociales que Determinan la Promoción del Campesino Chileno,* Université Catholique de Louvain, Collection de l'Ecole des Sciences Politiques et Sociales, No. 173, E. Warny, Louvain, Belgium, 1963, p. 182, quoted in United Nations publication cited in note 7 above.

11   Surely a misstatement. He probably meant 79. The correct figure is 76.

12   Msgr. Rafael Larraín, director of the Instituto de Educación Rural, in *La Voz, op. cit.*

13   At first glance one would imagine that advances should be accounted for here. Actually, they are included in the consumption which has already been subtracted to arrive at debt repayment capacity.

14   This calculation may be a bit unfair: land payments were delayed so colonists could have several years to get established, organize a cooperative, etc. The calculation is not made to be prematurely critical but to point out how many colonists will have to raise their incomes over 1963–64 to meet their increasing obligations.

15   As this is written, the readjustment system is being changed by INPROA to include also an index constructed from a list of selected wholesale products. Then the debt adjustment may be made either on the wheat index or on the wholesale price index, whichever is more favorable to the colonist. It is impossible to tell how much this will benefit colonists a priori. The fact that interest rate will be 5 percent instead of 6 percent and only $2\frac{1}{2}$ percent will be applied to the readjusted principal should lessen deficits that show up for some colonists later in this chapter, but not enough to change the conclusions reached.

16   Again we remind the reader that this assumes all factors equal to 1963–64 in 1964–65 when the first land payment is due. Modifications in the inflationary readjustment system made in 1964–65 by INPROA and detailed earlier will undoubtedly lessen the average deficit but it will not disappear entirely.

17   The comparisons in this section carry the same assumptions and restrictions as in the comparable section of the Los Silos analysis (Chapter 3).

18   Of course, no perquisites are given to individual colonists in the sense they are given to inquilinos. But some of the same benefits (i.e., house, grazing privileges, etc.) valued in our discussion of the situation before the reform are still available after. This means that if we are to compare incomes, we must include them again.

19 This figure is calculated from the schedule of the Ministry of Labor (referred to earlier) which values "grazing privileges" as a perquisite. This undoubtedly undervalues actual animal income. But this undervaluation is probably slight since a much higher percentage of these animals are horses than on Los Silos.

20 Map 3410–7100A.

21 Corporación de Fomento de la Producción, Ministerio de Agricultura, Universidad de Chile, *Insumos en la Agricultura, Año 1961–62,* Santiago, 1964.

22 Héctor Morales Jara, "Productividad Presente y Potencial en 96 Predios de la Provincia de O'Higgins y su Relación con el Tamaño de las Propiedades," unpublished thesis, Facultad de Agronomía, Universidad de Chile, Santiago, 1964, pp. 24, 48.

THE MELD:
ALTO LAS CRUCES
AND SAN DIONISIO

Chapter 5

What we have learned from Los Silos and Las Pataguas we will apply to Alto Las Cruces and San Dionisio. We won't make the same mistakes again.

—A member of the INPROA staff.

BOTH ALTO LAS CRUCES[1] and San Dionisio[2] were rented out for many years by the fundos' owner, the Archbishop of Santiago. When these properties came into the hands of INPROA at its founding, the Archbishop's Technical Committee had already begun the reform program: some colonists had been selected and a rudimentary cooperative, made up of all settlers, had been founded.

Both fundos were farmed under a combination sharecropping and rental system in 1963–64. At the close of the crop year, San Dionisio's colonists voted to continue this system another year. The Alto Las Cruces cooperative, on the other hand, opted for across-the-board rental in 1964–65. Parcelization will follow these intermediate steps, probably in 1966–67.

INPROA officials felt that the Las Pataguas system of establishing colonists immediately on parcels weakened its young cooperative by giving too much independence too quickly to farmers as yet unprepared for rational decision-making. They decided that putting several steps between settlement of a fundo and creation of private farms might foster cooperative ideas during the intermediate period, helping to make the cooperative into a bargaining organization. Besides, a centrally managed system would give INPROA controls over management during these intermediate steps, thus strengthening the colony economically.

INPROA officials recognized their dilemma: they had to tread a thin line in helping colonists, inexperienced in agricultural decision-making skills, to succeed economically without destroying their sense of participation in the colony.

As we shall see later, in the centrally managed, sharecropping pattern adopted for the major part of both farms, the original fundo fields were worked without physical division, meaning that many colonists had their wheat, for example, in one large field and had to cooperate in irrigating and harvesting it.

INPROA staff members were firm in their belief that only by becoming institutionally strong could the campesino organization become a self-reliant agency truly breaking with the existing social structure of Chilean agriculture and capable of acting one day without paternal surveillance.

Working through committees, the cooperative began, upon its formation, to make decisions on such non-technical issues as choosing fellow colonists and employees (the bookkeeper, for example), electing officials, punishing members who refused to do their share of the work, etc. Its meetings came to constitute a forum which helped crystallize colonists' desires for presentation to the INPROA staff.

For practical reasons, too, INPROA chose to economize on its actions as a service agency by dealing with a strong cooperative made up of all participants in the reform project and not with settlers individually. As it evolved, the cooperative would be the vehicle through which members would have to make decisions affecting their own destinies.

Some problems, however, could not be immediately resolved by a majority vote of members of the cooperative: amount of fertilizer to use, when to apply insecticides, whether or not to use seed disinfectants, etc. These techniques would have to be presented with the voice of authority at first—through the central management and also by way of supervised credit which could be withdrawn if advice were not followed. At the end of the 1963–64 crop year, on-the-farm courses in cooperatives, agricultural techniques, money management, etc., were added to the program to build up individual skills. Further, although in 1963–64 an INPROA technician largely divided his time between the two fundos, a separate resident technician was hired for both Alto Las Cruces and San Dionisio for 1964–65. This system was designed to teach colonists that new practices pay—in time, effort, and product. Adoption, reasoned INPROA officials, would follow.

We shall return to more details on the cooperative's accomplishments in 1963–64 and to a more thorough description of the land tenure pattern on the two fundos later in this chapter.

COLONIST SELECTION

No point system was used in the selection of original San Dionisio and Alto Las Cruces colonists. A subjective interview of former fundo occupants was administered by the Archbishop's Technical Committee in 1963. Replacements and new colonists were selected from Instituto de Educación Rural sources. Early settlers were largely chosen without much community involvement; after INPROA began functioning, however, its officials insisted on cooperative participation in picking colonists. INPROA maintained a list of campesinos applying for parcels. Therefore, some elimination of prospective colonists could be accomplished at the central office. (For example, campesinos from an entirely different area were removed from cooperative consideration.) Then candidates' names were submitted to the cooperative which summoned interested campesinos to appear personally before a selection meeting.

There were fifty-two original fundo residents on San Dionisio. Fourteen left before the reform got under way. Eight of these chose not to participate; six were dismissed, with the following reasons figuring in their dismissal: "drinks too much," "is too old to accept the responsibilities of a parcel," "doesn't want to work his land directly," "has already spread counterpropaganda against the reform."[3] Those who were expelled were given severance pay. By the beginning of the 1963–64 crop year, seventeen new colonists were brought in so that the fundo supported three more resident families than the year before, in addition to a number of sharecroppers who lived outside the fundo and farmed several hectare plots of sunflowers, corn, and beans. By the beginning of the 1964–65 crop year, eleven more permanent colonists had been selected by INPROA and four of the original colonists had been moved out by finding them other jobs on a nearby fundo, paying them an indemnification, and dismissing them.[4] The number of outside sharecroppers was correspondingly reduced in 1964–65. Final plans call for the farm's division into two parcels for seventy-three colonist families, with a possibility of two more parcels which, for the time being, would be held in reserve by the cooperative. When the seventy-three colonists are settled, the fundo will be supporting nearly 29 percent more resident families than before the reform.

Before reform, Alto Las Cruces supported ten families. In 1963–64 twelve colonists were settled there, half of them from the old fundo. Unfortunate accidents resulted in the death of two of these colonists during the crop year. Another colonist was expelled by the cooperative at harvest time in 1964. Five more settlers were selected at the beginning of the crop year 1964–65 and two more will be selected shortly to bring the farm up to its seventeen-family capacity. This will mean that the fundo after reform will support 41 percent more families than before.

PARCELIZATION

The Archbishop of Santiago still owns both Alto Las Cruces and San Dionisio. Through a deed in May 1963, however, he conferred in INPROA all rights to administer the fundos.

Plans for the parcelization of Alto Las Cruces were completed in September 1964, and INPROA applied to the Inter-American Development Bank, asking it for a loan for infrastructure.

Irrigation Problems: Alto Las Cruces. Infrastructure additions on Alto Las Cruces are complicated because the farm is divided into two distinct halves by a stream—not usable for irrigation purposes—and an accompanying marshy area. Thus divided into a north and south sector, the two parts of the farm receive irrigation water from two different canals of the Maule River.

In the north half, all water comes from the Sandoval Canal, which forks west and north from the Maule and, as it nears the northern boundary of the fundo, is almost parallel to it. At the time of reform, Alto Las Cruces held legal claim to a water supply insufficient to irrigate the entire fundo—only 14 *regadores* or an average of 131 liters per second. But in the absence of a water association, the fundo (and other nearby farms) merely took all the water needed for its cropping pattern.

Another related problem is lack of fertility, especially in the northern half of the farm. Taking advantage of the free water supply, the last renter had depleted the soil by raising rice without an adequate rotation and by not applying much fertilizer.

To insure that the north sector will have a permanent supply of water if a water association is organized and farms are no longer able to use whatever amount they need, the Archbishop is in the process of buying 150 shares of a canal near Talca to barter for an equal water flow in the Sandoval Canal.[5] Alto Las Cruces continues to use all the water it needs meanwhile, but when legal purchase is complete, these additional shares will total 220 additional liters per second.

Because the farm held fewer water shares in its south sector, a reservoir there evened out the water supply. Under the former rental system it fell into disrepair. This sector is watered by the smaller San Miguel Canal, which makes a more acute angle with the Maule than the Sandoval and runs parallel to the fundo's southern boundary. The fundo holds 5 percent of the rights of the San Miguel Canal Association which, in turn, owns half of the shares of the San Miguel Canal. These rights total about 74 liters per second.[6] Lately the Archbishop has entered into negotiations with the Irrigation Department of the Ministry of Public Works (Dirección de Riego del Ministerio de Obras Públicas), which owns a great part of the water rights in Sandoval Canal, to buy more regadores totalling 56 liters per second, but negotiations have not been completed. This additional water will probably be available when the canal to connect the Sandoval and San Miguel at their nearest point off the southeast corner of the fundo is completed by the Ministry of Public Works. Work on this connecting canal is in process.

Alto Las Cruces owns overflow rights (*derrames*) from neighboring fundos totalling probably 15 liters per second. Because of the low total amount of water,[7] the reservoir must be repaired to make the best use of the water that is available. It will have the capacity to store a flow of 145 liters per second during forty-four hours. The most expensive single item of the irrigation plan is rehabilitating the reservoir, which is expected to cost about 36 percent of the entire amount spent for rearrangement of the farm's irrigation system to fit the parcels.

Disrepair of the reservoir, coupled with a low initial water supply, was only part of the reason for the water scarcity in this sector. Minifundio operators off the eastern boundary of the fundo were pilfering water which belonged to Alto Las Cruces. INPROA has now obtained measured water dividers (marcos partidores) for them, thus giving the group of minifundistas a fixed amount and eliminating most possibilities of stealing an unlimited supply of water from that destined for Alto Las Cruces.

Repair of the reservoir raised the costs of irrigation on Alto Las Cruces substantially. It will be recalled, however, that the largest single item of expense on the Las Pataguas water project was the marcos partidores. Consequently, it was decided that on Alto Las Cruces (and also San Dionisio), a cheaper system of water shifts (turnos) would be more practical (see Chapter 4).

The Villorrio: Alto Las Cruces. Since the south sector of the fundo had been poorly watered, it was little used by the former renter. The bad state of repair of the houses here meant that all but one had to be demolished after INPROA took over. Eight more dwellings needed to be built to accommodate the nine planned parcels in the area.

INPROA was convinced from the Las Pataguas experience that a villorrio is an unwokable settlement scheme. Furthermore, Alto Las Cruces colonists voted to live on their land. Yet the INPROA planners realized that the stream might divide the community in two parts since it makes communications difficult between the distinct halves of the fundo. This would be especially true with respect to parcels 8 and 11 (Diagram I). Although they are quite near the planned cooperative buildings, the marshy area makes passage difficult and colonists on these parcels would have to use the eastern road to go to meetings or to have any contact with the remainder of the fundo. Furthermore, supplying electricity and drinking water to houses on dispersed parcels is difficult and expensive. A modified villorrio plan was finally decided upon. This plan groups the houses along the central eastern boundary of the fundo near the road which crosses the stream to connect with the north sector. It gives as many families as possible easy access to their land and puts the majority of the houses on the least fertile land in the south sector.

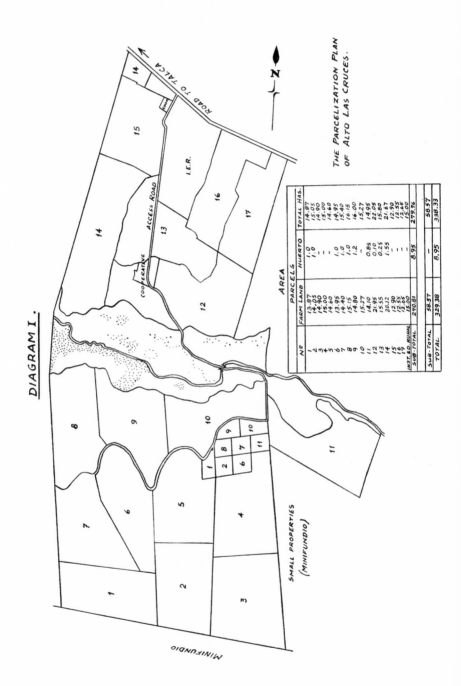

DIAGRAM I.

THE PARCELIZATION PLAN
OF ALTO LAS CRUCES.

N°	FARM LAND	HUERTO	TOTAL HAS.
1	13.87	1.0	14.87
2	14.05	1.0	15.05
3	14.90	—	14.90
4	15.00	—	15.00
5	14.60	—	14.60
6	13.95	1.0	14.95
7	14.40	1.0	15.40
8	15.15	1.0	16.15
9	14.80	1.2	16.00
10	15.27	—	15.27
11	14.10	0.85	14.95
12	21.95	0.10	22.05
13	15.55	0.25	15.80
14	20.12	1.55	21.67
15	12.90	—	12.90
16	12.55	—	12.55
17	12.65	—	12.65
INST. ED. RURAL	15.00	—	15.00
SUB-TOTAL	270.81	8.95	279.76
SUB-TOTAL	58.57	—	58.57
TOTAL	329.38	8.95	338.33

AREA PARCELS

The cooperative buildings are planned for a central location in the north sector, also on rather poor land. The nearby land in the stream bed might be brought into production some time in the future, but much labor will be needed to reclaim it. Strategic location of the cooperative and the land reserved for it in this area permits cooperative members themselves to do the necessary clearing job after a loan is obtained to pay for the technical drainage work. Only two new houses are necessary on the north part of the fundo.

Total Infrastructure: Alto Las Cruces. The total infrastructural bill for the fundo is estimated at E°166,343.85.[8] The farm (minus a parcel to be used by the IER) is valued at E° 163,033.05. The total cost of settling the seventeen families then will be E° 329,376.90. Of this nearly 51 percent can be attributed to new infrastructure:

Houses	23.5	percent
Fences and gates	4.6	"
Irrigation works	11.0	"
Roads	5.6	"
Electricity	3.1	"
Drinking water	2.9	"
	50.7	percent

On Las Pataguas only 20 percent of the cost of the reform was attributable to infrastructure (Chapter 4). Infrastructure on Alto Las Cruces will cost nearly E°9,800 per parcel holder settled; land will cost an average of E°9,600 a parcel (varying in size, depending on soil quality, from 12.55 hectares to 22.05 hectares).

Unlike Las Pataguas, however, infrastructure will not be included in each colonist's land bill. There will be a separate bill for infrastructure as installations are completed, since estimates may not coincide exactly with expenditures. (As pointed out in Chapter 4, this was not done on Las Pataguas and INPROA lost money as a result.)

Plans for San Dionisio. Plans for the parcelization of San Dionisio are not yet complete. It is known, however, that the cooperative will have to build fifty-three houses. Only twenty houses from the old fundo can be used and many colonists are living in prefabricated houses or two families to a house until the necessary plans are completed and the infrastructure loan from the Inter-American Development Bank obtained.

Most old but still usable fundo houses on San Dionisio are grouped along the public access roads. Here, too, the cooperative again vetoed a villorrio settlement, and houses dispersed on the parcels would simply have been too expensive. A type of modified hamlet settlement a bit different from that on Alto Las Cruces was decided upon.

On San Dionisio each house will be located on its parcel, but four houses will be grouped at adjoining corners of the respective plots. In this way four houses should be able to share a well and have a common warehouse, and electrical installations should be less expensive than in a completely dispersed settlement.

Only a trunk road exists on the fundo now. A U-shaped access road internal to the farm must be built and alterations made to the irrigation system (again based on turnos). Electricity and running water must be installed. Plenty of irrigation water from the San Dionisio and Machicura Canals is available, so there will be no complicated water purchase problems on this fundo as there are on Alto Las Cruces. There are plans for extending the irrigation system to the 257-hectare dry area at the base of the mountain as soon as possible. An estimate of these costs is not available at this writing, but per-colonist expenses are likely to be lower than on Alto Las Cruces.

TENURE SYSTEM: SAN DIONISIO AND ALTO LAS CRUCES, 1963–64

In the 50–50 sharecropping (medería) system on San Dionisio and Alto Las Cruces in 1963–64, INPROA supplied the land for which it, in turn, paid a cash rent to the Archbishop of Santiago. Operating expenses were split 50–50 with the colonists, but labor was completely at the cooperators' expense. Income was split 50–50 between the colonists and INPROA.

Each colonist was asked how much land he felt he could care for under a sharecropping system at the beginning of the 1963–64 crop year, the first year of the reform. INPROA worked out for the fundos the farming program which called for growing wheat, beans, corn, potatoes, and sunflowers.[9] Most of the wheat, however, was already planted when INPROA took over. Each colonist was assigned parts of large fields which represented the best compromise between his acreage desires, crops he wanted to grow, and the amount of cropping land actually available. Former fundo fields were not divided: a colonist may have had plots in four or five large fields, always knowing which part of the field was "his."

This system allowed INPROA to take advantage of any economies of size there might be in large fields and also to maintain centralized management over such matters as fertilizer application, insecticide use, etc., as well as planning of the farm's cropping pattern. The foremost advantage of the system seems to be that it economizes on scarce technical resources, but other economies are that the irrigation system does not need to be divided and that crops can be seeded with a large drill and harvested with a self-propelled combine.[10]

Each colonist had certain decisions to make on the portions of the fields which were his: when to weed, how to divide irrigation chores, etc. In wheat harvest, each sharecropper was given the option of combining separately and paying a higher harvesting fee or harvesting with other medieros who had their plots in the same field and dividing the yield by the number of hectares in medias he possessed. Most chose the latter alternative. Crops like potatoes and corn were harvested individually by hand. Sunflowers were cut by hand, heads were allowed to field-dry, and then were harvested with a combine.

Besides a plot on shares, all colonists could cash-rent (we will hereafter refer to "cash-rent" simply as "rent") a smaller piece of land—usually a cuadra—from INPROA. On San Dionisio they could grow sugar beets on this land according to specifications set forth by IANSA (Industria Azucarera Nacional S.A.), the national sugar beet company. Sugar beets were irrigated, weeded, and harvested by hand although they were planted by machine. Alto Las Cruces did not obtain a sugar beet contract in 1963–64. Since sugar beets are grown only on IANSA contract, colonists there could not raise sugar beets but, with no central management or control, could plant their rented acreage to crops of their choice.

On the two fundos, we attempted measurement of the same economic matters as on Los Silos and Las Pataguas. On San Dionisio we picked a random sample of fourteen cases out of the fifty-two settlers during 1963–64—about 27 percent—to interview in depth. On Alto Las Cruces we picked eight cases out of the ten 1963–64 colonists.

SAN DIONISIO: 1963–64

Can Colonists Pay Their Debts? Income accrued to a colonist
on San Dionisio from three sources: (1) half of all gross produce on
his sharecropped land after half of the operating expenses corresponding to his acreage were deducted; (2) all the net income from
his rented cuadra; (3) asignación familiar. The actual cash farm income of one rather typical colonist in 1963–64 is presented in Table
I to demonstrate our calculations in the subsequent section.

This colonist had 11 hectares in sharecropping and 1.56 rented
hectares of sugar beets. Total gross income on his sharecropped land
was E° 5,874.[11] Of this, he received half or E° 2,937. The other half
went to INPROA to pay land rent, management costs, land taxes, irrigation rights, etc. Of his half, this colonist kept out E° 464 worth of
wheat, potatoes, and corn for home consumption. Cash sales from his
portion of the sharecropping were E° 2,473 (E° 2,937 minus E° 464).

His gross income from sugar beets on rented land was E° 1,750,
while the total asignación familiar he received for his eight dependents was E° 472. His gross cash income (E° 2,473 plus E° 1,750 plus

TABLE I—CALCULATION OF NET INCOME FOR ONE CASE ON SAN DIONISIO 1963–64

(Acreage: 11 Hectares in 50–50 Sharecropping; 1.56 Cash-Rental Hectares)

	Gross Income						
	Total yield (1)	Hec-tares (2)	Price E° (3)	Total E° (4)	INPROA's half E° (5)	Sold by colonist E° (6)	Consumed by colonist E° (7)
1—Wheat	170 quintals	7.8	17.5	2,976	1,488	1,216	272
2—Potatoes	150 sacks	.8	10	1,500	750	710	40
3—Beans (for exportation)	12 quintals	.8	36	432	216	216	
4—Corn	35 quintals	.8	19	666	333	181	152
5—Sunflowers	12 quintals	.8	25	300	150	150	
Total		11		5,874	2,937	2,473*	464

a) * Gross cash farm income: sharecropping (Col. 6)   E° 2,473
b) Gross income for cash-rented 1.56 hectares of sugar beets   1,750
c) Asignación familiar (8 dependents)   472

Gross cash income   E° 4,695

TABLE I (continued)

	Operating Expenses			
Item	Total expenses (shares) E°	This colonist's portion E°	IN-PROA's portion E°	Total expenses on rented land (all paid by this colonist) E°
1—Outside labor: Permanent worker (year) E° 723 Weeding sugar beets 30 Harvesting beans 19 Harvest of sunflowers 15 Irrigator's wage 4	561.00	561.00		230.00
2—Meals for workers (calculated by schedule used by Ministry of Labor)	51.05	51.05		20.00
3—Interest (12%) on production advances (E° 230)	27.60	27.60		
4—Interest (12%) on consumption advances (E° 103)	12.36	12.36		
5—Interest on all seed and fertilizer: 12% of items 7, 8 and 11 below which total E° 318 (sharecropping) and E° 97 (rent)	38.16	38.16		12.00
6—INPROA's marketing fee—2% of sharecrop products sold (E° 2,473) plus 2% of E° 1,750 marketed from rented portion	49.00	49.00		35.00
7—Nitrate fertilizer—10 sacks (shares); 4 sacks (rent) at E° 8 a sack	80.00	40.00	40.00	32.00
8—Superphosphate fertilizer—8 sacks (shares) and 2 sacks rented portion at E° 15.87 a sack	127.00	63.50	63.50	32.00
9—Pesticide (prorated share)	66.00	33.00	33.00	9.00
10—Weed killer (prorated share)	100.00	50.00	50.00	
11—Seed: Potatoes E° 30 Wheat E° 312 Corn 10 Sugar beet 33 Beans 58.50 Sunflower 18.75	429.00	214.50	214.50	33.00

TABLE I (continued)

12—Rent of 1.56 hectares				250.00
13—Land tilling	48.00	24.00	24.00	20.00
14—Combining charges	275.00	137.50	137.50	
15—Cooperative administration	223.74	111.87	111.87	
Total	2,087.91	1,413.54	674.37	673.00

Total operating expenses (sharecropping)	E° 1,413.54
Total operating expenses (rental)	673.00
	E° 2,086.54
Gross cash income	4,695.00
Total operating expenses	2,086.54
Net income	E° 2,608.46

E° 472) amounted to E° 4,695. As was the case for many colonists, his greatest single operating expense (E° 862.05) was for outside labor he hired together with the meals he supplied (E° 561 plus E° 230 plus E° 51.05 plus E° 20). Lump-sum advances totalling E° 333 were given by INPROA through the cooperative in several installments. In addition, inputs in kind totalling E° 415 were loaned to this colonist. A 12 percent interest was charged on all loans.[12] INPROA also received a 2 percent fee for all goods it marketed.

As indicated previously, fertilizer, pesticide, weed killer, and most seeds were used in standard amounts under INPROA's guidance on the sharecropped portion. In addition, the national sugar beet company prescribed a standard amount of seed, pesticide, and fertilizer for the rented plot. The rent INPROA collected for this colonist's land was E° 250. The tractor used for harrowing purposes was rented from outside the cooperative as was the combine for the wheat and sunflower harvest. On the sharecropping enterprises this rental cost was divided with INPROA. The extent of use of this labor-saving equipment was also controlled by INPROA.[13]

Cooperative administrative expenses include part of the payment for asignación familiar as well as some other miscellaneous expenses. (Part of the contribution made to the government for asignación familiar payments came from INPROA's half of the harvest.) Table I shows that total operating expenses on the sharecropped and rented

TABLE II. SURPLUS OR DEFICIT AMONG A SELECTED SAMPLE OF SAN DIONISIO COLONISTS 1963-64

Case No. and number of hectares	Net cash income available to colonists (1)	Self-estimated family consumption expenses (2)	Debt repayment capacity (Col. 1 – Col. 2) (3)	Capital payments to make in 1963-64 (4)**	Deficit or surplus for 1963-64 (Col. 3 – Col. 4) (5)	Calculated family consumption (6)***	Debt repayment capacity using calculated consumption (Col. 1 – Col. 6) (7)	Deficit or surplus for 1963-64 assuming Col. 7 – Col. 4 (8)
B-1 16.02	E° 5,364	E° 1,328*	E° 4,036	E° 135	E° 3,901	E° 1,328	E° 4,036	E° 3,901
B-2 20.31	4,987	2,183*	2,804	135	2,669	2,183	2,804	2,669
B-3 8.59	776	1,621	– 845	135	– 980	1,698	– 922	–1,057
B-4 12.11	2,243	1,219	1,024	135	889	1,213	1,030	895
B-5 13.28	3,348	2,426*	922	135	787	2,426	922	787
B-6 12.50	2,608	736	1,872	135	1,737	2,426	182	47
B-7 14.45	3,522	898	2,624	455	2,169	1,940	1,582	1,127
B-8 15.63	3,874	1,208	2,666	285	2,381	1,940	1,934	1,649
B-9 11.72	1,755	866	889	315	574	1,940	– 185	– 500
B-10 16.41	3,051	2,919*	132	135	– 3	2,919	132	– 3
B-11 12.50	2,146	945	1,201	135	1,066	1,698	448	313
B-12 5.47	529	328	201	135	66	372	157	22
B-13 8.59	740	516	224	135	89	372	368	233
B-14 2.73	651	585	66	135	69	970	– 319	– 454
Total in E°	35,594	17,778	17,816	2,540	15,276	23,425	12,169	9,629
Average in E°	2,542	1,270	1,272	181	1,091	1,673	869	688

* These colonists could not make an estimate. Calculated figures (*** below) used.

** These vary because some colonists have miscellaneous outstanding debts to pay. The E° 135 shown for most is payment for machinery purchased by the cooperative.

*** Calculated on the basis of number of persons in the family from the study by Hernán Burgos Mujica, *Análisis Económico Agrícola para un Plan de Crédito Supervisado: Comuna de Navidad, Año Agrícola 1960–61*, Ministerio de Agricultura, Depto. de Economía Agraria, No. 19, p. 23. Based on theses by Elvira Matte de Cruchaga (1938) and Violeta Sívori A. (1950), Escuela de Servicio Social, Universidad Católica de Chile and norms established by the Servicio Nacional de Salud.

portion attributable to this case were E° 2,086.54 (E° 1,413.54 plus E° 673.00). Net income was E° 2,608.46 (E° 4,695.00 minus E° 2,086.54). All calculations of net cash income for the fourteen sample cases have been calculated in the same manner in the following analysis.

Income and Surplus: San Dionisio Colonists, 1963–64. In this section we will determine consumption and, subtracting it from net income, arrive at debt repayment capacity. Subtracting capital payments due, we will determine surplus or deficit. Table II shows these calculations. Cases are numbered B-1–B-14; the case we have described appears as B-6.

There are several reasons for variations in net cash income shown in column 1. Colonists differed in acreage farmed. Some colonists elected not to have a portion of sugar beet land (sugar beets yielded well in 1963–64). Some colonists kept back more than others for their own consumption. Some raised expenses considerably by utilizing a large amount of outside labor. Management techniques varied for such practices as weeding, irrigation, etc., over which colonists had control.

Consumption must be subtracted from net cash farm income to arrive at debt repayment capacity. To determine consumption, each colonist was asked to estimate his cash living expenses. Four colonists were unable to make this estimate. For these four, we calculated a consumption figure according to the National Health Service standards (referred to in similar calculations on Las Pataguas) and used this figure for the remainder of the computations in the table. As one measure of the accuracy of the remainder of the estimates, we used the NHS standards to calculate the living expenses for each of the ten colonists who did make an estimate. The total of the ten self-estimates (shown in column 2) was E°8,922. The calculated expenses for the ten families total E°14,596 (column 6). This difference is considerably greater than was the case for the Las Pataguas colonists. This seems to indicate either that colonists on San Dionisio are not consuming up to the minimum NHS standards or are not able to respond reliably to questions about cash living expenses (possibly because they do not have the year's experience nearer the money economy that colonists have on Las Pataguas). The former assumption is more likely, however. INPROA restricted advances on San Dionisio to a level lower than on Los Silos and Las Pataguas and probably colonists are indeed consuming below the calculated amount. Subtracting self-estimated family consumption from net income gives the debt repayment capacity of the cooperative members which is displayed in column 3. Only one negative number is recorded here.

The cooperative has purchased some machinery this year on which each cooperator was required to pay E° 135. With some other miscellaneous debts they have to pay this year (usually on individually owned draft animals), we have displayed the total 1963–64 capital expenditures of the fourteen randomly selected colonists in column 4. No land payment was due in 1963–64, of course, since colonists had not entered the land-purchase stage of reform.

Assuming that each colonist was able to give a more or less accurate idea of his consumption, the deficit or surplus corresponding to each colonist is shown in column 5. Using the calculated consumption figure, deficit or surplus is shown in column 8.

The average colonist shows a net farm income of E° 2,542 (column 1) and average capital debts of E° 181 (column 4). Average consumption, based on our two methods of calculation, varies from E° 1,270 to E° 1,673 (columns 2 and 6). Average surplus ranges from E° 688 to E° 1,091 (columns 8 and 5). This indicates that most colonists could probably have met a land payment in 1964 if the rate of land payments was roughly similar to those on Los Silos or Las Pataguas. Since we know that the rental paid to INPROA and the half of net income that accrued to INPROA from the sharecropped land were used to pay the rent the Archbishop required (5 percent of the value of the fundo), we can assume that the fundo is also capable of meeting necessary interest payments (which will also be 5 percent). In addition to interest, the part of the income accruing to INPROA pays the irrigation rights, land taxes, a few other expenses of the cooperative, and expenses of management.

How Did Members Spend Their Surplus? With the help of the cooperative, INPROA kept an accounting for each colonist. Lump-sum advances and in-kind advances were noted as they were loaned to each member. All of the operating expenses (like those shown in Table I), together with a prorated share of machinery the cooperative was purchasing, were deducted from the harvest corresponding to each colonist. On November 2, 1964, each colonist was given a lump-sum payment which represented his surplus from the 1963–64 crop year.

Fifteen colonists on San Dionisio were interviewed two weeks after receiving their lump-sum settlement to find out how it was spent. Although these were not the same colonists as in our original sample, both samples are of similar size and both were randomly chosen. Several conclusions can be drawn from the data we gathered on our second interview.

Table II shows that average surplus for a San Dionisio colonist ranged between E° 688 and E° 1,091. Lump-sum payments to the average colonist were E° 1,226. There are three possible explanations for a difference between our calculation and the average lump-sum settlement:

(1) Colonists planned to spend part of the lump-sum settlement on consumption when they received it. All of the consumption has already been subtracted from the range of E° 688 and E° 1,091 we established in Table II. Colonists certainly planned to make at least clothing expenditures with the cash they received at harvest time (just as when they were inquilinos, they bought clothes or food in bulk when they sold some produce from their chacras). The fact that they did not receive their settlements for the 1963–64 harvest until the 1964–65 crop year was underway merely delayed this part of their expenditure. Since our second interview revealed that family expenses (furniture, food inventory, home improvements, clothing) averaged 39 percent of the disposition of the lump-sum settlement, this means we must deduct 39 percent from the average lump-sum settlement to make it comparable to the range in Table II. This deduction puts average comparable surplus at E° 748, well within our established range.

(2) As noted previously, INPROA gave lower consumption advances on San Dionisio than on Los Silos or Las Pataguas. And unlike Los Silos no money was regularly coming in for the sale of milk (although it was for asignación familiar). If consumption was effectively restricted, we would expect the highest number in our range (E° 1,091) to more nearly reflect the real situation. (The least consumption has been subtracted.) Again we must remember that calculated consumption figures were used for four colonists because they could not estimate their needs. If these four figures had been known, they probably would have been lower than calculated consumption,

and the average might have been very close to the E° 1,226 calculation. Carrying this explanation to its next logical step, the 1964–65 consumption may more nearly reflect the calculated figure since the 39 percent spent on consumption from the 1963–64 lump-sum payment will really count as consumption for the 1964–65 year.

(3) Our average of E° 1,226 is too high. The bookkeeper of the cooperative, although he did not have exact figures at his disposal, estimated average surplus at E° 1,000.

Colonists spend quickly upon the receipt of their money because they are aware of how fast inflation depreciates currency. It does not follow that foolish expenditures are made. Most colonists we interviewed were aware of their capital needs—as they were of their consumption necessities—and made purchases when they received their funds.

About 41.5 percent of the average cash available was spent for farm expenses and capital between the date of the receipt of the cash and the time of our interview. As mentioned, about 39 percent had been spent for family expenses. Only about 19 percent of the average cash available had been saved.

Several planned uses of the amount saved were noted by our interviewees: (a) It will be used for consumption purposes later. (b) It will be used to pay labor so no advances need be requested. Only two from our sample indicated their willingness to do this. This frugality is not as rational as it seems. Inflation in the 1963–64 crop year ran nearly 40 percent while the subsidized credit rate, available through INPROA, was about 15.6 percent. Nonetheless, upon receiving their statements, a number of colonists were shocked at the amount charged for interest on advances. When we interviewed our original sample, few knew what their interest rate would be. (c) It will be used for entertainment. This response was as infrequent as (b).

We turn now to a comparison of income of colonists before and after the reform.

CHANGE IN INCOME UNDER THE REFORM: A COMPARISON

To compute a comparison of income available to the colonists now with income available before the reform, an important component is the net cash farm income arrived at in Table II. To that, however, we must add the amount of consumption in kind and perquisites. While the average total income of the colonists in their former situation was E° 1,028, after the reform it was E° 3,366, about three times higher. About two-thirds of the average E° 3,366 income in 1963–64 seems to have been used for the family's consumption.

Considering that colonists showed about enough surplus this year to make a land payment had one been required, we must conclude that, if everything else remains equal, consumption level should not be allowed to drift higher unless net income can be raised. Two factors indicate that, on the contrary, either net income must rise, or in the future more funds must be relied upon from the portion which in 1963–64 went to INPROA to make debt payments if consumption is maintained at its present level: (1) Asignación familiar will not be available when the colonists are assigned to individual parcels. (2) More colonists will be occupying the fundo. Unless the fundo is able to increase the acreage allowed in its sugar beet contract (not a very likely possibility), this high-yielding crop will not be available in acreages as large as in 1963–64 to raise colonists' income. In 1964–65, for example, all colonists elected to grow sugar beets, and this reduced the amount available to be allotted to each from 1.56 hectares to 1 hectare.

What are the possibilities of maintaining production on San Dionisio at its current level? Would it be possible to raise this level? We will turn to an investigation of these questions now.

CHANGE IN PRODUCTION UNDER REFORM AND
POSSIBILITIES OF RAISING NET INCOME

Reconstructed Farming Program: 1962–63. We have no documentation concerning production under the former renter, since he was unwilling to give us the data we needed. Furthermore, he rented several adjacent fundos and all were included in the same accounting.

We were able, however, with the help of a former field supervisor who stayed during 1963–64 to participate in the reform, to reconstruct the farming program for the 1962–63 crop year (the last under the renter) and compare it with this year's cropping pattern. As with most data collected in this manner, there were unsatisfying information gaps. However, we can say that the cropping pattern in 1963–64 was more intensive than in 1962–63. The neighboring farm, also rented by the same person, was cropped more intensively and his farming program had called for use of San Dionisio for pasture needs. This evidence and the recollection of former fundo residents who remained to participate in the reform seem to indicate that total production on San Dionisio rose in 1963–64 over production previously.

This short-term judgment based on one year's experience under reform is less than satisfying. San Dionisio seems to have relied to a great extent in 1963–64 on the accumulated fertility of the well-manured pasture land. But much of the fundo soil is a volcanic type which depletes easily. Furthermore, no clover or legume was planted either in 1963–64 or in 1964–65, because the farm was being prepared for subdivision. Only E° 32 a hectare was spent on commercial fertilizers on the fundo.

While production on rich soil can be temporarily raised by intensive cropping patterns and colonists initially benefit by the result, it does not necessarily follow that production will remain high. Production will depend, among other matters, upon the abilities of technicians to cope with the soil of the area and apply necessary inputs. This again underlines our assertion that good technicians must participate initially in reform efforts, teaching colonists the important practices they need to follow to maintain or raise production.

Production Potential. Perhaps a comparison of wheat production on San Dionisio and on a well-run neighoring farm might give some indication of production potential on San Dionisio.

Considering home consumption by colonists as well as grain sold, 29.75 quintals per hectare were produced on our sample area. On the entire farm, INPROA's records show that an average of 21.38 quintals were sold per hectare. (The latter figure does not account for home consumption, which we were able to calculate from our questionnaire material. This, in addition to sampling error, makes up for the difference in the two calculations.) Wheat production on the neighboring farm averaged 22 quintals per hectare. Half of the neighbor's wheat was planted with clover, so it seems that the differences in wheat production on these two fundos were not very marked in 1963–64.

Because the only well-managed farm we found which had relatively similar soil type and water supply had only wheat in common with San Dionisio, we will unfortunately have to confine our comparative analysis to this one case and crop. By observing that most

colonists showed a surplus in 1963–64 of about E° 1,000, the intensive cropping pattern in 1963–64 when compared to 1962–63, and
the similarity of wheat yields on San Dionisio compared to a well-
worked neighboring fundo, it seems quite likely that the immediate
problem on San Dionisio centers about maintaining crop production. Later, through judicious investments in cattle, poultry, feeder
pigs, etc., and obtaining a larger sugar beet contract, gross production could also undoubtedly be raised. Steps toward this kind of intensification are being studied by the cooperative.

Cutting Expenses. It might be possible to reallocate some labor
expenses to yield-increasing capital to maintain production at its
current level without raising expenses much.[14] When coefficients of
labor use in the input study[15] (this study was used in the Los Silos
and Las Pataguas cases) are utilized, they indicate that about 42
man-days per hectare are needed for the 170.31 hectares corresponding to our sample.

Our interviews show that 67 man-days per hectare were used on
our sample in 1963–64. Of this, 49.5 man-days per hectare were
family labor. Theoretically, then, it would be possible to cut labor
utilization to internal labor only, which would represent a savings to
our sample of E° 5,511—the total amount the fourteen colonists
spent on hiring outside labor in 1963–64.

Summarizing this economic analysis of San Dionisio, we have
shown that the average colonist showed a surplus in 1963–64 about
the size of a land payment. Part of INPROA's share of the income
was used to pay interest on the land debt this year. The other part
was used to pay irrigation rights, land taxes, and to reward the management factor. This income will all flow to the colonist when the
fundo has been parcelled out. At that time each colonist will have to
have developed a greater degree of management skill than he has
now, since the success of the fundo will depend more on his actions.

We can say with some confidence that total production on San
Dionisio after reform was greater than total production on the same
fundo the previous year. A good deal of the fundo's success in
1963–64 was due to high-yielding sugar beets. But we know that at
least some of this good production was due to reliance on the accumulated fertility of the soil.

Since colonists will not have asignación familiar and since the farm will be supporting more colonists under a parcelization scheme than it did in 1963–64, in order to continue to succeed economically colonists will have to take one or a combination of the following steps: (a) keep application of yield-increasing capital high to maintain this year's yields; (b) intensify the operation as soon as possible; (c) keep labor costs lower than in 1963–64.

THE COOPERATIVE AT SAN DIONISIO: 1963–64

As mentioned in the introduction to this chapter, much emphasis on San Dionisio in 1963–64 was placed on building an effective bargaining cooperative. In broad outlines, the cooperative is similar in organizational structure to that described on Los Silos.

Education poses constant difficulties for the new cooperative. Average literacy on the fundo has been somewhat upgraded by in-migration under the reform. Previously, the illiteracy rate was about 60 percent, but since most colonists selected from outside San Dionisio knew how to read and write, the illiteracy rate is now about 40 percent. This still places San Dionisio with the lowest level of literacy among the five Church properties. Previously, area children had to walk to school—an hour and a half in each direction—for a half day's instruction. During the year, however, San Dionisio built a school, hired two teachers, and, since April 1964, has been offering a full day of classes to over one hundred San Dionisio colonists' children and those from neighboring farms. All six primary grades are taught. Besides, courses for reading and writing are offered to adults each night. In 1965 or 1966 the government will probably begin paying teachers' salaries.

In-migration also brought some problems. Most council members in 1963–64 were elected from the new and more educated group, and as the year drew toward harvest jealousies arose among a group of old fundo residents who felt the newcomers had gotten too much power. The officers had allied themselves quite closely to INPROA's technicians and consequently some of the previous residents felt the council was not fulfilling its designated role as the cooperative's representative body. The rift did not crystallize until the year came to a close, however, and the cooperative operated quite smoothly until harvest time. The San Dionisio cooperative hired four and fired three bookkeepers in 1963–64. The last one came to his position in

April after most of the harvest was complete, and he found the books in a badly disorganized state.

In late August, during wheat planting, colonists stopped work for a day to protest because they still had not received their final accounting. This movement was headed not by the legitimately selected cooperative officers but by a rump-group whose members were occupants of the fundo prior to reform. It seems likely that a non-Christian Democrat politician holding office in the zone also had an influence over this group.

By October the rump-group persuaded the legally chosen council to travel to Santiago to demand their money. The cooperative had arranged to take the matter to a local judge if the money was not immediately forthcoming. INPROA argued both that the fundo records were so bad that its accounts, too, were disorganized and also that it preferred to wait a bit longer before turning the money over to the cooperative to permit a careful "investment plan" for the entire cooperative to be drawn up.

But the cooperative's position was uncompromising and convincing; lump-sum payments were distributed. Late receipt of the money and a complete lack of advance knowledge of the amount members would receive brought about some complaints similar to those described earlier on Las Pataguas. Even so, most colonists were quite satisfied with the amount they received.

Although it had not completed an investment plan, INPROA had, through the year, arranged for speakers to address the cooperative from time to time on matters of money management.

INPROA also suggested that if each cooperative member would contribute E° 70, two necessary projects could be undertaken. A team of workers could be contracted to go into the mountainous part of the fundo to cut fence posts, and work on the fundo road could be begun, thus hastening parcelization and alleviating the necessity of waiting until the Inter-American Development Bank loan could be culminated. Apparently anxious for parcelization, the cooperative accepted this suggestion by a wide majority and work began. All cooperative members began contributing their labor each Saturday to work on the fundo road at the beginning of 1965.

As noted earlier, the technician who had during 1963–64 divided his time between San Dionisio and Alto Las Cruces was assigned to San Dionisio permanently. Rather than giving his suggestions directly to the head of the cooperative's Agricultural Committee (who became thoroughly discredited as "INPROA's lackey" in the early part of the 1964–65 crop year), he plans to hire another technical person to work with the head of the Agricultural Committee to transmit his supervisory wishes.

To the extent that the emerging leadership of old fundo residents represents an integration of old and new elements, and not a permanent split, the cooperative will undoubtedly be benefited. Much also depends on the strength of several politicians in the zone. They are, there is little doubt, working through the old fundo residents to stir up discontent by dwelling on the themes that INPROA has been charging excessive rates of interest, that INPROA has creamed off more than the 2 percent marketing fee, and that INPROA has no intention of giving land titles after the sharecropping and rental period.

It is a hypothesis which we have not been able to explore adequately in this paper that middle-of-the-road land reform efforts will undoubtedly suffer attack both from the far-right and from the far-left, since both of these groups stand to gain from the failure of the reform.[16] Thus, a moderate land reform program prior to an across-the-board reform may be satisfactory only to the party which has made it.

In the case of Las Pataguas, we discovered that some neighboring landlords were highly critical of the colony and were willing to work against it. On Los Silos we discussed a few of the difficulties the project seems to have had with some previous fundo residents, apparently instigated by a Socialist alderman in the zone. We have just mentioned similar political activity with regard to San Dionisio. In addition to some of the fundo residents coming under the influence of political leaders, San Dionisio reported the only open invasion of an INPROA fundo during the first year of its existence. On December 29, 1963, the fundo was approached by a small group of neighboring dissidents who were apparently under the leadership of a Trotskyite group.

In December 1963 the paper *Rebelde*, the Chilean Trotskyite organ, reported a meeting of the Interprovincial Congress of Campesinos held October 26–27 in Talca.[17] The congress concluded that "only a violent agrarian reform impelled by the campesinos would give the land to those who really want it." Among other matters, the congress also agreed "unanimously" that the government should:[18]

1. Take over lands, properties, tools, machinery, seeds, etc., and give them to the workers without charge. Facilitate the establishment of long-term credits without interest in order to buy necessary implements and labor supplies.
2. Proceed to the expropriation of fundos, transferring them to campesinos in case of any conflicts between landowners and workers.
3. Initiate a real reform program by immediate expropriation of these fundos: *San Dionisio,* San Luis, San Juan de Dios, La Unión, San José (all in Linares Province) and Pirazzo Bramadero, *Alto Las Cruces,* Esmeralda, Mariposa, and La Suiza (in Talca Province). This should be the first step. All private farms should follow.

Late in December, then, armed with copies of the *Rebelde,* false titles and other documents, the invaders appeared on the fundo. They stated that their intentions were to occupy the dry part of the fundo to exploit mines there. The "invasion" was handled poorly—so poorly that when the caravan of trucks arrived, police had already been called and were awaiting the luckless group. Their leaders were immediately detained.

The hapless invasion was, in the long run, merely a propaganda victory for INPROA as it merited a story and editorial in *El Mercurio* (January 8), a story in *La Tercera de la Hora* (December 30), and a story in *La Provincia* (December 31). Further, it proved that new colonists were not going to give up their land easily. There apparently was no support internal to San Dionisio for the movement. And the experience seemed to unite the group living on San Dionisio against what they still consider to be a common enemy.

The mere fact that the cooperative is becoming an organization capable of taking its own actions and defending its own interests (requiring even INPROA to be on guard so that its rights are not infringed) is testimony to changes wrought the past year on San Dionisio. For most members, this is the first organization of its type to which they have belonged. During its first year, the cooperative has: (1) grappled with one of its most serious social problems—illiteracy —by installing a school on San Dionisio; (2) begun to integrate two groups—in-migrants and previous residents; (3) discharged bookkeepers it felt were doing an unsatisfactory job; (4) protested successfully to INPROA and received the lump-sum payments for the 1963–64 harvest after threatening to take the matter before a local judge; (5) voted to establish a fund with which it could begin necessary infrastructural improvements; (6) come to an apparent realization that a united position before INPROA redounds to everyone's benefit; (7) protected itself against an invasion.

TENURE STRUCTURE ON SAN DIONISIO: 1964–65

Few changes in tenure structure in 1964–65 over 1963–64 have been made on San Dionisio. Colonists voted down moving to a step which would involve rental of the entire fundo.

In order to build more self-discipline into the system, committees of colonists have been appointed to manage each large wheat field. A forty-two-hectare wheat field, for example, has a seven-man settler committee assigned to it which decides when to irrigate and then divides the necessary work. Wheat fields are undivided in 1964–65 and colonists do not know which exact plot is theirs. The wheat was planted with a large drill, as in 1963–64, and will be harvested with a self-propelled combine. Each colonist gets the yield corresponding to half of six hectares after half of the non-labor operating expenses are deducted. If he has not cooperated by doing his share of the work, the cooperative may vote to dock some of his income. This is one example of building incentives into a cooperative structure.

Sunflowers were omitted from the farming program in 1964–65 since yield in 1963–64 was low. Also on 50–50 shares, each of the sixty-two members of the cooperative with land rights in 1964–65 has a plot of potatoes and corn. These are also machine planted and the amount of fertilizer and seed disinfectant used is standard for all. Again, each colonist is responsible for the working of his own land, weeding and irrigating the growing crop, and harvesting.

As mentioned previously, the acreage allowable under the IANSA contract was not increased in 1964–65. Since harvest in 1963–64 was so good, all colonists elected to have sugar beets in 1964–65 and the per-colonist acreage was correspondingly reduced.

ALTO LAS CRUCES

Can Colonists Pay Their Debts? As with San Dionisio, each colonist on Alto Las Cruces had part of his land in mediería and could have besides at least one rented cuadra. As mentioned previously, these colonists, unlike those at San Dionisio, could plant their rented plots to whatever they chose (except sugar beets, since the fundo did not have an IANSA contract). Many of the colonists used the rented land for growing crops which the family planned to consume. Few sold any of this produce as cash crops. Since the calculation of net income for each colonist on Alto Las Cruces has been made in precisely the same manner as in Table I, we shall not repeat a case here. We shall also omit mentioning the assumptions and the detailed reasoning which accompanied the analysis of other cases. Two colonists suffered losses in net income, as noted in Table III, column 1. They registered very low yields coupled with extremely high expenses.

Five colonists show a negative debt repayment capacity, and the average debt repayment capacity was E° —303. Required capital payments (E° 419) averaged higher than on San Dionisio. Capital expenditures (in Table III, column 5) represent only E° 45 each for cooperative capital bought; the remainder is for draft animals purchased which must be paid off this year.

Two colonists, who marketed some produce from their rented cuadra and kept operating expenses down, show a surplus (column 6), but the average for all colonists shows a deficit of E° 722.

If calculated consumption (column 2) were used instead of self-estimated consumption (column 3) the losses would be more pronounced since the sum of column 3 (excluding C-2 who was not able to make an estimate) was E° 10,015 while the sum of column 2 (again excluding C-2) was E° 14,189.

We turn now to a comparison of income of colonists before and after the reform. Average income (cash plus perquisites) under the reform was E° 2,345, about E° 800 more than the year previous to reform. Cash that went for consumption purposes in 1963–64 seems to have been higher on Alto Las Cruces than San Dionisio, ranging from about E° 1,678 to E° 2,200. (Table II shows that on San Dionisio the comparable range was E° 1,270 to E° 1,673.) In part, this was due to the fact that average family sizes were larger—on Alto Las Cruces eight people as contrasted with six on San Dionisio. In part, it seems to have been due to higher pre-reform consumption habits on Alto Las Cruces that were carried over into the post-reform situation.

All—or nearly all—of the net cash income on Alto Las Cruces was probably spent on family consumption in 1963–64. Furthermore, home consumption of in-kind production and perquisites was higher by about E° 150 than on San Dionisio. Again we must remember that colonists consumed rather than sold most of the produce from their 1.56 rented hectares.[19]

TABLE III—SURPLUS OR DEFICIT AMONG A SELECTED SAMPLE OF ALTO LAS CRUCES COLONISTS: 1963–64

Case and No. of hectares	Colonists' net cash income (1)	Calculated family consumption (2)*	Self-estimated family consumption or Col. 1 if colonists unable to estimate (3)	Debt repayment capacity (available cash) assuming self-estimated consumption when available (Col. 1 – Col. 3) (4)	Capital payments to make (1963–64) (5)	Deficit or surplus for year (Col. 4 – Col. 5) (6)
C-1 25	E° 2,074	E° 3,628	E° 2,923	E° – 849	E° 595	E° –1,444
C-2 20.70	1,168	3,409	3,409**	–2,241	380	–2,621
C-3 19.92	932	3,409	1,830	– 898	45	– 943
C-4 16.02	3,469	1,698	887	2,582	265	2,317
C-5 20.70	– 523	1,328	1,131	–1,654	353	–2,007
C-6 18.16	3,185	2,426	839	2,346	325	2,021
C-7 28.13	1,096	970	787	309	765	– 456
C-8 19.53	– 404	728	1,618	–2,022	623	–2,645
Total 168.16	10,997	17,596	13,424	–2,427	3,351	–5,778
Average 21.02	1,375	2,200	1,678	– 303	419	– 722

* Calculated on the basis of number of persons in the family from the study by Hernán Burgos Mujica, *Análisis Económico Agrícola para un Plan de Crédito Supervisado: Comuna de Navidad, Año Agrícola 1960–61*, Ministerio de Agricultura, Depto. de Economía Agraria, No. 19, p. 23. Based on theses by Elvira Matte de Cruchaga (1938) and Violeta Sivori A. (1950), Escuela de Servicio Social, Universidad Católica de Chile and norms established by the Servicio Nacional de Salud.

** Could not make an estimate. Calculated figure used in this case.

If this project is to succeed economically, it would appear that family consumption will have to be lowered while debts are being paid off. If average consumption had been E° 750 lower this year, the average colonist would still have been better off than before the reform and there would have been little deficit. Still there would have been no surplus which would have permitted them to make a land payment had one been required.

Possibility of Raising Net Income. Are there possibilities of raising net income on Alto Las Cruces? It is impossible to compare the situation of Alto Las Cruces this year with that of any neighboring fundo, since there are too many variables involved. With Los Silos, Las Patagaus, and San Dionisio, we were able to state with some confidence that fundos could be selected for comparison which had more or less similar soil types and no special irrigation problems. As pointed out in earlier sections of this chapter, Alto Las Cruces is a special case. For years much of the fundo was planted to rice and fertility dropped. Besides impoverished soil, there were many irrigation problems which were not rectified before the 1963–64 crop year began. These two factors—soil type and irrigation—which we could match satisfactorily on neighboring fundos to make our case previously, cannot be assumed comparable in the case of Alto Las Cruces.

There would be little disagreement that if production is to be raised, the irrigation system must be improved. Further, the E° 5,984 spent for commercial fertilizer on the land covered by our sample (approximately E° 36 a hectare), although slightly above San Dionisio's expenditure (E° 32 a hectare), certainly was not enough to compensate for the much lower initial fertility of the fundo. Indicating the problems of education which remain in practical matters on Alto Las Cruces, only two of our sample felt fertilizer use sufficiently important that they had used it on their rented cuadra over which they made most of the management decisions.

We may again look to labor use to suggest another possible cut in operating expenses. The input study[20] shows that 38.3 man-days of labor per hectare is average for the zone for the same combination of crops as grown on our sample of Alto Las Cruces. Our data show that 33.72 man-days of labor per hectare were already available in our Alto Las Cruces sample. Yet our interviews show an average of

54 man-days a hectare actually used. The contracted portion of this labor was paid E° 5,778. Comparison with the study standard of 38.3 man-days seems to indicate some outside labor will need to be hired in future years, but probably not as much as in the 1963–64 crop season.

When so many Alto Las Cruces colonists were presented with financial settlements showing deficits in 1963–64, there were understandable complaints. Impoverished soil, irrigation irregularities, high labor expenditures, and absence of a high-yielding cash crop (like sugar beets on San Dionisio) seem to have brought on Alto Las Cruces' problems and emphasized the necessity of doing better the next year to colonists. To some, however, it meant disillusionment so extreme that they threatened withdrawal from the cooperative. A sugar beet contract was obtained for 1964–65. This should raise cash sales and colonists should benefit from the type of instruction that IANSA gives and the inputs that it makes available.

The Cooperative: Alto Las Cruces. As on San Dionisio, the Alto Las Cruces cooperative showed a great deal of development during its first year of operation. It voted to proceed with renting in 1964–65. The farm was not to be divided into parcels during rental. Crops would be planted in large fields so that large planting and harvesting equipment could be used. Row crops were to be managed in the same manner as on San Dionisio. The rental payment due INPROA was to be prorated to each colonist depending on the acreage he had. Well past planting time in the 1964–65 crop year, however, the cooperative had not agreed on what rental payment it would make, regarding the original amount set by INPROA as too high.

SUMMARY: SAN DIONISIO AND ALTO LAS CRUCES

(1) INPROA is attempting to apply at Alto Las Cruces and San Dionisio what it learned on Los Silos and Las Pataguas. The dialogue between the cooperatives and INPROA seems to be improving, so that the cooperatives are at least influencing INPROA policy to a greater extent than on Las Pataguas.

(a) INPROA is moving more gradually toward private property than it did on Las Pataguas, using longer intermediate steps of centrally managed sharecropping and rental. (There was only a single year of sharecropping on Las Pataguas, and it was not centrally managed.) During these steps, INPROA can maintain control of the technical phases of the cooperative's operation and work toward building up both the cooperative and the farming skills of its members. The cooperative can vote on how long it wishes each step to last. Although both farms used a system of mediería coupled with a small rented plot in 1963–64, only Alto Las Cruces voted to move to the rental phase in 1964–65. Parcelization plans are limited by the speed with which the Inter-American Development Bank loan is received, since subdivision as currently conceived cannot proceed without large infrastructural expenditure loans which must come largely from outside the country. In the case of San Dionisio, the cooperative itself will underwrite some initial infrastructure in the absence of other funds. Upon parcelization, INPROA will have to rely heavily on supervised credit to force compliance on technical matters. Hopefully, the intermediate period will have also stimulated adoption of some key practices.

(b) Unlike Las Pataguas, where the irrigation system was adapted to small parcels by using measured water gates (marcos partidores), a cheaper system of turnos will be used as the irrigation system is adapted to small plots on Alto Las Cruces and San Dionisio.

(c) A modified villorio system has been adopted which combines some of the economies and social advantages of hamlet settlement and gives as many settlers as possible the opportunity to live on their land. On Las Pataguas attempts to establish the villorio system showed that colonists preferred living on their land. This experience, plus the expressed desire of each cooperative, has influenced INPROA's decision on this matter.

(d) On Las Pataguas the infrastructural costs were added to the land bill. The actual expense of infrastructure was more than the estimated cost plus its readjustment for inflation, so that INPROA lost some money in the process. On Alto Las Cruces and San Dionisio the land and the infrastructure bills will be separate. INPROA will bill colonists for infrastructure as it is completed and actual costs are known.

(2) Infrastructure on Alto Las Cruces will account for about 51 percent of the cost of settling colonists. A similar calculation cannot yet be made for San Dionisio, since its parcelization plans are not as far along.

(3) The fertile land of San Dionisio, intensively cropped, contributed to the economic success of the fundo in 1963–64. But this volcanic soil depletes easily. Intensive farming and the fact that no legume was seeded with wheat in 1963–64 underscore the importance of fertilizer application in subsequent years if a drop in productivity is to be avoided.

(4) Irrigation problems and a depleted soil worked against Alto Las Cruces colonists this year. At San Dionisio colonists grew sugar beets on a small plot of land they rented; on Alto Las Cruces they used production from rented land to increase their consumption. This is likely to be remedied in 1964–65 since Alto Las Cruces now has a contract to grow sugar beets, but the data from Alto Las Cruces illustrate the strong desires which exist among Chilean campesinos to increase their consumption.

(5) Total production on San Dionisio seems to have risen since the reform. We have no data on which to base a similar statement on Alto Las Cruces. But after the irrigation system is fixed and legal processes to get more water rights are completed, much land that was inadequately watered previously on Alto Las Cruces will undoubtedly be brought into production.

(6) Average income of colonists on San Dionisio before the reform was E° 1,028. This income rose to E° 3,366 after the reform. Approximately two-thirds of this was consumed by the families. The remainder was used for cooperative capital payments, individual capital purchases, and individual savings.

Average income for colonists on Alto Las Cruces before the reform was E° 1,535. After the reform it was E° 2,345. All of this, it appears, was consumed.

On both Alto Las Cruces and San Dionisio it seems likely that family consumption could be reduced to meet some investment needs and still leave families better off than before. That this is a painful and hard-to-achieve alternative should be admitted, however.

(7) On both fundos some savings could be realized by reducing hired labor.

(8) Both fundos are supporting more families now than before the reform.

We have lacked, in the last three chapters, necessary perspective to complete our analysis. Each of the experiments in agrarian reform which we have described was a recent one, and each has been analyzed for the short period of one year. In each we have qualified our results somewhat because of the short time-period involved.

We have, however, other land reform laboratories open to us in Chile: the programs of the government and of a private Italian settlement company. Each of these has settled farmers on parcels of land— INPROA's professed goal. How have inquilinos and medieros who received farms years ago under this program progressed? What have their problems been? We shall turn in Chapter 6 to a selected sample of these farmers to attempt to discover answers to these questions.

NOTES

1 342.7 hectares including a marshy area that may be reclaimed one day.
2 1,127 irrigated and 257 irrigable but now dry hectares. This does not include 1,900 hectares of mountain land largely unfit for farming.
3 Files of San Dionisio.
4 Two of these were dismissed because they were bachelors; the cooperative and INPROA insist on married couples and give some preference to large families.
5 The likelihood of an association being formed is great since Alto Las Cruces is in the area of the "Maule Norte," a regional development project of the Chilean government now in its planning stages.
6 The reader will note that in describing water rights in the Sandoval Canal we referred to "regadores" of water and in San Miguel to "shares" of water. Regadores is an old measure and the quantity of water a regador represents usually varies from canal to canal and within one canal according to the time of year. (But if regador is not qualified by an explanation it refers to 18 liters per second of the Maipo River.) A share is a percentage of all the water in one canal, which also varies according to seasons. In old land titles, water rights are usually expressed in regadores while in new titles, when water associations are organized, water rights are expressed in shares. To complicate matters, shares are sometimes sold for a certain number of regadores.
7 Even assuming the fundo is able to obtain the new rights, this half of the farm will have claim to only 145 liters per second in comparison with 351 liters per second for the north part.
8 Instituto de Promoción Agraria, "Proyecto Específico Alto Las Cruces" (mimeographed), Santiago, August 1964. See page 40 ff.
9 No sunflowers were grown on Alto Las Cruces.
10 This might also have been a diseconomy. As we will see, ample labor existed on the fundo—perhaps enough so that there was little justification for the mechanization of these operations.

11 Again, the author makes no attempt to round off the figures in the following sections.

12 Actual interest was higher for fewer months. Twelve percent for twelve months is a reasonable average.

13 Otherwise colonists might have made uneconomical use of rented machinery (a cost they shared with INPROA) instead of hiring labor (since colonists bore 100 percent of hired labor costs).

14 Here again, all of the restrictions and assumptions to this approach enumerated in Chapter 3 hold.

15 Corporación de Fomento de la Producción (CORFO), Ministerio de Agricultura, Universidad de Chile, *Insumos Físicos en la Agricultura, Año 1961–62*, Santiago, 1964.

16 Celso Furtado has made this point discussing the difficulties SUDENE, the Northeast Brazilian Development Agency, has had with its land reform program, ". . . there are extremists—those of the right who really believe that the problems can be solved without deep changes. And there are others who don't want to see your experiment work because they think it is not large enough a change. Both extremes will work against you." Personal interview with Furtado, July 7, 1964.

17 *Rebelde*, "Combativo y Unitario Congreso de Campesinos Se Realizó en Talca," Santiago, December 1963, p. 1.

18 *Ibid.* (Italics in point three are the author's. Alto Las Cruces was mentioned too, but it escaped "invasion.")

19 This difference was even more pronounced when only in-kind crop consumption is considered. It averaged E° 582 on San Dionisio and E° 764 on Alto Las Cruces—a difference of E° 182.

20 CORFO, Ministerio de Agricultura, Universidad de Chile, *op. cit.*

THE GOVERNMENT
COLONIZATION PROJECT:
A PERSPECTIVE   Chapter 6

The Constitution assures to all inhabitants of the Republic: . . . the in-
violability of all property without any distinction. . . . The exercise of the
right of property, however, is subject to the limitations or rules that
demand the maintenance and progress of the social order; this means
that the law will be able to impose obligations or public utility services
which favor the general interests of the state. . . . The state will promote
the convenient division of land into family property.
                    —*The Constitution of Chile.* September 18, 1925.

TO PUT our discussion of INPROA into perspective, we must search for
and document other departures from the traditional land tenure system in Chile which established inquilinos or medieros on their land
long enough ago to afford some insights into their successes and fail-
ures. To that end, we turn to earlier colonization efforts of the Caja
de Colonización Agrícola.

Given the basically unchanged structure of land tenure existing in
Chilean agriculture, it should be a valid assumption that Church
landholders or CORA parcel holders will confront the same sort of
problems as those encountered by fundo workers who became Caja
colonists. Should a broader reform be possible in Chile one day, its
administrators also might benefit by a close look at some problems
which former landless laborers had upon being awarded property.

Since the main purpose of this chapter is to describe the current
situation of islands of former inquilinos or medieros who are now
established as colonists, we selected for close scrutiny colonies in
which settlers had been given their land at least twelve years ago.

METHODOLOGY AND SAMPLE CHOICE

We picked twelve colonies at random—eight within the central nucleus, three colonies to the north, and one to the south—on which to interview. We stratified our sample to represent colonies of differing sizes (vis-à-vis number of settlers) and geographic dispersion.

On eight of these we attempted to ascertain the background of the original 544 colonists so we could determine how many former inquilinos or medieros were available for depth interviews.[1]

Of the 544 parcels studied, 108, or 19.8 percent, had initially been assigned to inquilinos or medieros. By the time of our interview 82 inquilinos or medieros remained and this percentage had dropped to 15. Twenty-six parcels had been sold for varying reasons—many because parcel holders had died and left no heirs but some because the colonists found they could not make a living on their land. Considering the entire universe of our sample, 263 out of 544 parcels had changed ownership. This indicates that a higher percentage of parcels changed hands considering the universe (263 out of 544 or 48.4 percent), than considering only former inquilinos and medieros (26 out of 108 or 24 percent).[2]

Of the original 544 parcels, a percentage breakdown of owners' former occupations reveals additionally that: 4.6 percent were professionals; 10.8 percent had worked for the Caja de Colonización Agrícola; 9.9 percent had worked for another government agency; 8.4 percent were engaged in some sort of business; 10.7 percent had been fundo employees; 16.7 percent had been engaged in some other form of agriculture (owner of another parcel elsewhere) a fundo owner, or Ingeniero Agrónomo, for example); and 9.9 percent of the colonists were remembered by our informants simply as "they came from elsewhere," or "they had never worked in agriculture," but were neither inquilinos nor medieros. The percentage of parcels reserved for community use was 9.2.

On these eight colonies, 212, or 39 percent, of the parcels are now owned by absentee landlords. On the average, one or two colonists per colony were originally assigned two parcels. Today 11.2 percent of the parcels, or 62 parcels, have come into the hands of less than half that number of owners, indicating some tendency toward uniting of parcels through purchase.

The fact that only 15 percent of the original inquilinos or medieros remained—82 out of 544—considerably cut the universe we could pick for depth interviews. Of these, we drew twenty-one colonists, or about 26 percent. Later we added nine more colonists (who met our requirement of being inquilinos or medieros prior to settlement) located on the four colonies in our sample on which we did not gather background information for all colonists.

Parcels were originally established as family units—small enough so no labor in addition to that of the family would need to be contracted except in rush seasons, and large enough to provide a decent family living. They were equalized on the basis of soil type and irrigation possibilities, and average about sixteen hectares in the central nucleus.

The purpose of the following analysis of thirty former inquilinos or medieros who were settled on parcels at least twelve years ago is to: (1) detail the current system of land tenure under which the parcel is being farmed, (2) determine each colonist's cash income situation, and (3) enumerate some of the colonists' current economic problems.

CLASSIFICATION OF LAND TENURE SYSTEMS ON THIRTY SELECTED PARCELS

The law under which colonies were founded prevents issuing more than one title per property. Its intent is to prevent a minifundio problem.[3] Although this makes a *de jure* division impossible, we found a de facto division quite common.

The thirty cases studied in 1964 lend themselves to the following land tenure system classification:

1. Parcels farmed as a unit: single management. (18)
    (a) Family: in community without inquilinos, medieros, or other permanent workers. (7)
    (b) Family: acting as medieros of owner (their father or mother). (3)
    (c) Non-family mediería. (2)
    (d) Family: with inquilinos or other non-mediería permanent workers. (6)
2. Parcel farmed in divided fashion: pluralistic management. (9)
    (a) Heirs farming separately with medieros or inquilinos in at least some sections. (5)

(b) Mediero from outside the family farming at least one section while owner farms the remainder. (1)

(c) Owner has non-family mediero and his sons work as medieros of mediero. (1)

(d) Family: acting as medieros of owner. (2)

3. Owner recently deceased; family has reached no agreement as to disposition of parcel. (3)

In our sample, eighteen parcels are farmed as one management unit, while nine are physically divided in some manner, each section of the parcel under different management. In three cases, the family is in a state of indecision over the disposition of the land since the owner has recently died and no equilibrium situation has been reached. Of those parcels worked under single management, seven are farmed by the family without other hired workers. The most common case is that there are older, unmarried sons who provide much of the labor but most management decisions are made by the parcel owner. Usually, operating expenses are paid by the owner and he receives all of the income. He provides for his sons during the year and possibly pays them something extra at harvest time.

A mediería arrangement is a more formal variation of the same system. Three cases were found where family members are share-croppers for their father or mother (the parcel owner) while the farm remains undivided. Married sons are likely to sharecrop since this system gives them a more formal claim on the parcel's income. In this arrangement, the parcel holder expects his sons to provide all of the labor, most of the management, and half of the operating costs. The owner gets 50 percent of the gross income at the end of the year and the sons divide the other half. Since parcel holders need not supply labor, this system is often used in cases where the landowner is too old for physical labor but still wants to maintain control over his land. In two of these cases, labor and management are provided by non-family sharecroppers.

We found six undivided parcels utilizing the labor pattern of Chilean fundos. The former mediero or inquilino is now fulfilling a patronal role, making all of the management decisions and acting as overseer. Labor is supplied by permanent laborers, resident or non-resident, who are paid in cash and often get about the same perquisites that might be given on a fundo. Most frequently, however, inquilinos working for colonists get a lower cash salary and fewer perquisites than inquilinos in the neighborhood working on fundos.

Of the nine farms worked in divided fashion, seven also involve some labor by either inquilinos or medieros, and hence retain the traditional structure but on an even smaller scale than above.

Five of these parcels had been divided because of the owner's death. In some cases, sections of the parcels are farmed personally by heirs who built a house on their part; on others, families still live together in the original parcel house but farm their land as completely separate accounting units. In other cases, parcel fragments are managed separately, while working capital—like horses or a simple plow or harrow—are owned in common. Women heirs, if they had some management experience previously, may have set up an inquilino on their part. If they had no management experience or if they do not live on the parcel themselves, they may have a sharecropper who supplies the labor, management, and half of the operating expenses and collects 50 percent of the income. There are combinations of these systems within the same parcel. For example, upon one parcel holder's death his wife took over half of the twenty-one-hectare unit, half of which she farms personally and the other half of which she works with a mediero. Each of the three children got a sixth of the parcel. The son farms his sixth himself; one daughter has set up a sharecropper on her portion and the other daughter rents out her fraction.

We found one instance of a mediero from outside the family farming one section of a parcel while the owner farmed the remainder. In another case the farm was physically divided among all sons, but to relieve the owner of all responsibilities he has put a mediero from outside the family in charge and each of his sons is a sharecropper to the mediero. This case is most difficult to classify within our system of "unitary" and "pluralistic" operation since some management functions are retained by the trusted mediero from outside the family and some by the sons.

In still another two cases, we found sons operating their own sections of the parcel but acting as sharecroppers for their father. Thus they made management decisions and paid 50 percent of the operating expenses, collecting the other half from the owner. Gross income was split 50–50.

That parcels now support more families than they did originally seems to be caused by several interrelated factors: (1) The economy is growing too slowly to accommodate family members who might seek off-the-farm employment. Forty-seven new families (sons and daughters of the original landholder) now live on the same parcel as the 24 living original owners. As we might suspect, instances of division among family members is higher in oldest colonies. The 14 settlers on the 6 colonies founded between 1931 and 1942 averaged 1.95 "new related families" per parcel. The 16 colonists on the 5 colonies founded between 1945 and 1953 were supporting an average of 1.25 "new related families" per parcel. (2) Education in the countryside is so poor that even if jobs are available off the farm the families of parcel holders are ill-prepared to take them. The average number of years of formal schooling of children over twelve studied is about four. This says nothing about the quality of their education, which is certainly below what a comparable number of years of schooling in the city would provide. The problem is aggravated by the fact that parcel holders lack a knowledge of techniques which would result in more productive use of labor on their farms. Only 12 of these 30 farms meet their full labor need from family labor; 7 of these do so by using the labor of more than one family with kinship ties to the owner. The other 18 parcel holders employed a total of 33 inquilinos, sharecroppers, or other permanent laborers. In most cases where workers were hired, there was ample family labor available (a total of 37 families on these 18 parcels). The result is either increased operating costs to the parcel holder (in case he has inquilinos) or division of income (if he has medieros). This suggests that the parcel holder may be forced by the economic system, characterized by large numbers of laborers whose marginal product approaches zero, to shelter more workers than principles of maximization would dictate. Besides, a farm owner may feel his status so improved by landownership that he can hire laborers just as his former patrón made use of a contracted labor force. This also seems to imply that the colonization program has done little to break the traditional social pattern existing in Chilean agriculture.

On the 30 parcels originally assigned to 30 families, 104 families now earn the major part of their income. There is some indication that this is a continuing trend. The older colonies have more families supported per parcel than newer ones. The 14 parcels on the older group of colonies studied were supporting 55 families, or an average of 3.93 families per parcel. The 16 farms on the newer group of colonies were supporting 49 families, or an average of 3.06 families per parcel. To clarify and expand upon these points, we must turn to the income situation on these parcels.

INCOME ON THIRTY SELECTED PARCELS

The fact that so many people are attempting to make a living on one "family-sized" parcel of land makes an economic study of the farms extremely difficult. On each of the 30 parcels we studied, we attempted to obtain income information by identifying the one person most knowledgeable about the operation. The usual case was that the parcel was supporting so many families that our informant did not know the economic situation of the remainder of the families. In some cases, we were able to piece together the information we needed by asking the other families in question for the data; in others, their absence from the farm at the time of our interview or their reluctance to give us the figures we needed made that impossible. Thus, we were not able to get data on the entire parcel's operation from 12 of our respondents and had, in these cases, to concentrate on detailing the income for but one of the families living there. These parcels supported six inquilinos or permanent workers and 34 other families in addition to the family from which we elicited data. This equals 52 families or 4.3 families per parcel.

In the 18 cases in which we gathered cash income data for the entire parcel, 52 families were supported in addition to the one interviewed—12 inquilino and 40 other families. These 40 were usually families of grown children or medieros from outside the family. In these 18 cases, the average parcel supported 2.9 families.

For each case we gathered information on all income which accrued to the parcel holder from (a) sale of crops; (b) sale of animals or animal products; and (c) miscellaneous sales or inventory additions. We found the inventory portion of (c) to be very minor, largely because parcel holders tend to add capital only if surplus is left over at the end of the year. We included no produce consumed in kind, since in this analysis we are seeking a measurement of cash position. Items included in operating expenses were similar to those detailed in former chapters.

Total net cash farm income in 1963–64 for the twelve "one-family" cases studied was E° 14,272, averaging E° 1,189 per family. Six families found it necessary to work outside the parcel to augment their income. They earned E° 3,654. Averaging this figure over the twelve cases adds another E° 305, bringing average cash income per family to E° 1,494.

These twelve families estimated the cash needed for consumption purposes during the year at E° 23,407 or an average of E° 1,950. Since average cash income totaled only E° 1,494, colonists either estimated their consumption too high or went into debt. It is quite obvious that these twelve families are consuming most of their cash income; there was no average surplus (net income minus family consumption) for the "one-family" units studied.

Total net cash farm income in 1963–64 for the eighteen entire parcels studied was E° 60,626 averaging E° 3,368 per parcel. On eleven farms some income was added to this by family members who worked outside the parcel. E° 16,958 was earned in this manner averaging, over the eighteen cases studied, E° 942 per farm. Average cash income per farm, considering income earned on the farm and brought in from working elsewhere, was E° 4,310.

Inquilino support and wages and perquisites for workers has already been subtracted from this calculation as an operating expense. But forty families depend directly on the E° 77,584 which is the total net income (E° 60,626 plus E° 16,958) accruing to families living on the eighteen parcels. A rough estimate of the amount of the average income available per family produces a figure of about E° 1,939.[4]

The cases for which we had one-family data averaged a net cash income of E° 1,494. We noted previously that there were more families per parcel in this group (4.3 compared with 2.9). Where there were fewer families per parcel there was a higher net cash income available to each—E° 1,939. This is certainly not surprising. But does a surplus remain even in the latter situation? While we were able to tabulate income figures for an entire parcel, attempts to elicit self-estimated cash consumption for every family living there were unsatisfactory. While one person may have been able to provide information on the overall management of the farm, no one person could detail the consumption needs of all families living there.

We may, however, turn once again to our "one-family" data for an estimation of cash used for consumption purposes. If consumption per family among the forty families on the eighteen farms we studied was as high as estimates for the twelve families (E° 1,950 per

family), consumption for the forty families would have been E°
78,000 (E° 1,950 times 40). Since total cash income for the eighteen
farms was E° 77,584, consumption at this level would leave nothing
for surplus.

Considering that some of the forty families are sharecroppers and
would not be likely to consume at as high a level as the twelve parcel
holders, chances are good that their average cash consumption was
more or less in line with the E° 1,494 average income available to
them. This figure would set cash income at E° 59,760 (E° 1,494
times 40) and mean that in our sample of forty, about a E° 17,824
surplus would be available (or an average of about E° 446 for each
of the forty families). We noted that there was a deficit in the comparable average considering "one-family" data.

Considering that in our sample "one-family" net income ranged
from E° 1,494 to E° 1,939, income for parcel holders in our sample
was about three or four times the average inquilino's cash income
and 50 to 100 percent above that of very highly paid inquilinos
(mentioned in Chapter 3). This calculation does not consider consumption in kind of products grown on the farm which, although
we did not attempt a measurement, we established earlier (in the
case of INPROA projects) is undoubtedly higher for colonists than for
even the best-rewarded inquilinos. Of course, inquilinos are given
perquisites as part of their incomes. Yet most of these same regalías
are still available to colonists: house, grazing rights, garden, etc.
Only minor items would still not be available: bread, firewood, a
free noon meal, etc.

But concluding that colonists are better off than inquilinos does
not answer another more interesting question: Are parcel holders
doing well? In seventeen out of the thirty cases we studied, colonists
had to depend at least partially on income they earned outside their
farm. Even so, the vast majority of our sample are living at little better than subsistence levels. As more years pass, income is divided
among more and more families. Surplus for investment purposes is
lowered accordingly. Besides a de facto subdivision of parcels which
has split income among many families, what are other factors responsible for the average poor performance of the parcels studied?
We shall proceed by listing some difficulties of parcel holders. These
problems are not mutually independent. In the long run they seem

to indicate a lack of education; in the short run, a lack of technical assistance.

PROBLEMS OF INQUILINOS AND MEDIEROS AS PARCEL HOLDERS

Extensive Land Use. Our thirty cases represent 736.86 hectares (considering now total farms); of this, 379.80 hectares, or 51.5 percent, are devoted to pasture. Excluding the two largest parcels located in a livestock-raising area of Chile, the total land area drops to 442.86 hectares, but the land in pasture still occupies 152.80 hectares and the percentage of land in pasture drops to 34.5. Of the twenty-eight cases in question, the average parcel contained 15.8 hectares, of which 5.5 hectares were devoted to pasture. The majority of the seeded area was usually devoted to wheat.

This extensive use of land, it may be hypothesized, is also a carryover from colonists' experience on a fundo where, as farm workers, they learned many of the agricultural practices they use today. Few of them have ever had instructive visits by extension or Caja personnel, or admit to seeking out such information. Their best source of technical farming information is probably their own experience—unadulterated by new learning—under a patrón.

In addition, there are other possible reasons parcel holders stated for this high percentage of land in pasture:

(1) "There is not enough water to irrigate the entire parcel." This may be true—or partially true—in some cases but the interview used involved a personal inspection of each parcel and the visit revealed that a vast majority of pasture land was irrigated or irrigable.

(2) "The pasture is improved." Only about ten hectares in our sample were seeded to improved pasture—that is, to a stand of from one- to three-year-old alfalfa or clover. (From Linares south this included only a two-year stand of clover, since alfalfa usually freezes out after the first year.)

(3) "The non-seeded portion of the parcel is land incapable of supporting row crops." Again, for some of the land in natural pasture this is probably true. Yet through judicious applications of fertilizer and other inputs, even poor land can be brought into production. While large extensions can afford to omit poorest land from cropping, it can be argued that small parcels cannot. It should be

noted that risks are attendant upon investment in these inputs, however, and it seems that parcel holders are afraid to invest in untried inputs when they are not certain their decision will not push them below subsistence income levels. Input prices in Chile do tend to follow produce prices, however, so it is doubtful that we could argue that fertilizer would not pay if correctly used.[5]

(4) "No more crops could be marketed if they were grown." In the central nucleus colonists can depend on an organized market for their wheat, beans, corn, sugar beets, and sunflowers.

(5) "The pasture is needed for the farm's animals." A relatively few animals (247) graze on a high percentage of the farms' total area (51.5 percent) or about three animals per hectare.

In the majority of the cases studied, in the estimation of the author, the amount of land in pasture could, conservatively speaking, be cut by one-half, the remaining pasture improved somewhat for the animals the parcel holder owns, and per-parcel net income increased accordingly. But colonists simply do not know of alternatives to the present extensive farming system practiced on the parcels.

Lack of Use of Conventional Inputs and Working Capital. Interviews showed that four of the parcel holders we visited used no fertilizer and five spent under E° 100 on it. That this represents an extremely low rate of fertilizer use is accentuated by the fact that eight of the parcel holders we interviewed farm in the La Serena area on land that is nearly pure sand. They must use generous applications of fertilizer or nothing will grow. Not considering these eight cases and using the artificial limit of E° 100 to indicate fertilizer adequacy, 41 percent use either no fertilizer or merely a token amount. Nearly all colonists have a vague notion what crop rotation is—they tend to move crops from one part of their parcel to another. But a legume is not always included in the rotation scheme. Those in the south part of the central nucleus tend not to seed anything in the years in which the soil is "resting" (colonists' usual term); they merely rely on white clover to come up by itself on irrigated land. Nearer Santiago, a number of parcel holders seeded clover or alfalfa with wheat but grazed it soon after the wheat was cut, thus killing the legume stand. Subsequently, they left the soil to "rest" without any cover—save weeds—for five or six years. In the cases studied in the central nucleus, only two cases were found where a successful rotation was used.

The Caja de Colonización Agrícola declared itself as offering the following credit program to colonists: (a) two-year credit for seeds and fertilizer; (b) five-year credit for animals and tools; (c) ten-year credit for fences, machinery, fruit trees, chicken houses (and other small farm industries), irrigation, and general improvements; (d) fifteen-year credit for permanent improvements; and (e) under certain conditions, twenty-year credit for house construction.[6] None of this credit was supervised and because of a lack of funds, the Caja was not able to keep up its lending program. By 1959 a quantity equal to only 6 percent of its operating budget was designated for loans.

The situation today has doubtless improved somewhat. Even so, seventeen out of the thirty colonists interviewed used no short-term credit for fertilizer or seed expenses in 1963–64. They usually indicated an awareness of the possibility of getting a loan but used the following excuses for not obtaining it:

(1) "There is too much red tape (*tramitación*) involved in obtaining credit." We heard this general statement modified: (a) "I have formally asked for credit. They told us they would come with the money but nobody has come. And I'm not going to ask again." (b) "I was told I could get credit when a group of officials visited my parcel. I was merely to go to the office and pick it up. But I have gone several times and each time been told to come back later. Each trip takes nearly all day and I can't afford to keep going back."

(2) "We have tried credit in years past, but defaulted."

(3) "They won't loan us money because it is against the law to subdivide our property. Although there is but one title, the inspector who came noticed that we live in several houses on the parcel so he wouldn't give us credit."

(4) "We would never use credit under any condition."

Those thirteen among our interviewees who received credit in 1963–64 borrowed an average of E° 250 from the Banco del Estado (Bank of the State) or the new Instituto de Desarrollo Agropecuario (INDAP—Institute of Agricultural Development) created by the Agrarian Reform Law of 1962. The Banco del Estado charged about 17–18 percent interest in 1963–64 and INDAP charged 12 percent. Both interest rates are negative since inflation last crop year was about 40 percent. Once acquainted with credit, users are often habitual borrowers, realizing that operating on borrowed money is a *"buen negocio"* (good business). Three colonists used credit for the first time in 1963–64 under the INDAP program.

Some credit is given in cash, some in kind. Cash was merely granted at the beginning of the crop year and paid back with the harvest. In-kind credit—fertilizer and seed—was picked up at the central office and money was remitted by colonists at harvest time. No visits to parcels were recorded by officials of the lending institution in any of the cases. Medium- and long-term credit was unknown among our interviewees. Twelve colonists used no seed disinfectants, weed killers, or pesticides.

There has been little substitution of capital for labor on the parcels studied. Four of the thirty had a tractor with some implements. Twenty-two farmed with E° 3,000 or less working capital (not including buildings). The general case was that the parcel holders farmed with several horses and a crude plow and harrow; only the most fortunate had a horse-drawn cart for trips to town.

Lack of Technical Help. Only seven of the thirty established parcel holders we visited had ever received an extension-type visit from Caja personnel or from any other agency.[7] Even in 1964, before the new government took over, few CORA technicians were available to give new colonists extension assistance. Of 537 CORA staff members in June 1964, only 159, or about 30 percent, were professional and technical. Only 32 professional and technical people were stationed at twelve provincial offices from Tarapacá to Magallanes. In contrast, nearly four times that number, 127 professionals, were stationed in the Santiago offices. (Some of these are in charge of colonies near Santiago, however.) Of 378 administrative and service personnel, 62 are located in the provinces. Five times that number are stationed in Santiago.

Of the 537, 81, or about 15 percent (about half of the professional staff), have had some specialized agricultural training. Fifty-three of these hold the degree of Ingeniero Agrónomo. The remaining 28 hold the Práctico Agrícola degree. (The training of a Práctico Agrícola is similar to a high school education in vocational agriculture.) Most of the 32 professional and technical people stationed in the provinces have had some formal agricultural education. The remainder of CORA's technical and professional staff—most of which is Santiago based—is made up of civil or building engineers, topographers, accountants, and lawyers.

Originally, an attempt was made to determine how many colonists were once either inquilinos or medieros by visiting the provincial CORA offices. Few could supply us with the data we requested either on the occupation of the colonists who originally obtained parcels or on the number of inquilinos who persist today. And we thus had to rely on informants on each colony. Since former fundo residents—especially medieros and inquilinos—would be those needing the most technical advice under an extension program, should one be carried out, the very fact that they could not be identified by the provincial office seems to be another indication that no such program is available.[8]

Lack of Cooperative Organization. Some lack of centralized technical help could presumably be made up by a strong cooperative organization which could bargain to obtain cheaper inputs and sell production advantageously. Furthermore, a well-organized cooperative could be a vehicle through which technical help within each colony might be mobilized.

Sixty-six cooperatives were established on the 116 Caja colonies when they were founded. Interrelated factors hampered their effectiveness from the very beginning. Little capital was supplied by the Caja. Heterogeneous backgrounds meant that members had little in common. Leadership, if it developed at all, tended to be provided by the most educated and wealthiest colonists because there were usually more of them, and a wide social and economic gulf separated them from former inquilinos and medieros who were also colonists and cooperative members. A loose organization usually developed. More affluent colonists had less need for a cooperative since they usually had economic interests elsewhere to provide some of their livelihood. One by one, the most difficult functions to be performed by a cooperative—those dealing with buying and selling advantageously—fell by the wayside. A sense of loyalty to or participation in the organization never developed. The cooperative had no control whatsoever over its own membership—colonists were selected by the Caja de Colonización Agrícola.

Little emphasis was placed on institution building. In some cases, an able person was promised two parcels if he would come to the colony and act as a "manager." It was not unusual to find the manager not getting along well with the cooperative—or at least not having much contact with it. In most cases the manager regarded his cooperative position as a sinecure and his major interest was to obtain land promised him.

The CIDA report notes:

Regarding another important aspect, colonies as a social community, the failure has been complete. The marked heterogeneity of the colonists, which implies a diversity of interests difficult to unite, and the little attention given by the Caja to community development, has resulted in the social disintegration of the group. Each colonist—separated from his own group—has arrived at this new nucleus with a heritage of experience and traditional attitudes which has impeded obtaining the hoped-for results. There are cooperatives, but in name only.[9]

THE ITALIAN COLONIZATION EFFORTS IN LA SERENA[10]

A brief digression is necessary to explain another colonization plan, beneficiaries of which have been considered together with those colonists of the Caja de Colonización Agrícola in former sections of this chapter. All but two colonists were indeed Caja colonists. But in 1951, the Caja de Colonización Agrícola introduced an important change into its newly founded La Serena colonies: more foreign settlement. These colonists have been included in our previous analysis because they met our selection requirement: even though they lived in Italy formerly, they were medieros prior to receiving a parcel.

One facet of this foreign settlement plan developed into the program of the Compañía Italiana Chilena de Colonización (CITAL) which today has forty-nine Italian-born colonists on three non-Caja colonies in its charge.

One of President Gabriel González Videla's (1946–52) favorite projects was the regional development of his home city, La Serena, in Coquimbo Province. As Pike has noted:

Probably the most impressive accomplishment of the González Videla term was the transformation wrought in the president's hometown, La Serena. This beautifully situated coastal city at the northern edge of the central valley was turned into a model community. Slums were cleared, handsome new buildings were erected, and many fine schools, particularly well-equipped technical schools, were constructed. La Serena today is one of the most hopeful sites in all of Chile. Had the Radicals won the 1952 presidential elections, they intended to carry out a similar revamping of Iquique.[11]

Plan La Serena, as it was originally conceived, was an integrated effort to beautify and industrialize La Serena. It was designed to provide an increased number of social services—education, health services, etc.—extend the paved portion of the Pan-American highway through Coquimbo Province, take advantage of the natural beauty of the seaside location to attract tourists (by restoring the Spanish-type architecture of La Serena and encouraging the construction of resort-type settlements near the sea), and surround the city with a green belt of small farmers to supply food to the industrial center.[12]

The agricultural portion of Plan La Serena ultimately settled some seventy families along the Pan-American highway to the north and south of La Serena.

Previously, the some 2,500 hectares which made up these colonies were called the *"vegas* [meadows] of La Serena." Even though the official name of the settlement is Presidente González Videla, residents still refer to their colony as Vega Norte and Vega Sur. Since this area was nearly pure beach sand, the land had not been farmed previous to Plan La Serena.

The colonizers reasoned that since the land would present special difficulties, it might be wise to bring in settlers for at least some of the parcels from outside of Chile, where the tradition of family farms was strong. From this idea grew González Videla's plan to bring twenty Italian families to intersperse with the Chileans in Vega Sur and a like number of Germans for Vega Norte.

Nearly all of the Italian settlers for the south sector were picked from Trent, which, until 1918, belonged to Austria. This area of Italy was hard-hit economically after the war. Surplus labor piled up here as soldiers returned just as it did in many parts of Europe. Trent was a minifundio zone where tracts of land had gotten extremely small through subdivision from generation to generation. Many settlers had two jobs in order to subsist and varying systems of sharecropping were common.

When the Instituto Nacionale di Credito per il Lavoro Italiano All' Estero (ICLE—this translates National Institute of Credit for Overseas Italian Workers) attempted to fill González Videla's request for settlers, they sent twenty willing Trentan families. The settlers were given some operating credit and Italian-style houses were nearly all built for them by the time they arrived in Chile. In total, ICLE put up about 60 percent of the necessary capital for the Italian portion of the Caja project. At least some of ICLE's support at the time came from the Marshall Plan.

When the Italian settlers arrived they found that La Serena was quite different from the clay soil and mountainous terrain they had known in Trent. Although most of their houses were awaiting them, the sandy, marshy land had not been cleared or even levelled. Much of the soil was too saline to be used and mountain water had to be brought nearer not only to irrigate the perpetually dry soil, but to flush its salt content back into the ocean. Colonists also had to learn how to cope with a climate that permitted two seedings a year and a soil totally devoid of organic matter.

The agricultural conditions in La Serena could scarcely have been more foreign to the new arrivals. In the face of these problems, it is remarkable that all twenty families remained on their land. A few old people returned to Italy but they always left family members behind to maintain the land parcels. Some concentration of lands has gone on as the twenty Italian colonists who were each assigned one parcel now own thirty parcels in the area.

In contrast, many of the twenty families of German settlers established in Vega Norte failed. They arrived sixteen days after González Videla left office and since Carlos Ibáñez, González Videla's successor, had little interest in his predecessor's favorite project, few Chilean funds were forthcoming. Furthermore, the selection process for these colonists was completely different. A doctor was contracted to go to Germany and select the twenty colonist families. He picked them from refugee camps in various sections of Germany, relying mainly on like physical characteristics for his judgment. Many of those he brought had little interest and background in agriculture.

Houses were not yet constructed for the Germans when they arrived since they had no supportive agency as strong as ICLE (although there was a German settlement company) working in their behalf. While colonists had been led to believe that they would find green farms when they arrived in Chile, they were especially surprised to find nothing but a sandy plain that, to them, looked more like a desert than a farming community. For the first year, they lived in an abandoned mining camp.

Eighteen families eventually staged a sit-in strike in the German Embassy in Santiago, demanding repatriation. Eventually, about 120 people returned to Germany and in 1956 the German Colonization

Company was liquidated. Only six German families yet remain in Vega Norte; of them, only two work in agriculture today. The other four are absentee landlords who have found more lucrative jobs elsewhere and who maintain their parcel as an investment.

The Italian colonization in Vega Sur resulted in the founding of the Compañía Italiana Chilena de Colonización in which ICLE, CORFO and CORA now hold shares. CITAL, founded in August 1951, purchased another series of small fundos several miles to the east of La Serena and eighty Italian families were brought in to settle Colonia San Ramón and twenty to settle nearby Colonia Mirador. Since many of the new colonists had farmed with perhaps less than a half hectare in Italy, CITAL presumed that from six to eight hectares would be sufficient for them in Chile.

This program had to act rapidly since upon CITAL's founding there remained only a little over a year of González Videla's term as president. Colonists were selected as quickly as possible in Italy —usually not from the same villages. In many cases, the original persons selected decided they could not come at the last minute and bribing prospects with little desire to come was necessary as a last resort to fill the colony. Many had little experience in agriculture and their common bond was that they were unemployed in Italy and anxious to begin their life anew elsewhere.

The land these settlers found when they arrived was almost as sandy as that nearer the sea on Vega Sur. Besides, the land was unusually rocky. The stones had to be laboriously picked up each year at seeding time only to be replaced by an almost equal number each subsequent year. For one reason or another, by 1955 more than half of the families had left and the parcels had been reorganized into thirty-six farms by CITAL. Parcels on San Ramón which no Italian settler wanted were sold to Chileans at a public auction.

These parcels, and twelve more CITAL sold to Italian colonists in Linares Province (fundo San Manuel in Parral), unlike those in the Vega colonies, were sold with a mortgage that was readjustable for inflation. An index based 60 percent on the rise in the price of wheat and 40 percent on the rise in the price of milk is constructed each year to determine the adjustment. Of the Italians who left the La Serena area, twenty remained in Chile. Some got loans from ICLE to return to Italy and a smaller group of six families was sent to Brazil where ICLE—again unsuccessfully—attempted to settle the fami-

lies on another farm. In 1964 ICLE authorized a loan of $190,000 to
purchase another fundo for the twenty original Italian families who
work as renters or sharecroppers near Santiago. This matter is still
in the stage of negotiation.

There is some evidence that the Italian settlers are becoming ac-
climated to their new country. For instance: (1) nearly all of them—
even the original settlers—speak Spanish; (2) a number of the second
generation have married Chileans; and (3) many have taken out
Chilean citizenship.

On the other hand:

(1) There is little evidence that the older settlers have much contact with Chileans. Chileans who live on the colony seem to have respect for the Italians who live there, but are also convinced that they
received better parcels and, because of that, are more successful. (As
explained previously, in San Ramón the poorest of the parcels were
sold and Chileans bought them.) Those Chileans living on Vega Sur
seem to think that the Italians got a better deal because their houses
were already built while at least some Chileans had to build their
own.

(2) Most of them speak either Italian or their European dialect
within their families.

(3) Italian regional dishes still form the basis of their diet—a corn
dish called *polenta,* for example, is as common among the Trentan
group as the soup called *cazuela* is among the Chileans.

(4) Many still have Italian periodicals sent to them.

(5) Although they usually indicate they will stay in Chile, they all
have plans to go to Italy to see their relatives "when they can afford
the trip." Many have visited Italy and brought back glowing reports
of how much better the situation is there now. Upon hearing these
rumors, some openly wish they had waited out the bad days in Italy.
"As soon as I get enough money I'll return to stay," is commonest
among oldest residents who would like to "return to Italy to die"
and younger settlers who are feeling crowded off the parcel by their
brothers.

(6) There is very little evidence that practices begun in the Italian
families have been adapted by the Chileans living nearby. This is
probably due in large part to the heterogeneous nature of the Chilean settlers in the Vega and the relative geographical isolation of
the Italians on San Ramón and Mirador. In Vega Sur, for example,

as in most old Caja projects, many parcels are owned by Chileans who are absentee landlords. Of the Chilean owners who live on their parcels, few farm them personally.

This author was able to locate only one Chilean inquilino who was awarded a parcel on Vega Sur. He admired his Italian neighbors but admitted to having little to do with them.

The transference of techniques seemed more pronounced in the opposite direction as three of the six Italians interviewed had inquilinos of their own. (Although sharecropping was common in Trent, inquilinaje was not.) Still, there was a higher percentage who worked their land personally than in all the Chilean colonies studied.

NOTES

1 This approach differs from the one used in the excellent study of the colony Pedro Aguirre Cerda in 1959. See Ministerio de Agricultura, Dirección General de Producción Agraria y Pesquera, Departamento de Economía Agraria, *Estudio de la Colonia Pedro Aguirre Cerda (El Tambo) de la Caja de Colonización Agrícola,* Santiago, 1959. This study investigates the economy of this colony in depth, usually not separating colonists on the basis of their background.

2 On Colony Pedro Aguirre Cerda, "of the 89 original colonists who received 96 parcels, only 36 kept their property and some have purchased neighboring parcels. The 53 property holders who sold their parcels have been replaced by 35 new colonists so that now there exists a tendency toward larger properties since the 96 parcels are in the hands of 71 persons." *Ibid.,* p. 115. (This colony was founded in 1942 and the study written in 1959.) Now, each property transfer must be approved by the council of CORA and, according to the current agrarian reform legislation (Law 15,020), each parcel buyer must have the same qualifications as new colonists.

3 This law supersedes the usual inheritance laws in Chile which provide that in most cases where no will is left half of the estate goes to the surviving wife and the other half is divided equally among the children. There are, of course, many complex exceptions to this general case.

4 Of course, this is only a rough measure. The owner of the parcel would probably get more than one fortieth; sons would probably get less; outside medieros less than sons; etc.

5 Peter Dorner, "An Open Letter to the Chilean Landlords," published in Spanish in *La Nación* (Chile), June 21, 1965.

6 Joaquín Leiva and Sergio Maturana, "Documentación Sobre Aspectos Específicos de los Programas Nacionales con Enfasis en la Creación de Nuevas Unidades" (II), paper presented at the Segundo Seminario Latino-

Americano Sobre Problemas de la Tierra, Montevideo, November–December 1959 (mimeographed), pp. 27, 58–59.

7 The study of Pedro Aguirre Cerda affirmed that 25 percent of its colonists had received the visits of "one or more experts," Ministerio de Agricultura, *op. cit.*, p. 115.

8 For more elaboration on this point applied to an earlier age in the Caja's history, see Edmundo Vilensky Marinot, *La Caja de Colonización Agrícola*, Editorial Jurídica de Chile, Santiago, 1951, who concludes: "The role of the agencies of the Caja de Colonización Agrícola that operate in different provinces does not correspond to the role they should have. They are just 'red-tape' offices with no authority which do not offer technical help because they lack personnel . . . ," p. 100. This is undoubtedly less true now than when Vilensky's paper was written. As late as 1959 the Caja employed only 43 technical people. Now they employ about 3.5 times that number. The ratio of technical people to administrative personnel has remained about the same, however, 1:3.3. See Leiva and Maturana, *op. cit.*, p. 28.

9 CIDA borrador, "Chile," p. 308.

10 The information for the following section has been gathered from interviews with colonists in La Serena and from personal interviews with Sr. Cristóbal Unterrichter, with FAO until 1965 and formerly with Instituto Nacionale di Credito per il Lavoro Italiano All' Estero in La Serena; Sr. Carlos Portales, CITAL, and Sr. Duncan MacIver. Manager, CORA, La Serena.

11 Fredrick Pike, *Chile and the United States 1880–1962*, University of Notre Dame Press, Notre Dame, Indiana, 1963, pp. 247–48.

12 See Presidencia de la República, *Plan de Fomento y Urbanización para las Provincias de Chile: La Serena*, Santiago, 1951.

IN CONCLUSION:
IMPLICATIONS FOR AGRARIAN
REFORM IN CHILE Chapter 7

The necessity for agrarian reform in Chile answers to two facts which can be doubted by no one. First . . . this is a social and moral objective. The second fact is the need for obtaining an increase in the physical production of foodstuffs and new materials. . . .
—Radomiro Tomic, leading Chilean Christian Democrat theorist and now Ambassador of Chile to the United States. September 3, 1964.

Through land reform aimed at increased production, taking different forms in each country, we can provide those who till the soil with self-respect and increased income, and each country with increased production to feed the hungry and to strengthen their economy.
—President Lyndon B. Johnson. March 16, 1964.

REFORM, AS we have noted time and again in this study, is an exceedingly complex issue since it alters traditional institutions which, until the moment of change, form the very framework of the lives of its participants. Neither campesinos nor the institutions set up to administer reform on a bureaucratic level have much experience in coping with problems brought on by institutional change. Yet knowledge of difficulties which reform brings should not discourage the reformer, who must learn pragmatically—even from short-run experiences—what the problems are and how they may be solved or circumvented.

TYPES OF ECONOMIC ORGANIZATION FOR REFORM

We have noted that INPROA's and CORA's programs commit them to establishing family farms. For its part, INPROA now regards its cooperative farming experience on Los Silos and centrally managed sharecropping and rental on San Dionisio and Alto Las Cruces as intermediate training steps leading to individual proprietorship. Yet there is no reason to believe that Chile need settle on either cooperative farming or family farming. As Dorner has asserted, "There is room for and indeed need for diversity, depending always on the circumstances now existing." Although family farms may be feasible in one area, "under other circumstances [they] may be a complete failure. The same can be said of any other alternative."[1]

Since alternatives may be clarified and refined with experimentation, it is indeed unfortunate that Chile has had little experience with cooperative farming in its central nucleus. Los Silos is one of the first cooperatively farmed fundos in Chile's history. For this reason it is especially lamentable that the experimental program on Los Silos seems due for termination in favor of individual farms. One can only hope that their experiments with cooperative farming, based on some of the lessons of Los Silos, take its place. If government officials are serious about an eventual system involving cooperative management as an alternative to the current land tenure structure, more trial laboratories are needed in Chile. To attempt to model a large reform program drawing from the little experience Chile has had and from successful foreign systems (where the cultural milieu is different) may result in costly and avoidable errors.[2]

If the government really wants to attempt cooperative farming—even as an intermediate step between the fundo and the private parcel—it will have to do more than iron out the inherent technical problems of the system. Cooperative farming as a policy for reform will initially have to counter a great deal of adverse public opinion and political pressure. Even INPROA tends to condemn cooperative farming, largely because of the economic difficulties on Los Silos in 1963–64. More dangerous because it is usually based on lack of evidence, some abhorrence to cooperative farming is on prima facie grounds. The family farm is somehow surrounded with an almost sacred aura because of its success in North America. Politically, cooperative farming is condemned by rightists partly because it could probably move faster than parcelization and, more obviously, because there is an automatic association with the far-left of any ideas that smack of collectivism.

An advance sample of the political pressure cooperative farms are likely to encounter is found in an editorial responding to the speech in which CORA's new executive vice-president revealed his favorable attitude toward cooperative farming. Even though immediately after President Frei's inauguration *El Mercurio* had supported the new government, on this issue it was clearly in opposition:

Aspirations of raised productivity have not been fulfilled by experiences of co-operative farming in which the fundo is considered co-owned by its members. Even a shallow understanding of the psychology and customs of our campesinos is enough to foster all sorts of doubts about work discipline, about policies of owning capital and receiving remuneration, and over the custody of goods in this type of collective property.[3]

Since, as we have indicated, the choice does not seem to be between family farms *or* cooperative farming, and organization for reform purposes may vary even within one country's reform program, we have not argued the merits of individual versus collective ownership in Chile. We would be remiss, however, not to resummarize and compare some of the conclusions about reform that emerge from earlier analyses. Since parcelization is currently the most feasible political alternative and since our study is based on cases where the family farm is or will be the predominant tenure form, these concluding remarks are weighted in this direction.

Systems which involve cooperative farming encounter the following difficulties when compared with individual units which we have documented. Technical mistakes are more costly. Since decisions are made centrally, a wrong decision usually means a loss for all participants in the reform. It is much more difficult to build meaningful economic incentives into a cooperative system. It is very easy for one individual member of a cooperative to reason that all functions of the cooperative will be performed just as efficiently if he, one member in a group, shirks his responsibilities. Perhaps the statement of debts given to each cooperator on INPROA-directed fundos will help him to realize the seriousness of a loss another year. Perhaps the committee system established for the working of large fields on San Dionisio will prove successful. Or maybe the system of docking members who do not work conscientiously (according to cooperative vote) will help the cooperatives to function more effectively.

On the other hand, cooperative systems seem to have these major advantages: they preserve the economies of size that exist in large fields and permit work to be done with large machines (if indeed this is an economy since the labor factor is so abundant).[4] They permit the present irrigation system—very expensive to reorganize—to be utilized. They may economize on scarce technical resources.

Parcelization, when compared to centrally managed schemes, also has certain difficulties. Infrastructure—both social and economic overhead capital—is extremely expensive and the surveys that accompany land division, as it is currently conceived, are very costly. Infrastructure and parcelization added about 20 percent to the cost of reform on Las Pataguas and about 50 percent to reform on Alto Las Cruces. The higher figure in the latter case was due largely to irrigation problems. The comparable figure on current government projects is running about 50 percent. Many times parcel owners, inexperienced as managers, are not prepared to make rational economic decisions when they are awarded their parcel. Heretofore, patrones and higher-level fundo empleados have tended to make most of the decisions that need to be made. It is doubtful that large equipment could be used as efficiently on small parcels. On the other hand, parcelization seems to offer clearest economic incentives to reform participants.[5] It would seem that parcelization would be at its best as a land reform instrument if a campesino organization— effective enough to contribute to its own infrastructural necessities —were developed. Only the basic infrastructure should be supplied —reform beneficiaries should be encouraged to build their own roads and make their own irrigation system revisions (as part of a co-operative plan of work and based on study, of course). Colonists can erect their own fences and even construct their own houses and granaries. This would lower original costs to parcel holders, mean less expense for the reform agency, and give colonists some sense of participation in their own future.

CAMPESINO ORGANIZATION: AN IMPORTANT FACTOR IN REFORM

In Chile, quite unlike Mexico, Bolivia, and Cuba in Latin America, the traditional land tenure system is still very much intact. Viable campesino organizations pressing for reform had been suppressed in Chile, at least prior to the Frei inauguration in 1964, due to laws discouraging them. The heterogeneity of agriculture, the class structure of the society, and differing policy desires of campesinos have also played a part. In the absence of (or at least supplementary to) voluntary groups to express campesino desires, organizations must be set up by the reform agency to relay the wishes of the beneficiaries of the reform to its administrators in some orderly, systematic fashion.

As campesino organizations or cooperatives become effective, they can act as a vehicle through which inputs and technical assistance are channelled. Due to the scarcity of technicians in a developing country, it is unlikely that any broad-scale reform will allow continuous and direct contact between the agency performing extension functions and each participant in reform. If campesino leaders are trained, they, in turn, can learn to pass information and techniques on to members. It is not even necessary that the country rely solely on Ingenieros Agrónomos (there is only one for each 5,000 persons in the agricultural labor force in Chile) for technical agricultural assistance to cooperatives. Lower-level technicians with but one or two years in college or even trade school and with as heavy an emphasis on extension methods as on technical agriculture could perform an invaluable service and would not be separated by such a vast social distance from the people served.[6]

In addition to these functions, the campesino group can, in time, develop into an organization that has "self-help" attributes (i.e., San Dionisio's cooperative voting to collect E° 70 from each member to proceed with infrastructure).

Since the success of a reform agency-campesino organization arrangement is predicated on good communications internal to each and one with the other, every effort should be made to facilitate feedback by making each organization conscious of the other's structure and functions. In addition to a badly functioning organization —or one that is simply too young to operate effectively—one bottleneck to communications is the existing social system in Chile. If reformers are not careful to avoid it, the patrón-inquilino relationship tends to grow back (or perhaps it has never been eradicated) in the "reformed" situation.

On Los Silos and Las Pataguas, we noted a tendency for the technical person to be regarded as a patrón. Social divisions on Las Pataguas between huerteros, parceleros, and hijueleros maintained the old system. On projects of the Caja de Colonización Agrícola, cooperatives did not function smoothly largely because of social rifts. An inquilino or mediero, when awarded land, tended to set up another inquilino on his new farm. On Los Silos, even an elected member of the cooperative—a campesino himself—was voted out of power partly because of the gulf that had developed between him and other cooperators. Some of this relationship is still evident as INPROA deals with the respective campesino cooperatives it organized. Institutions are not changed easily and, especially in a traditional society where wealth and power are still in the hands of the landlords, old patterns of social relations tend to persist.

This does not mean that it is impossible for communications feedback to occur between the reform agency and the campesino organization. On the contrary, once this difficulty is known and understood, overcoming it should not be an insuperable problem. As feedback between agencies improves, the reform agency has a responsibility to modify some of its policies based on pressures from campesino groups. On the other hand, the reform agency has an impelling responsibility to veto some of the cooperative's actions because of its obligations and restraints: (a) it has only limited funds; (b) it has obligations and limitations placed upon it by lenders and donors; (c) it has a number of cooperatives within its program—if demands of one infringe upon the rights of others the reform agency must veto or modify the action; (d) the land reform agency represents a concentration of technical knowledge which gives staff members professional obligations, i.e., if the cooperative wants to supply a certain amount of fertilizer and the professional is aware that the amount is not sufficient or of the wrong quality for optimal production, his duty is to veto the cooperative's decision.

There are indications that the campesino organizations in INPROA's charge and INPROA itself have strengthened and communications have improved during 1963–64. This interplay between institutions and the learning process it involved have brought about the following policy modifications.

(a) The cooperative voted to have each house built on parcels on both San Dionisio and Alto Las Cruces. This request simply involved too high an outlay of funds. Yet INPROA heeded the cooperative's request and kept in mind the failings of a villorrio (hamlet) settlement system on Las Pataguas. Therefore systems were designed to allow most colonists to live on their land while retaining some of the advantages of the villorrio.

(b) The amount set for the rent of Alto Las Cruces was judged as too high by the campesinos' cooperative. While this action will probably result in lower rent for the cooperative, INPROA is responsible for making rental payments to the Archbishop. INPROA is certainly not free to lower the rental without considering its own financial responsibilities if it is to remain solvent.

(c) INPROA lost money as the result of adding infrastructure estimates to land costs and giving the entire bill to colonists before infrastructure was complete. Learning from this experience on Alto Las Cruces and San Dionisio, INPROA plans to bill infrastructure separately from land when actual costs are known.

(d) The cooperative on San Dionisio demanded lump-sum settlement payments for their 1963–64 harvest. INPROA was delayed partially because of its bookkeeping procedures, but partially because it wanted to devise a rational scheme for investment for cooperative members. Action of the cooperative was non-compromising and carried the threat of a possible legal suit, and INPROA was forced to comply.

This interplay between two institutions involved in land reform is important. As a result of demands made through their cooperative, members and the service agency learn. This give-and-take seems to be the essence of a pragmatic approach to land reform—one which can settle issues as they arise. It is quite different from the early Caja de Colonización Agrícola in which Caja-cooperative-campesino contact was infrequent. INPROA's approach does not always function smoothly. Indeed, we have cited instances where it seems obvious that the institutions involved still do not understand each other. Considering their youth, this is to be expected. But INPROA is conscious of the necessity for good communications and strong cooperative organization. In order to assist the cooperatives to develop into bargaining organizations, INPROA is doing the following:

(a) Allowing the cooperative (in large part) to choose its own landholding members (exception: Las Pataguas). Realizing that unless a reform program begins with inquilinos or other landless laborers it has done little toward reform, most new landholders were old fundo residents and the majority of colonists were either inquilinos or medieros.

(b) Attempting to give all members equal land rights (except, again, on Las Pataguas where INPROA realized earlier mistakes and is now trying to rectify the situation by encouraging hijuela operators to withdraw from the cooperative and by making more land available for purchase by huerteros).

(c) Placing a person skilled in cooperative techniques on each fundo under reform.

(d) Splitting up the fundo into parcels only after a number of years of centralized management during which members are dependent on the cooperative for many of their needs. This is regarded by critics as a mere extension of the patronal system; in fact, it seems to be a rational step during which campesinos are trained for the trying experience of becoming landholders. Besides, in this intermediate period they come to rely more on the cooperative as an institution that can help them with problems they could not cope with alone.

ECONOMIC COMPONENTS OF REFORM

Reform tends to raise the incomes of campesinos immediately. Although we analyzed only a short, early period in the history of the INPROA fundos, we were able to show that the income of new landholders was, on the average, increased two or three times under the reform system.

In addition to supporting campesinos with a better standard of living than formerly, reform makes it possible for the fundos to support more families. When the reform on the four Church fundos studied has settled all families now planned for, the farms will be supporting 182 families or 23 percent more than prior to the reform. In 1963–64 the four fundos averaged 12 percent more families than before the reform.

It was quite obvious that total production on all of the Church farms studied was greater after reform. Even so, production on each —with the possible exception of San Dionisio—was lower than potential. And even on San Dionisio, where great reliance was placed on accumulated fertility of the soil, production may not remain high. This meant that in a number of cases colonists will not be able to cover their new debts—land payments and necessary capital. More intensive farming seems to be the most obvious remedy for production below potential. In order to raise productivity, more yield-increasing inputs will have to be applied and the farm will have to be better managed.

There are other ways in which current debts can be paid; in each case they involve more sacrifices than does raising productivity:

(a) Since consumption of campesinos rose with income under reform, consumption could be cut back, thus leaving members better off than they were previous to the reform and better off than even the best-paid inquilinos in Chile. We noted that consumption in 1963–64 on Los Silos was E° 2,158, on Las Pataguas about E° 3,317, on San Dionisio E° 2,222, and on Alto Las Cruces E° 2,345. On Las Pataguas, where the entire plot was under individual management, family consumption was highest, possibly indicating another advantage for centralized management early in the reform process. There is some indication also that home consumption of goods the colonist raises is lower when the farm is centrally managed.

(b) One way of raising net income might be to cut back on the amount of hired labor used until it is possible to intensify the operation. This means that individuals would have to become more efficient. All evidence points to the fact that much more labor than average was used on the farms under reform. The defect of this recommendation is that one way effects of a reform can be spread to a larger group is through employing labor. Calling for a cut in labor supply reduces this beneficial effect of reform. On the other hand, once the farm is worked more intensively and the individual campesino is solvent enough to make his land and capital payments, he should be better able to employ the superabundant labor which exists more productively than at present.

THE IMPORTANCE OF DEVELOPING ENTREPRENEURSHIP TO REFORM'S SUCCESS

Merely giving the campesinos land will not turn them into entrepreneurs. Comparing the development of entrepreneurial ability with the task of effecting a reform in the first place, T. Lynn Smith has called bringing about a widespread distribution of land ownership "child's play in comparison with the one of developing the necessary managerial skills on the part of the heads of families whose only roles previously have been the limited ones of the agricultural laborer."[7]

Stating that campesinos have not learned how to make rational technical decisions regarding their own land does not say they are incapable of being taught.[8] Quite the contrary, as we have shown in the case of San Dionisio, campesinos probably learn quickly how funds, once available, can be wisely spent. On the other hand, if no direction is given them, the decisions they make may merely copy the system they know best—that of the latifundia which hires abundant outside labor and involves extensive farming.

Colonists sold land under the direction of the Caja de Colonización Agrícola tended to remain at a subsistence level at least partly because of the paucity of technical help they were given. Showing the participants in reform how to produce, how to keep accounts, and supplying them with credits they need to purchase inputs, indeed, helping them to make decisions—even through coercion for a time—are important components of successful reform. Once colonists are settled on their land, the responsibilities of the reform agency are only beginning unless a country is willing to sacrifice marketed agricultural production to campesinos' consumption.

The Los Silos experience seems also to point out that the campesino leader and the technician cannot be the same person—at least initially. But this should change as campesino leaders learn the techniques they need to become successful managers.

LARGE-SCALE REFORM VS. ISOLATED EFFORTS

There would probably be definite economies of size involved if reform occurred on a large scale rather than as an isolated effort.

Larger marketing institutions and other organizations serving campesinos could be developed, thus economizing at least on technical and organizational and administrative talent. (Of course, there is a point beyond which a larger organization becomes less efficient as bureaucracy becomes more cumbersome.) Larger campesino organizations would probably be feasible. Again this could economize on technical and leadership talent and would mean that administrative units could be nearer an optimum size. Social and economic overhead capital might be usable by a number of fundos, thus lowering its per-settler cost.

Large-scale reform does not bring the same political problems and pressures as isolated reform efforts either. Since land reform is such a politically charged issue, a colonization effort which represents a center solution may be under attack from the far-right and the far-left. The left claims that the program does not go far enough; the right claims that independent campesinos cannot possibly succeed.

Then too, and more importantly, if reform proceeds slowly, landowners who see the handwriting on the wall may neglect their fundos even more than previously, exacerbating still further the inelasticities in food supply. "Should the transition to the new system be prolonged, the large-scale agrarian reform, when it comes with its own inherent costs, will, in addition, have to be carried out in a production context already impaired by having been subjected to the prior lengthy period of costly and debilitating uncertainty."[9]

A quicker reform will enable all concerned to determine the nature of the post-reform situation and return to a more stable situation with its pressing problems of raising production.[10]

PRIVATE VS. GOVERNMENT REFORM

Land reform which proceeds as a private effort rather than a government program runs into distinct problems, intimately related with problems presented in the last section, since it is not able to easily attract land to its program. INPROA's program, although extremely valuable as an experiment, is necessarily small, depending on Church property and external funds. It has no funds to purchase land and no power to expropriate. Then, too, land must be sold to colonists at near-commercial value with some possible reductions to reward laborers who formerly worked there at extremely low wages. The Church (or any other private organization) will not—and cannot be expected to—reduce the price of land in the absence of a fear of expropriation. The Church is responsible for maintaining the value of the possessions of its faithful, many of which come into its hands as a trust to support some specific Church benevolence.

A government reform should channel some of the campesinos' new earnings into productive investments in the economy as a whole, while offering incentives to campesinos for investing in their own property and holding down luxury consumption. Thus campesinos could pay for their property regardless of how land was obtained for the reform. Some of this payment might be excused if the campesino invests in land improvements on his farm and the annual amount due could be delayed in bad crop years. Mortgage amortizations could successfully substitute for a real estate tax (whose benefits to campesinos would be less obvious). These payments would tend, through mechanisms as sure as taxation, to draw surplus production from the farm into overall development purposes. Furthermore, there is some evidence that campesinos will tend to regard their tenure as more secure if they have paid for their land as they are accustomed to paying for other goods.[11] A dearer good will probably merit more interest, and hence personal investment, than one that is cheap and does not involve sacrifice. Of course, if the land were taken by a series of peasant uprisings, selling land to campesinos might be politically impossible.

Another difficulty of reform under private auspices is that infrastructural funds are more difficult to obtain than for a governmental agency. The large Inter-American Development Bank loan to INPROA was blocked by the office of the President of the Republic prior to the election of September 1964. It is quite possible that government and private institutions may find themselves competing for external funds, in which case the governmental agency is most likely to be favored.[12]

REFORM: AN INTEGRAL PART OF DEVELOPMENT

Land reform must be regarded as an integral part of the economic development program of Chile. We have seen how a few isolated plots given out by the government to inquilinos or medieros do not result in an economically successful enterprise. In the face of lack of off-the-farm jobs and educational deficiencies in the countryside, grown sons and heirs are forced to remain on the parcel, thus dividing income among more and more families.

In the short run an agrarian reform in Chile must aim to employ people more productively on the land. As the economy develops, industries must draw rural people off the land. And goods offered must be those for which campesinos are willing to raise their own production (and hence their cash incomes) to purchase. If an overall development program is not implemented and if agriculture does not move in the direction of a more intensive cropping pattern, it is difficult to imagine that an agrarian reform will result in anything but a minifundio problem, subsistence farming, and havens for the unemployed or underemployed.

NOTES

1 Peter Dorner, "Land Tenure, Income Distribution and Productivity Interactions," *Land Economics*, Vol. 40, No. 3, August 1964, p. 253.

2 Cooperative farming is, of course, a rather ambiguous term. The Los Silos experiment, described in this study, is one type of cooperative farming. In the same sense, San Dionisio and Alto Las Cruces may also be considered cooperative farming. Another possibility is the corporate structure de-

scribed in Peter Dorner and Juan Carlos Collarte, "Land Reform in Chile: A Proposal for an Institutional Innovation," *Inter-American Economic Affairs*, Vol. 19, No. 1, Summer 1965, pp. 247–54.

While experience with cooperative farming is rare in the central nucleus, it is true that Chile has at least two experiences with communal property outside its major farming area to draw on. One of these is the *comunidades agrícolas*. The comunidades are found particularly in the province of Coquimbo, just north of the central nucleus. See CIDA borrador, "Chile," pp. 254–83 and Patricia Cañón Valencia, "Las Comunidades Agrícolas de la Provincia de Coquimbo Frente a una Reforma Agraria: el Caso de Mincha," unpublished thesis, Facultad de Agronomía, Universidad de Chile, Santiago, 1964. The other type is found in the Araucanian Indian reservations of the south. See CIDA borrador, "Chile," pp. 166–78; 183–93 and Alejandro Palacios Gómez and Patricio Pinto Pérez, "Estudio Socio-Económico de la Agricultura Indígena en la Provincia de Cautín," unpublished thesis, Facultad de Agronomía, Universidad de Chile, Santiago, 1964. Inheritance has played a major role in these two instances and institutions have grown up over centuries. In most cases title to these properties is joint, but land is farmed individually save some pasture land which may be common. Yet policy makers who are aiming at some kind of cooperative arrangement cannot afford to overlook a careful study of these experiences.

Of course there exists a body of literature on the collective ejido in Mexico. See, for example, Juan Ballesteros Porta, *Explotación Individual o Colectiva?* Instituto Mexicano de Investigaciones Económicas, Mexico City, 1964; Nathan L. Whetten, *Rural Mexico,* University of Chicago Press, Chicago, 1948, pp. 207–39; Charles J. Erasmus, *Man Takes Control,* University of Minnesota Press, Minneapolis, 1961, pp. 183–305; Clarence Senior, *Land Reform and Democracy,* University of Florida Press, Gainesville, 1958. Some information also exists on the proportional profit farms in Puerto Rico.

3 *El Mercurio,* December 17, 1964, p. 3.

4 Long argues that labor-saving capital is often uneconomic in underdeveloped countries where there is superabundant farm labor for which the marginal product approaches zero. Erven J. Long, "The Economic Basis of Land Reform in Underdeveloped Economies," *Land Economics,* Vol. 37, No. 2, 1961, pp. 113–23.

Also, the long-run average cost curve in agriculture reaches its increasing phase with greater firm size more quickly than in industry. Any positive effects of economies of size are soon overbalanced by a more clumsy organization. Opportunities for division of labor are less than in industry since the seasonality of agricultural chores precludes simultaneous "assembly line" task performance. And management difficulties are more complex due to the spatial spread of agricultural work over a large area and the variety and non-routine nature of decisions to be made. See John M. Brewster, "The Machine Process in Agriculture and Industry," *Journal of Farm Economics,* Vol. 32, February 1950, pp. 69–81.

5 Raup has asserted that investments of an individual owner's time (and that of his family) and capital are undoubtedly greater and incentives to produce more clearly defined when each farmer has undisputed land rights to his own plot of land. Philip M. Raup, "The Contribution of Land Reform to Agricultural Development: An Analytical Framework," *Economic Development and Cultural Change,* Vol. 12, No. 1, October 1963. The point is closely related to the idea that secure tenure leads to the surest development of accretionary capital in agriculture, an argument presented by Raup.

   Some scholars argue that yeoman owner-operators help to promote the development of a much needed "middle class," the basis of a true democracy and an egalitarian society. See for example, T. Lynn Smith (ed.), *Agrarian Reform in Latin America,* Alfred A. Knopf, New York, 1965. See Smith's introductory essay, pp. 3–62 and the article by Salvador Camacho Roldán, pp. 80–84.

6 Lately the United States has found that subprofessionals can be effective antipoverty workers. About 15,000 slum residents who show promise have been recruited from welfare roles or ranks of the unemployed, put through short courses, and set to work doing jobs for which professional social workers are not essential: helping the needy find jobs or housing, assisting slow learners, or simply directing families to social workers or agencies that can help them. This helps to fill the gap of about 10,000 needed social workers. Besides, since their knowledge of poverty is firsthand, they seem to have a special ability to communicate with the poor. Utilizing subprofessionals for training in cases of agrarian reform should be carefully explored by countries since training funds are so scarce. Scanty reports reaching the United States seem to indicate that literacy teams in Cuba have been rather successful in teaching Cuban campesinos to read and write.

7 Smith, *op. cit.,* p. 11.

8 For a cogent statement on this point see Marion R. Brown, "Sources of Information for New Land Owners." in D. T. Myren (ed.), *Communications in Agricultural Development,* Proceedings of the Inter-American Symposium on the Role of Communications in Agricultural Development, Mexico City, October 13, 1964, pp. 101–7.

9 William P. Glade, "The Alliance for Progress as an Instrument of Socialization," in William V. D'Antonio and Fredrick B. Pike (ed.), *Religion, Revolution and Reform: New Forces for Change in Latin America,* Frederick A. Praeger, New York, 1964, p. 214.

10 *Ibid.*

11 The reader may want to explore some of the possibilities of taxation in greater depth. See, for example, John D. Strasma, "Market-Enforced Self-Assessment for Real Estate Taxes," *Bulletin for International Fiscal Documentation,* Vol. 19, Nos. 9 and 10, Amsterdam, September and October 1965.

12 As mentioned previously, however, INPROA did finally receive the funding —but not until November 8, 1965.

Selected
Bibliography

BOOKS AND BULLETINS

Alba, Víctor, *Alliance without Allies: The Mythology of Progress in Latin America,* Frederick A. Praeger, New York, Washington, London, 1965.

Alexander, Robert J., *Labor Relations in Argentina, Brazil, and Chile,* McGraw-Hill, Inc., New York, San Francisco, Toronto, London, 1962.

Alexander, Robert J., *Today's Latin America,* Anchor Books, Doubleday and Company, Inc., Garden City, New York, 1962.

Amunátegui Solar, Domingo, *Historia Social de Chile,* Editorial Nascimento, Santiago, 1932.

Ballesteros Porta, Juan, *Explotación Individual o Colectiva?* Instituto Mexicano de Investigaciones Económicas, Mexico City, 1964.

Barros Arana, Diego, *Historia General de Chile,* Vol. VII, ed., Rafael Gover, Santiago, 1886.

Barros Arana, Diego, *Riquezas de los Antiguos Jesuítas de Chile,* Editorial Ercilla, Santiago, 1932.

Bishops of Chile, *El Deber Social y Político,* Secretaría General del Episcopado de Chile, Santiago, 1962.

Boizard B., Ricardo, *La Democracia Cristiana en Chile,* Editorial Orbe, Santiago, 1963.

Borde, Jean and Mario Góngora, *Evolución de la Propiedad Rural en el Valle de Puangue,* Vols. I and II, Editorial Universitaria, Santiago, 1956.

Brown, Lester R., *Increasing World Food Output: Problems and Prospects,* Foreign Agricultural Economic Report No. 25, United States Department of Agriculture, Economic Research Service, Washington, D.C., April 1965.

Burgos Mujica, Hernán, *Análisis Económico Agrícola para un Plan de Crédito Supervisado: Comuna de Navidad Año Agrícola 1960–61*, Ministerio de Agricultura, Departmento de Economía Agraria, Santiago, 1962.

Butland, Gilbert J., *Chile: An Outline of Its Geography, Economics and Politics*, Royal Institute of International Affairs, Oxford University Press, London and New York, 1951.

Castillo V., Jaime, *Las Fuentes de la Democracia Cristiana*. Editorial del Pacífico, Santiago, 1963.

Chonchol, Jacques, *El Desarrollo de América Latina y la Reforma Agraria*, Editorial del Pacífico, Santiago, 1964.

Cohen, Alvin, *Economic Change in Chile, 1929–30*, University of Florida Press, Gainesville, 1960.

Congresos Internacionales Demócrata-Cristianos, Editorial del Pacífico, Santiago, 1958.

Domínguez, Oscar, *El Condicionamiento de la Reforma Agraria*, Université Catholique de Louvain, Collection de l'Ecole des Sciences Politiques et Sociales, Number 173, E. Warny, Louvain, Belgium, 1963.

Elliot, G. F. Scott, *Chile: Its History and Development, Natural Features, Products, Commerce and Present Conditions*, Charles Scribner's Sons, New York, 1907.

Ellsworth, P. T., *Chile: An Economy in Transition*, The Macmillan Company, New York, 1945.

Erasmus, Charles J., *Man Takes Control*, University of Minnesota Press, Minneapolis, 1961.

Frente de Acción Popular, *La Política Agropecuaria del Gobierno Popular*, Imprenta Horizonte, Santiago, 1964.

Gay, Claudio, *Historia Física y Política de Chile: Agricultura*, Vol. I, E. Thunot y Cía., Paris, 1863.

Góngora, Mario, *Origen de los Inquilinos de Chile Central*, Editorial Universitaria, Santiago, 1960.

Halperin, Ernst, *Nationalism and Communism in Chile*, Massachusetts Institute of Technology Press, Cambridge, 1965.

Hirschman, Albert O., *Journeys Toward Progress*, Twentieth Century Fund, New York, 1963. (See especially the chapter "Inflation in Chile.")

Hirschman, Albert O., ed., *Latin American Issues: Essays and Comments*, Twentieth Century Fund, New York, 1961.

Houtart, François and Emile Pin, *The Church and the Latin American Revolution* (translated from the French by Gilbert Barth), Sheed and Ward, New York, 1965.

Inter-American Development Bank, *Social Progress Trust Fund: Third Annual Report—1963*, Washington, D.C., 1964.

James, Preston E., *Latin America*, third edition. Odyssey Press, New York, 1959.

Jobet, J. D., *Precursores del Pensamiento Social de Chile,* Editorial Universitaria, Santiago, 1955.

Magnet, Alejandro, *El Padre Hurtado,* Editorial del Pacífico, Santiago, 1957.

Mamalakis, Markos and Clark Winton Reynolds, *Essays on the Chilean Economy,* Richard D. Irwin, Inc., Homewood, Illinois (a publication of the Economic Growth Center, Yale University), 1965.

Martin, Gene Ellis, *La División de la Tierra en Chile Central,* Editorial Nascimento, Santiago, 1960.

McBride, George McCutchen, *Chile: Land and Society,* American Geographic Society, New York, 1936.

Messner, Johannes, *La Cuestión Social,* Ediciones Rialp, Madrid, 1960.

Ministerio de Agricultura, Corporación de Fomento de la Producción Universidad de Chile, *Insumos Físicos en la Agricultura 1962–63,* Santiago, 1964.

Ministerio de Agricultura, Departamento de Conservación y Administración de Recursos Agrícolas y Forestales, *Agricultura Técnica,* No. 2, Santiago, December 1958.

Ministerio de Agricultura, Departamento de Economía Agraria, *La Agricultura Chilena en el Quinquenio 1956–1960,* Santiago, 1963.

Ministerio de Agricultura, Departamento de Economía Agraria, *Aspectos Económicos y Sociales del Inquilinaje en San Vicente de Tagua Tagua,* Santiago, 1960.

Ministerio de Agricultura, Departamento de Economía Agraria, *Estudio de la Colonia Pedro Aguirre Cerda (El Tambo) de la Caja de Colonización Agrícola,* Santiago, 1959.

Parsons, Kenneth H., Raymond J. Penn, and Philip M. Raup, *Land Tenure* (Proceedings of the International Conference on Land Tenure and Related Problems in World Agriculture in 1951), University of Wisconsin Press, Madison, 1956.

Partido Demócrata Cristiano, *El Libro de la Tierra: Movimiento Nacional de Liberación Campesina,* Santiago, 1964.

Pepelasis, Adamantios, Leon Mears, and Irma Adelman, *Economic Development: Analysis and Case Studies,* Harper and Brothers, New York, 1961.

Phipps, Helen, *Some Aspects of the Agrarian Question in Mexico,* University of Texas Press, Austin, 1925.

Pike, Fredrick B., *Chile and the United States, 1880–1962,* University of Notre Dame Press, Notre Dame, Indiana, 1963.

Pike, Fredrick B., ed., *The Conflict Between Church and State in Latin America,* Alfred A. Knopf, New York, 1965.

Pinto Santa Cruz, Aníbal, *Chile: Un Caso de Desarrollo Frustrado,* Editorial Universitaria, Santiago, 1962.

Powelson, John P., *Latin America: Today's Economic and Social Revolution,* McGraw-Hill Book Company, New York, Toronto, and London, 1964.

Presidencia de la República, *Plan de Fomento y Urbanización para las Provincias de Chile: La Serena,* Santiago, 1951.

Sadie, Johannes L., *Población y Mano de Obra en Chile 1930–1975*, CORFO/ CELADE, Santiago, 1962.

Schurz, William Lytle, *Latin America*, E. P. Dutton and Co., Inc., New York, 1963.

Senior, Clarence, *Land Reform and Democracy*, University of Florida Press, Gainesville, 1958.

Servicio de Seguro Social, *Manual de Instrucciones del SSS. 1961–62*, Unidad No. 23393 en el Registro de Propiedad Intelectual de la Biblioteca Nacional, Santiago.

Silva Cotapos, Carlos, *Historia Eclesiástica de Chile*, Imprenta San José, Santiago, 1925.

Smith, T. Lynn, ed., *Agrarian Reform in Latin America*, Alfred A. Knopf, New York, 1965.

Subercaseaux, Benjamín, *Chile: A Geographic Extravaganza* (tr. of *Chile: Una Loca Geografía*), The Macmillan Company, New York, 1943.

Tannenbaum, Frank, *Ten Keys to Latin America*, Alfred A. Knopf, New York, 1962.

United Nations, Department of Economic and Social Affairs, *1963 Report on the World Social Situation*, E/CN.5/Rev.1; ST/SOA/52, New York, 1963.

United Nations, Economic Commission for Latin America, *Social Development of Latin America in the Post-War Period*, E/CN. 12/660 (published in Spanish and English), Mar del Plata, Argentina, May 1963.

United Nations, Organización Internacional del Trabajo (ILO), *Informe al Gobierno de Chile Sobre la Formación Profesional Agrícola*, OIT, OTA/ Chile/R.7, 1963.

Universidad de Chile, Instituto de Economía, *La Economía de Chile en el Período 1950–1963*, Vols. I and II, Santiago, 1963.

Véliz, Claudio, ed., *Obstacles to Change in Latin America* (especially Osvaldo Sunkel, "Change and Frustration in Chile," pp. 116–44), Oxford University Press, London, New York, Toronto, 1965.

Vicuña Mackenna, Benjamín, *Historia de Santiago*, Vol. II, Santiago, 1869 (second edition, Editorial Nascimento, Santiago, 1924).

Vilensky Marinot, Edmundo, *La Caja de Colonización Agrícola*, Editorial Jurídica de Chile, Santiago, 1951.

Villain, Jean, *L'Enseignement Social de l'Eglise*, Spes-Paris, Paris, 1953.

Vitale, Luis, *Esencia y Apariencia de la Democracia Cristiana*, Arancibia Hnos., Santiago, 1964.

von Gestel, C., *La Doctrina Social de la Iglesia*, Editorial Herder, Barcelona, 1961.

Warriner, Doreen, *Land Reform and Development in the Middle East: A Study of Egypt, Syria, and Iraq*, Oxford University Press for the Royal Institute of International Affairs, 1957.

Whetten, Nathan L., *Rural Mexico*, University of Chicago Press, Chicago, 1948.

Wolf, Eric, *Sons of the Shaking Earth*, University of Chicago Press, Chicago 1959 (Phoenix Edition, 1962).

Worcester, Donald E. and Wendall G. Schaeffer, *The Growth and Culture of Latin America*, Oxford University Press, London and New York, 1956.

ARTICLES AND CONFERENCE PRESENTATIONS

Becket, James, "Land Reform in Chile," *Journal of Inter-American Studies,* April 1963, pp. 177–211.

Bray, James O., "Demand, and the Supply of Food in Chile," *Journal of Farm Economics,* Vol. 44, No. 4, November 1962, pp. 1005–20.

Bray, James O., "La Intensidad del Uso de la Tierra en Relación con el Tamaño de los Predios en el Valle Central de Chile," No. 24, *Revista Finis Terrae,* Santiago, 1960, pp. 47–62.

Brewster, John M., "The Machine Process in Agriculture and Industry," *Journal of Farm Economics,* Vol. 32, February 1950, pp. 69–81.

Brown, Marion R., "Sources of Information for New Land Owners," in D. T. Myren, ed., *Communication in Agricultural Development,* Proceedings of the First Inter-American Symposium on the Role of Communications in Agricultural Development, Mexico City, October 13, 1964, pp. 101–7.

Carroll, Thomas, "Reflexiones Sobre la Distribución del Ingreso y la Inversión Agrícola," *Temas de BID,* No. 2, Washington, D.C., August 1964, pp. 19–40.

Collarte, Juan Carlos, G. A. Palacios, and P. P. Pinto, "Desarrollo Histórico de la Agricultura Chilena—Período Prehispánico—1830," Seminario en Economía Agraria, Facultad de Agronomía, Universidad de Chile, Santiago, unpublished, 1961.

Cox, Isaac Joslin, "Chile," in A. Curtis Wilgus, *Argentina, Brazil and Chile Since Independence,* Vol. III, Russel and Russel Inc., New York, 1963, pp. 277–414 (copyright 1935 by George Washington University Press).

Dorner, Peter, "Land Tenure, Income Distribution and Productivity Interactions," *Land Economics,* Vol. 40, No. 3, August 1964, pp. 247–54.

Dorner, Peter and Juan Carlos Collarte, "Land Reform in Chile: A Proposal for an Institutional Innovation," *Inter-American Economic Affairs,* Vol. 19, No. 1, Summer 1965, pp. 3–22.

Dorner, Peter and William C. Thiesenhusen, "Relevant Research Programs to be Conducted in Developing Countries," *Journal of Farm Economics,* Vol. 46, No. 5, December 1964, pp. 1095–105.

Glade, William P., "The Alliance for Progress as an Instrument of Socialization," in William V. D'Antonio and Fredrick B. Pike, ed., *Religion, Revolution and Reform: New Forces for Change in Latin America,* Frederick A. Praeger, New York, 1964, pp. 197–223.

Kaldor, Nicholas, "Problemas Económicos de Chile," *Trimestre Económico,* Vol. 26 (2), No. 102, Mexico City, April–June, 1959, pp. 170–221.

Keller R., Carlos, "Minifundios y Latifundios," *Chile: Su Futura Alimentación,* Editorial Nascimento, Santiago, 1963, pp. 13–63.

Landsberger, Henry A., "Obstáculos en el Camino de un Movimiento Sindical

Agrícola: El Estudio de un Caso," Instituto de Organización y Administración (INSORA), University of Chile, paper presented at the VII Congreso Latinoamericano de Sociología, Bogotá, July 1964.

Long, Erven J., "The Economic Basis of Land Reform in Underdeveloped Economies," *Land Economics*, Vol. 37, No. 2, 1961, pp. 113–23.

Pearse, Andrew, "Agrarian Change Trends in Latin America," paper given at the First World Congress of Rural Sociology, Dijon, France, 1964.

Penn, R. J. and Jorge Schuster, "La Reforma Agraria de Venezuela," *Revista Interamericana de Ciencias Sociales*, Vol. 2, No. 1, Unión Panamericana, Washington, D.C., 1963, pp. 29–39.

Pike, Fredrick B. and Donald W. Bray, "A Vista of Catastrophe: The Future of United States–Chilean Relations," *Review of Politics*, Vol. 22, No. 3, July 1960, pp. 393–418.

Raup, Philip M., "The Contribution of Land Reform to Agricultural Development: An Analytical Framework," *Economic Development and Cultural Change*, Vol. 12, No. 1, October 1963, pp. 1–21.

Raup, Philip M., "The Role of Research in Agrarian Reform," *Agrarian Reform and Economic Growth in Developing Countries*, United States Department of Agriculture, Economic Research Service, Washington, D.C., March 1962, pp. 52–63.

Seers, Dudley, "A Theory of Inflation and Growth in Underdeveloped Countries," *Oxford Economic Papers*, June 1962, pp. 173–95.

Silvert, K. H., "A Political Sketch of Chilean History from 1879," American Universities Field Staff Letter, West Coast South America Series, New York, January 1957.

Silvert, K. H., "An Essay on Social Structure," American Universities Field Staff Letter, West Coast South America Series, New York, November 1956.

Smith, T. Lynn, "Values Held by People in Latin America Which Affect Technical Cooperation," *Rural Sociology*, Vol. 21, No. 1, March 1956, pp. 68–75.

Strasma, John, "Market-Enforced Self-Assessment for Real Estate Taxes." *Bulletin for International Fiscal Documentation*, Vol. 19, Nos. 9 and 10, Amsterdam, September and October 1965.

Thiesenhusen, William C., "Un Experimento de Reforma Agraria," *Desarrollo Económico*, Vol. 2, No. 1, Primer Trimestre 1965, pp. 19–23.

United Nations, Economic Commission for Latin America (CEPAL), "Rural Settlement Patterns and Social Change in Latin America," *Economic Bulletin for Latin America*, Vol. 10, No. 1, 1965.

Vekemans, Roger, "Análisis Físico-Social de la Situación Prerevolucionaria de América Latina," *Mensaje*, No. 115, special number, third edition, Santiago, 1963, pp. 67–75.

Yale Law Journal, "Notes and Comments, the Chilean Land Reform: A Laboratory for Alliance-for-Progress Techniques," Vol. 73, No. 2, New Haven, December 1963, pp. 310–33.

Zavala, Silvio, "The Frontiers of Hispanic America," in Walker D. Wyman and Clifton B. Kroeber, eds., *The Frontier in Perspective*, University of Wisconsin Press, Madison, 1965, pp. 35–58.

MANUSCRIPT

Comité Interamericano de Desarrollo Agrícola (CIDA), "Estudio Sobre Tenencia de la Tierra en Chile," draft copy (mimeographed), Santiago, 1964. (See also the excellent bibliography prepared by CIDA, pp. 494–522 of this report.)

LEGISLATION

Diario Oficial, Law 5,604, Santiago, February 16, 1935.
Diario Oficial, El Reglamento de Ley 5,604, Santiago, May 27, 1935.
Diario Oficial, Decreto con Fuerza de Ley No. 397 (to Law 5,604), Santiago, August 5, 1935.
Diario Oficial, Decreto con Fuerza de Ley No. 76, Santiago, February 24, 1960.
Diario Oficial, Law 15,020 (Ley de Reforma Agraria), Santiago, November 27, 1962.
Díaz Salas, Juan, *Código del Trabajo*, Vol. VII, comprende desde Febrero de 1954 hasta Marzo de 1956, Editorial Nascimento, Santiago, 1956.

CHURCH ENCYCLICALS

Pope John XXIII, *Mother and Teacher (Mater et Magistra)*, 1961, in *Social Action Digest*, Vol. 4, Nos. 8 and 9, August and September, 1961.
Pope Leo XIII, *On the Condition of Workers (Rerum Novarum)*, 1891, excerpts in William Ebenstein, *Great Political Thinkers, Plato to the Present*, Rinehart and Company, Inc., New York, 1951, pp. 832–33.
Pope Pius XI, *On Reconstructing Social Order (Quadragesimo Anno)*, 1931, excerpts in William Ebenstein, *Great Political Thinkers, Plato to the Present*, Rinehart and Company, Inc., New York, 1951, pp. 832–33.

UNPUBLISHED THESES

Cañón Valencia, Patricia, "Las Comunidades Agrícolas de la Provincia de Coquimbo Frente a una Reforma Agraria: el Caso de Mincha," Facultad de Agronomía, Universidad de Chile, Santiago, 1964.
Carvallo Drién, Marcelo. "Land Tenure and the Development of Chilean Agriculture," Master's thesis, University of Wisconsin, Madison, 1963.
Chonchol, Jacques, "Informe Pericial, Tasación y Cálculo de Rentabilidad del Fundo 'Los Silos'," Facultad de Agronomía, Universidad de Chile, Santiago, 1948.

Collarte, Juan Carlos, "Análisis de una Alternativa de los Sistemas de Tenencia de Tierra en Chile," Facultad de Agronomía, Universidad de Chile, Santiago, 1964.

de la Paz Gajardo, Mónica, "Estudio Socio-Económico de Puntilla de Pirque," School of Social Work, Universidad Católica de Chile, Santiago, 1961.

Mires Girones, Naddyne and Carmen Palavecino H., "Análisis de Algunos Aspectos Sociales de los Obreros Agrícolas de las Comunas de Florida, Puente Alto y Pirque en el Año 1955," School of Social Work, Universidad de Chile, Santiago, 1955.

Morales Jara, Héctor, "Productividad Presente y Potencial en 96 Predios de la Provincia de O'Higgins y su Relación con el Tamaño de las Propiedades," Facultad de Agronomía, Universidad de Chile, Santiago, 1964.

Ossio S., Hugo, "El Crédito Agrícola Supervisado en Chile," Memoria para optar al Diploma de Graduado en Economía Agraria, Programa de Estudios Económicos Latinoamericanos para Graduados, Universidad de Chile, Santiago, 1964.

Palacios Gómez, Alejandro and Patricio Pinto Pérez, "Estudio Socio-Económico de la Agricultura Indígena en la Provincia de Cautín," Facultad de Agronomía, Universidad de Chile, Santiago, 1964.

Seeger Stein, Helmut, "Informe Pericial, Tasación y Cálculo de Rentabilidad del Fundo 'Los Silos de Pirque'," Facultad de Agronomía, Universidad de Chile, Santiago, 1952.

Sternberg, Marvin J., "Chilean Land Tenure and Land Reform," Ph.D. thesis, University of California, Berkeley, September 1962.

Thiesenhusen, William C., "Experimental Programs of Land Reform in Chile," Ph.D. thesis, University of Wisconsin, Madison, 1965.

THE PRESS: ARTICLES AND RELEASES

The Atlantic Monthly, "Chile," October 1962.

The Atlantic Monthly, "Chile," January 1963.

Burks, Edward C., "Church Demands Reforms in Chile," *The New York Times,* November 4, 1962.

Burks, Edward C., "Rate of Growth Is Rising in Chile," *The New York Times,* April 21, 1963.

Clarín, "La Cooperativa 'Los Silos' Se Defiende de Acusaciones," Santiago, July 12, 1963.

Clarín, "Reforma Agraria sin Campesinos en el Fundo 'Los Cuatro Silos'," Santiago, July 9, 1963.

Corporación de la Reforma Agraria, "The Chilean Agrarian Reform," Press Release, Santiago, August 1963.

Dorner, Peter, "An Open Letter to the Chilean Landlord" (tr. of an article originally appearing in *La Nación,* Santiago, June 21, 1965).

Ercilla, "La Iglesia Abre el Surco de la Reforma Agraria," Santiago, July 4, 1962.

Goodsell, James Nelson, "Chile: Parcelling Out the Land," *Christian Science Monitor,* July 21, 1964.

Gross, Leonard, "The Catholic Church in Latin America," *Look,* October 9, 1962.

Heister, Ed, "The New Revolution in Latin America, A Re-armed Church Battles the Reds," *Parade,* July 7, 1963.

Inter-American Development Bank, "BID Otorga Asistencia Técnica para Facilitar la Parcelización de Tierras de la Iglesia Católica en Chile," Press Release, CP-14-64, Washington, D.C., February 20, 1964.

Inter-American Development Bank, "Inter-American Bank Lends $1.5 Million to Aid Church-Sponsored Agrarian Reform in Chile," Press Release, NR-59/65, Washington, D.C., November 8, 1965.

El Mercurio, "Adquisición de Nuevos Fundos Privados Hará la Corporación de la Reforma Agraria Este Año," Santiago, January 2, 1964.

El Mercurio, "El Cardenal Silva Henríquez Advierte Sobre Peligro del Comunismo en América Latina," carried on the AP wire from *L'Osservatore della Domenica,* Santiago.

El Mercurio, "Corporación de la Reforma Agraria Entregó Conjunto Habitacional Indígena," Santiago, September 15, 1964.

El Mercurio, "Fueron Entregados a sus Nuevos Propietarios Parcelas y Huertos Familiares de Hacienda Kennedy," Santiago, April 12, 1964.

El Mercurio, "Gobierno Hará 100.000 Nuevos Propietarios en Seis Años con Aplicación de Reforma Agraria," Santiago, November 19, 1964.

El Mercurio, "Programa para el Desarrollo Regional y Reforma Agraria en la Provincia de Talca," Santiago, August 28, 1964.

El Mercurio, "Reforma Agraria" (editorial), Santiago, December 17, 1964.

El Mercurio, "Reforma Agraria se Basa en Factores de Orden Humano, Cívico, Social, y Económico," Santiago, December 15, 1964.

El Mercurio, "Reparto de Tierras en Virtud de la Ley de Reforma Agraria," Santiago, May 3, 1964.

Meyer, Ben F., "Monseñor Raúl Silva Henríquez Elogia Resultados de la Reforma Agraria de la Iglesia en Chile," AP dispatch, *El Mercurio,* Santiago, July 11, 1963.

Morales Benítez, Otto, manuscript prepared for publication in *El Tiempo,* Bogotá, received by the International Development Foundation, Inc., New York, October 8, 1963.

Nevins, Rev. Albert, "Chile: Nation on a Tightrope," *South Pacific Mail,* Santiago, February 21, 1964.

Peruvian Times, "Chilean Farm Workers Get More Land," Lima, May 3, 1963, reprinted from *The Catholic Herald of London,* February 15, 1963.

Pizarro, Eduardo Silva, "Reajuste al Valor de las Parcelas," *El Mercurio,* Santiago, September 15, 1964.

Poblete Troncoso, Moisés, "Cuarenta Años de Legislación Social Chilena," *El Mercurio,* Santiago, September 7, 1964.

La Provincia, "Se Pretendió Dar Un Golpe de Ocupación Ilegal del Fundo San Dionisio," Linares, Chile, December 31, 1963.

Rebelde, "Combativo y Unitario Congreso de Campesinos Se Realizó en Talca," Santiago, December 1963.

Skelly, John T., "Chilean Spokesman Sees Success," *Latin American Times,* October 4, 1965.

Thiesenhusen, William C., "Latin American Land Reform," *The Nation,* January 24, 1966, pp. 90–94.

UNPUBLISHED REPORTS

Corporación de Fomento de la Producción, CORFO, Chile: National Economic Development Program, 1961–70" (mimeographed), Santiago, January 1961.

Corporación de Fomento de la Producción, CORFO, "Cuentas Nacionales de Chile, 1958–1963" (mimeographed), Santiago, June 1964.

Corporación de la Reforma Agraria, "Ref: Eleva Proyecto de Parcelización del Sector No. 1 del Grupo Los Alamos No. 1230" (mimeographed), Santiago, September 11, 1963.

Dorner, Peter, "Problems in Chilean Agriculture and Land Reform," prepared for AID (mimeographed), Santiago, 1964.

Instituto de Promoción Agraria, "Estudio de Parcelización Hacienda 'Las Pataguas'" (mimeographed). Santiago, 1963.

Instituto de Promoción Agraria, "Informe de INPROA" (mimeographed), Santiago, 1963.

Instituto de Promoción Agraria, "Institute for the Promotion of Agricultural Development" (mimeographed), Santiago, June 10, 1963.

Instituto de Promoción Agraria, "Proyecto Específico Alto Las Cruces" (mimeographed), Santiago, August 1964.

Instituto de Promoción Agraria, "Proyecto INPROA-AID," request for grant (typewritten), Santiago, 1964.

Instituto de Promoción Agraria, "Proyecto PL 480 AID-INPROA" (mimeographed), Santiago, July 30, 1964.

Leiva, Joaquín and Sergio Maturana, "Documentación Sobre Aspectos Específicos de los Programas Nacionales con Enfasis en la Creación de Nuevas Unidades" (II), paper presented at the Segundo Seminario Latino Americano Sobre Problemas de la Tierra (mimeographed), Montevideo, November–December 1959.

Ministerio de Agricultura, Departamento de Economía Agraria, "Sinopsis de la Agricultura Chilena, 1961–63" (mimeographed), Santiago, August 1964.

Puga, Gonzalo and Hugo Jordán, INPROA, "Plan de Trabajo e Inversiones," transmitted to Mr. John Robinson, AID Director (mimeographed), Santiago, July 13, 1964.

Rochac, Alfonso and Casto Ferragut, "Informe Preliminar Sobre Reforma Agraria de la Iglesia Católica en Chile" (mimeographed), Washington, D.C., 1964.

Troncoso, Hernán, "Trade Union Freedom," English translation of a pamphlet originally published by Acción Sindical Chilena (ASICH) and prepared for the Congreso Nacional de Abogados de Concepción (dittoed), Santiago, 1957.

United States Department of State, Foreign Service Dispatch, "Chile: Agrarian Land Reform," No. 863 (mimeographed), June 15, 1960.

United States Department of State, Unclassified Airgram, AIDTO A-667, "Agrarian Reform Program of the Catholic Church in Chile" (mimeographed), Washington, D.C.

United States Department of State, USAID, "Rural Cooperative Development Institute, INPROA," Project Number 513-13-140-159, Agreement Number INP-1-64, Pro-Ag (dittoed), Santiago, June 30, 1964.

La Voz, "Obispo de Talca Entregó Tierras," No. 261, Santiago, August 5, 1962.

Index